Quality Management
and Qualification Needs 1

Johannes Köper
Hans Jürgen Zaremba

Quality Management and Qualification Needs 1

Quality and Personnel Concepts of SMEs in Europe

With 40 Figures
and 22 Tables

Physica-Verlag

A Springer-Verlag Company

658.4012
K83q
VOL. 1

Johannes Köper
Hans Jürgen Zaremba
Institut für Wissenschaftstransfer
durch wissenschaftliche Weiterbildung (IfW)
Universität Bremen
Fahrenheitstraße 1 (BITZ)
28359 Bremen
Germany
ifw@uni-bremen.de

ISBN 3-7908-1261-7 Physica-Verlag Heidelberg New York

Die Deutsche Bibliothek – CIP-Einheitsaufnahme
Quality management and qualification needs / Johannes Köper; Hans Jürgen Zaremba. –
Heidelberg: Physica
1. Quality and personnel concepts of SMEs in Europe; with 22 tables. – 2000
   ISBN 3-7908-1261-7

This work is subject to copyright. All rights are reserved, whether the whole or part of
the material is concerned, specifically the rights of translation, reprinting, reuse of illustra-
tions, recitation, broadcasting, reproduction on microfilm or in any other way, and storage
in data banks. Duplication of this publication or parts thereof is permitted only under the
provisions of the German Copyright Law of September 9, 1965, in its current version,
and permission for use must always be obtained from Physica-Verlag. Violations are liable
for prosecution under the German Copyright Law.

Physica-Verlag is a company in the specialist publishing group BertelsmannSpringer
© Physica-Verlag Heidelberg New York 2000
Printed in Germany

The use of general descriptive names, registered names, trademarks, etc. in this publication does not imply, even in the absence of a specific statement, that such names are
exempt from the relevant protective laws and regulations and therefore free for general
use.

Cover design: Erich Kirchner, Heidelberg

SPIN 10747727   88/2202-5 4 3 2 1 0 – Printed on acid-free paper

Editorial

Leonardo da Vinci

This publication is part of the project "Survey and analysis of new work requirements and qualification developments in the context of quality management in SMEs as a basis for a forecast of requirement profiles for preventive further training strategies. A comparative study of the metalworking and food-processing industries". This project has been carried out by the following research network. The project and the publication have been carried out with the support of the European Commission in the context of the LEONARDO da Vinci programme, which is an action programme of DG XXII - Education Training and Youth. This document does not necessarily represent the Commission's official position.

Research network

Institut für Wissenschaftstransfer durch Wissenschaftliche Weiterbildung (IfW), Universität Bremen, Germany
Johannes Köper
Hans-Jürgen Zaremba
Franz Betuker

Lifelong Learning Institute Dipoli, Helsinki University of Technology, Finland
Seija Hämäläinen

University Libraries
Carnegie Mellon University
Pittsburgh, PA 15213-3890

National Technical University of Athens (NTUA), Greece
Dr. Daphne Lipowatz

Centre for Quality & Services Management, University College
Dublin (UCD), Ireland
Brian Fynes
Seán de Búrca

Centro Interdisciplinar de Estudos Económicos (CIDEC),
Lisbon, Portugal
Henrique Marçal
M. Mendes
Mário Vicente
Alberto Peres Alves

College of Applied Engineering and Maritime Studies, Chalmers
University of Technology, Gothenburg, Sweden
Dr Matts Carlsson
Tuula Bergquist

Centre for the Study of Education and Training (CSET),
Lancaster University, United Kingdom
Dr. Murray Saunders
Joan Machell

Contents

Introduction

These studies are results of the project "Survey and analysis of new work requirements and qualification developments in the context of quality management in SMEs as a basis for a forecast of requirement profiles for preventive further training strategies. A comparative study of the metalworking and food-processing industries". This project has being carried out within the framework of the programme LEONARDO DA VINCI of the European Commission (GD XXII) and funded by the European Union. These studies are based on surveys and analyses conducted between December 1995 and November 1997 in metalworking and food-processing small and medium-sized enterprises (SMEs) in seven partner countries of the European Union: Federal Republic of Germany, Finland, Greece, Ireland, Portugal, Sweden and the United Kingdom.

For the benefit of vocational training new abilities to be taught and new organisational conditions of training in the interplay of training providers and companies must be in the centre of interest. The present studies therefore concentrate on questions about the *quality capability of companies and employees*.

- How, for example through which work organisation, do companies produce quality?

- What do employees must do for it?

- What do employees need to know and be able to implement?

- What answers do companies find in their personnel development and in external training provision?

The studies seek to identify the needs and tasks of vocational training in a developing company practice. Other than quantitative surveys of the introduction of standardised systems and techniques of quality management, the underlying investigation therefore was focused on the concrete implementation practice of quality management and on the training practice of small and medium-sized enterprises. Therefore, expert interviews with managers and, as intermediate step of the analysis, individual-company evaluation were chosen as methodology of the investigation.

The sector studies are a synthesis of these expert interviews in the companies which have been evaluated in case studies on individual companies and with quantitative and qualitative methods at a sectoral level.

The analysis of quality and personnel concepts in small and medium-sized enterprises does not only identify examples of good practice and promising tendencies. It also identifies weak points and barriers in usual quality systems as well as in quality concepts and personnel policy of companies as well as in present vocational training provisions. Both are thus presented for a wide discussion.

Quality, as it is also shown in the present sector studies, is a cross-sectional task, cross-departmental in the companies, between companies in their market relationships and in the constant dealing of companies with the expectations of consumers and the public. Accordingly, quality capability of companies and employees can hardly be secured in vocational training by introducing new specific skills or a group of specific skills for certain occupational groups, as for example with regard to a new technology. Therefore, the authors intend to address a wide target group with their findings: political planers, developers and providers of vocational training as well as actors in the economy at in- and extra-plant levels.

Project design

The project was based on the following hypotheses:

Quality management, vocational qualification and European vocational training

1.   Quality management is a lasting strategic task of companies in the globalised customer market. Quality management represents an identical standard for the competition of enterprises acting in different company cultures in the European Union. Furthermore, it represents a new basis of confidence for new customer-supplier relationships in the single market. Both are crucial especially for SMEs because their competitive strength is the ability to react quickly to market and customer demands with products of high quality.

2.   Qualified employees are required for the quality capability of enterprises. If quality is not to be checked at the end of the process anymore, but is to be responsibility at each stage of the production of products and services, the forms of work need to be changed and the contents enlarged. In order to meet the new job requirements, staff needs appropriate qualifications. These qualifications comprise specialist and generic qualifications, quality system knowledge and process competence as well as social key qualifications. Enterprises have to re-discover and develop the human resources, which represents a European locational advantage. On the part of the employees in Europe, direct responsibility in their work plays an increasingly important role for motivation and work satisfaction, and

their capability to take on extended tasks is getting more important for their employability.

3.   The certificate according to ISO 9000 proves the fulfilment of the standards by the enterprise. This standardised quality assurance does not reveal much about the concrete internal implementation practice which generates the concrete skill demands on the employees. Effective quality systems are enterprise-specific. They have to be integrated in the corporate strategy and philosophy, materialise in concepts of product, process and customer orientation and concern the company organisation and process strategies, which depend on many factors, as well as the work organisation of the enterprise.

4.   Quality capability and customer orientation of the employees - this could be a practical focus of European vocational training; a concrete task at which the different vocational training cultures and structures in the European countries can prove their efficiency and be renewed. This task lies in the development of innovative training strategies that support internal personnel development for a comprehensive quality management. This approach presupposes enterprises that change to learning organisations, and vocational training bodies that support this development with suitable training provisions.

The following figure shows the **research aims** related to these hypotheses:

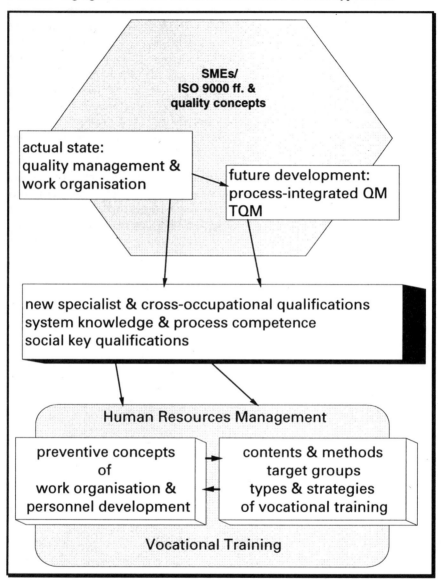

Figure 1: Research aims

To reach these aims the research has carried out the following steps of survey, evaluation and analysis:

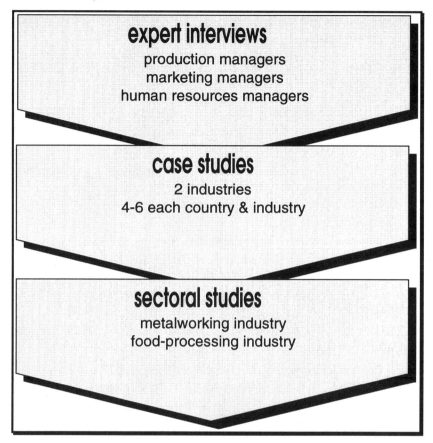

Figure 2: Research steps

Survey design

The research network decided for the following methodology:

- predominantly qualitative survey and analysis by means of
- expert interviews with management staff to be
- evaluated in company case studies as the basis for the
- sectoral evaluation.

Expert interviews with executives in marketing, process planning and human resources in each company should allow to identify in *company practice* both function-specifically and cross-functionally the tasks and difficulties in the implementation of quality management in small and medium-sized enterprises.

The essential specifications for this design of the survey were:

- Enterprise-specific quality systems and their implementation are management tasks. The management has the relevant expert knowledge regarding the difficulties and ways of the certification process, the concrete implementation of quality management in enterprises, the further development of quality management in the practice of enterprises. The expert interviews were to identify this existing management competence in SMEs.

- The imperative of quality management that quality is a cross-departmental management task. Therefore, by interviewing managers from different functions, the survey intended to analyse the implementation of the quality loop in SMEs.

- The impact orientation of the inquiry. Answers of executives who implement quality- and personnel-related aims of their companies, document not only *what* is done in the companies but also *how* it is done. Here lies the valuable possibility to transfer the dialogue of the researchers *with* the managers to a dialogue *between* the managers.

The interviews were conducted on the basis of a questionnaire/interview guide with standardised, semi-standardised and open-ended questions.

Evaluation in company **case studies** should allow to identify in *company practice* impacts of quality management on human resources, requirements and measures of personnel development.

The essential specifications for this design of the survey were:

- Companies and their production practice must be the concern of training needs researchers: How do companies *produce* quality? What do employees need to *do* therefore? What do employees need to *know* therefore? It is the concrete internal implementation practice where skill needs of the employees take effect.

- Effective quality systems improve the organisation of companies, improve processes and work. This defines new work requirements. And new work requirements define necessary new qualifications of staff.

The following figure illustrates the **survey design**:

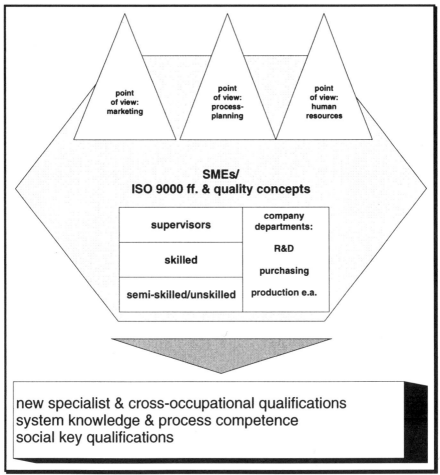

Figure 3: Survey design

The differentiation according to company departments and hierarchic levels served to answer open questions regarding the repercussions of quality management on previous departmental and hierarchic structures in the companies:

- Does the implementation of quality management define new work requirements and skill profiles as being rather interdepartmental or department-specific?

- Are the resulting new job and skill profiles rather specific to the levels of authority or cross-hierarchical

- Which special job and skill requirements can be identified for which target groups?

Guidelines for a problem-representative sample

The survey was not intended to deliver *quantitatively* representative results. It was aimed at *qualitatively* oriented surveys and analyses for the forecast of skill and training needs.

Guideline for the selection of companies and the composition of the survey sample was that they represent typical quality management and qualification cases and problems SMEs are facing due to the implementation of quality management.

The diagram shows the outline of the sample according to criteria:

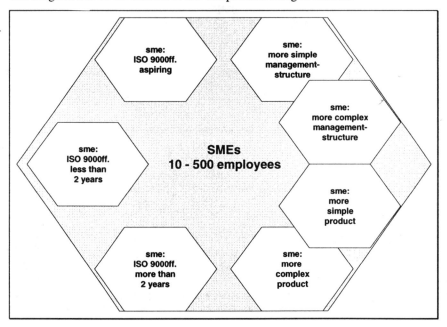

Figure 4: Outline ot the sample

The size class of 50 - 500 employees had been decided in the planning phase of the research project. There had not yet been a uniform European definition of small and medium-sized enterprises. According to the new definition of small enterprises, the size class of 10 - 49 has been included in the investigation in the course of the design review.

Database

Metalworking industry:	Food-processing industry:
The study is based on the survey of 34 SMEs which have been evaluated in case studies.	The study is based on the survey of 33 SMEs which have been evaluated in case studies.
There have been surveyed:	There have been surveyed:
6 companies in the Federal Republic of Germany	5 companies in the Federal Republic of Germany
4 companies in Finland	4 companies in Finland
6 companies in Greece	5 companies in Greece
4 companies in Ireland	5 companies in Ireland
4 companies in Portugal	3 companies in Portugal
6 companies in Sweden	5 companies in Sweden
4 companies in the United Kingdom	6 companies in the United Kingdom
A total of 94 experts was interviewed in these companies. 32 were marketing managers, 34 production managers, 28 personnel managers.	A total of 90 experts was interviewed in these companies. 28 were marketing managers, 33 production managers, 29 personnel managers.

Figure 5: Database

Part 1: Metalworking

Metalworking SMEs: Target group and sample

Metal goods and mechanical engineering in Europe
Reasons for the selection of the sectors

1. The metalworking industry is a European key industry for the European single market as well as the global market.

2. The range of products and their use, the structure of the customers and the production technology traditionally make high demands on the quality assurance of companies. This corresponds with a high density of standards both nationally and in Europe (i.e. mechanical engineering regulation) and with sector-specific aspects in the development of the otherwise cross-sectoral ISO 9000 ff (ISO 9004-1) standards. The range of products and their use, the structure of the customers and the production technology make also extraordinary demands on the implementation of modern comprehensive quality systems as to the adaptation to sector-specific management systems (i.e. configuration management in plant engineering and construction) and operational processes.

3. The sector has a high demand for personnel and qualification and thus resorts to the traditional advantage of the location due to the high level of qualification of the European workforce. This advantage has to be secured and improved if the new requirements of the global customer markets are to be met.

*

Metal goods (NACE 31)

> *"The EU is not only the world's most important producer of metal goods but can also present higher growth rates than their fiercest competitors, the USA and Japan. (...) The sector is characterised by a comparatively low rate of concentration. About 98% of the enterprises employ less than 100 people. These small enterprises account for 56% of the employees and almost 35% of the turnover of this sector. (...) Since the early eighties the sector has heightened productivity by increasing automation of the production process. (...) Consequently, there is a greater demand for a skilled workforce in this area. Although the enterprises increase the rate of mechanisation in production, most sectors of the metal goods industry continues to be labour-intensive."*

Panorama of the EU Industry 1993, European Commission (editor), Luxembourg 1993

> *"The metal goods industry, in which numerous small enterprises operate, is quite an important sector with some 2 million employees (...). Due to fierce international competition, EU producers are being forced to rationalise and to improve the quality of their products (...). The competitiveness of the EU producers is based primarily on the supply of products that are technically flawless, of high quality and designed especially for the requirements of the customers."*

Panorama of the EU Industry 95-96, European Commission (editor), Luxembourg 1995

Mechanical engineering (NACE 32)

> *"The EU is now the world's biggest machine market after outnumbering the US market volume in the eighties. The lead of the EU is even more obvious in mechanical engineering because it is - contrary to the USA - a strong net exporter. (...) A breakdown according to company size shows that small and medium-sized enterprises dominate in mechanical engineering. They are usually highly specialised, their production is dominated by individual and small batch production because the market segment they provide for does not allow large scale production despite intense export activities. Mechanical engineering is a labour intensive industry. (...) In order to accomplish its production task it requires not only a large number of engineers but also a specialised workforce. The availability of these qualifications is, therefore, a general locational condition for successful machine production. During upswing periods there are regularly shortages in recruiting personnel because the labour market does not provide the required specialist personnel as readily as demanded.*

Panorama of the EU Industry 1993, European Commission (editor), Luxembourg 1993

> *"The mechanical engineering industry is one of the leading manufacturing sectors in Europe, contributing around 8% to the total industrial production (...) characterised by small and medium-sized enterprises (...). The mechanical engineering industry in the EU is still highly competitive at an international level (...). This competitiveness is based above all on advanced technology, high quality and the competence to provide customised solutions (...). Due to the use of high technologies and the increased application of system solutions, the customer needs increasingly also services such as consulting, training, software and maintenance (...). Therefore, an especially qualified staff is needed, as it exists to a large extent in European companies, but not in competing companies in third*

countries (...). The advantage of the location still counts here, which the EU countries possess due to the high qualification of their workforce."

Panorama of the EU Industry 95-96, European Commission (editor), Luxembourg 1995

"Key success factors for operating successfully in the engineering industry are as follows:

- *Marketing: The development of the industry requires marketing support to identify opportunities and growth areas matched to firm's capabilities.*

- *Highly Skilled Personnel: The pressures on firms and personnel brought about by new manufacturing concepts and techniques mean that greater reliance must be placed on shop floor operatives.*

- *Technology: Technology is a critical factor in the industry. The trends towards miniaturisation and ASIC's mean that in high technology change sectors companies must be at or near the leading edge in order to survive. This applies generally in the Office and Data Processing, Electrical Equipment and Instrument Engineering sectors. In the remainder of the sectors specific techniques, such as CAD, CAM, CNC, are generally more important.*

- *High Added Value: Competition must be based on higher added value products rather than depending on low labour costs as a source of competitive advantage.*

- *Quality: Quality is vitally important and refers not only to the product quality but also to the quality of the underlying systems and support services such as marketing and administration.*

Centre for Quality & Services Management, University College Dublin, Sectoral Report, 1996

Overview of the sample
"Metalworking SMEs in 7 European partner countries"

The sample of the survey is not a representative average of small and medium-sized enterprises of the EU metalworking industry.

This is because all surveyed companies deal actively with quality management, are certified according to ISO 9000 or seek certification.

On an average, the surveyed companies represent progressive strategies for competitiveness at the business location Europe.

Table 1: Countries/enterprises according to products, total number of employees, ISO certificate (Metal industry)

Code no. & country	Products	Company size	State & of type certification	
111 F R Germany	Systems for automobile assembly	167 employees	certification < 2 years	ISO 9001
112 F R Germany	Cramps and nails in magazine	90 employees	certification < 2 years	ISO 9002
113 F R Germany	Equipment, transportation equipment for food industry	20 employees	aspiring certification	ISO 9001
114 F R Germany	Drive technology	22 employees	aspiring certification	ISO 9001
115 F R Germany	Ships, logistics	520 employees	certification > 2 years	ISO 9001
116 F R Germany	Fittings for industrial use	40 employees	certification > 2 years	ISO 9001
211 Finland	Coating machines, rolls, calendars, length cutters	38 (1250) employees	certification > 2 years	ISO 9001
212 Finland	Post-processing equipment to the graphic arts industry and components	26 employees	aspiring certification	ISO 9002
213 Finland	Gearwheels, special gear boxes, fine adjustment actuators, gear assembly	55 employees	certification > 2 years	ISO 9002
214 Finland	Open gear units and drives and segmented girth rings for industrial use	145 employees	certification > 2 years	ISO 9001
311 Greece	Accessories for military use	146 employees	certification > 2 years	ISO 9001

Code no. & country	Products	Company size	State & of type certification	
312 Greece	Metallic equipment for heating and water supply	47 employees	certification < 2 years	ISO 9002
313 Greece	Moulding pump products	260 employees	aspiring certification	ISO 9002
314 Greece	Air-conditioning machinery	170 employees	aspiring certification	ISO 9001
315 Greece	Mechanical engineering, metal construction, and machinery manufacturing	300 employees	certification > 2 years	ISO 9002
316 Greece	Centrifugal power pumps	61 employees	certification < 2 years	ISO 9001
411 Ireland	Chassis, cover products for the computer and telecommunication markets	150 employees	certification > 2 years	ISO 9001/2
412 Ireland	Electronic enclosures, cables, harnesses especially for mainframe computers and data storage	130 employees	certification > 2 years	ISO 9002
413 Ireland	Security cabinets	15 employees	aspiring certification	ISO 9002
414 Ireland	Injection moulded linear bushing components	49 employees	certification < 2 years	ISO 9002
511 Portugal	Automobile radiators	181 employees	certification > 2 years	ISO 9001
512 Portugal	Vessels and tanks, heat exchangers, condensers, evaporators, reactors, columns, complete installations	85 employees	certification > 2 years	ISO 9001

Code no. & country	Products	Company size	State & of type certification	
513 Portugal	Wood-working tools	130 employees	aspiring certification	ISO 9001
514 Portugal	Food industry equipment	431 employees	certification > 2 years	ISO 9002
611 Sweden	Thermal printers, EAN code printers	110 employees	aspiring certification	ISO 9001
612 Sweden	Heavy motor vehicle industry	125 employees	certification < 2 years	ISO 9002
613 Sweden	Spring units for furniture and Volvo Truck Co.	186 employees	aspiring certification	ISO 9002
614 Sweden	Espagnolettes	205 employees	certification > 2 years	ISO 9001
615 Sweden	Clips	110 employees	certification < 2 years	ISO 9001
616 Sweden	Plastic injection moulding	53 employees	certification < 2 years	ISO 9002
711 United Kingdom	Fabricated machine parts	44 employees	certification > 2 years	ISO 9001
712 United Kingdom	Sheetmetal and painted components	120 employees	aspiring certification	ISO 9002
713 United Kingdom	Fabrication and pressure vessels	110 employees	certification > 2 years	ISO 9001
714 United Kingdom	Aerospace, nuclear; special machine tool component manufacture	50 employees	certification > 2 years	ISO 9002

From the 34 surveyed companies 8 fell in the group of 10-49 employees, 21 in the group of 50-249, and 5 in the group of 250-500 employees.

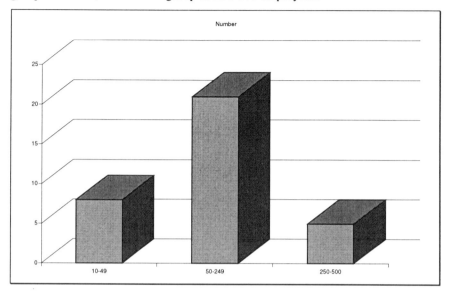

Figure 6: Number of companies / sizes (employees) in the metal industry (Total = 34)

From the 34 surveyed companies 10 still sought ISO certification, 5 of which for ISO 9001 and also 5 for ISO 9002.

8 companies were certified for less than 2 years, 3 of which according to ISO 9001 and 5 according to ISO 9002.

16 companies were certified for more than 2 years, 11 of which according to ISO 9001 and 5 according to ISO 9002.

A certificate according to ISO 9003 was not represented in the sample.

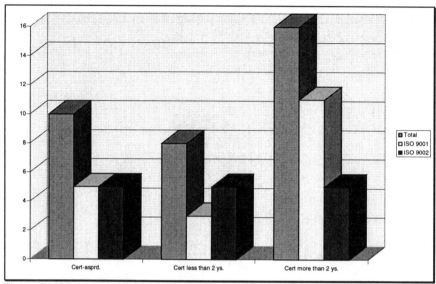

Figure 7: Number of companies / type and state of certification (aspiring/less than 2 years/more than 2 years) in the metal industry (Total = 34)

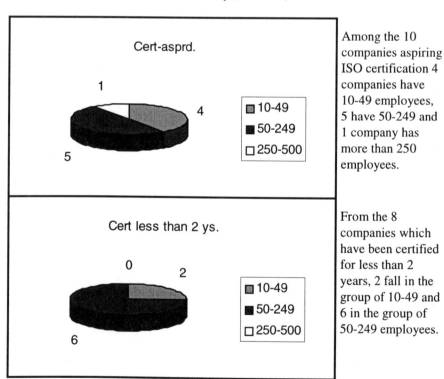

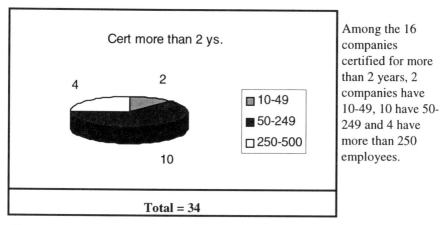

<table>
<tr><td>

Cert more than 2 ys.

4   2

10-49
50-249
250-500

10

Total = 34

</td><td>

Among the 16 companies certified for more than 2 years, 2 companies have 10-49, 10 have 50-249 and 4 have more than 250 employees.

</td></tr>
</table>

Figure 8: Sizes (employees) / state of certification in the metal industry

The sample

The following brief descriptions are extracts from country-specific overview studies on metalworking small and medium-sized enterprises and from the individual-company case studies of the project partners.

Federal Republic of Germany

The metalworking and mechanical and electrical engineering industries were in 1996 with 3.49 million employees the largest industrial employers in Germany. According to the data of 1994 (Federal Statistics Office), the companies in the group of 10-499 employees in the sector of metal products (NACE 31) with 9,489 companies and 583,933 employees account for about 18.6% of the companies and about 8.3% of the employees in the mining and manufacturing industries, and in the sector mechanical engineering (NACE 32) with 7,691 companies and 600,691 employees for about 15.1% of the companies and about 8.5% of the employees. Traditionally, the mechanical engineering industry represents a key sector in Germany. About 60% of the mechanical engineering business was done in international business in 1996.

Since the beginning of the nineties, the German metalworking industry is in a restructuring process with crisis features. Between 1991 and 1993 production contracted for instance in mechanical engineering by about 20%. The suppliers of capital goods were particularly hit by the general decline in economic activity. In addition, in 1995 the upward revaluation of the currency had a negative effect on the export. While in 1991 there were still about 1.5 million people employed in the mechanical engineering industry, until 1996 this number had been reduced to only 950,000 people. Under an increased international competition from the USA and

Japan as well as from new industrial countries, a restructuring is taking place in two directions: concentration on system solutions for individual customers under integration of micro-electronics in Germany and transfer of serial production to more cost-effective locations.

In the middle of 1996 about 15,500 companies were certified in Germany according to ISO 9000. An exact allocation of the certificates according to sectors and size of companies could not be identified. Taking a list of the market leader of certifiers from 1996 as a basis, 8% of the certificates go to the metalworking and 8% to the mechanical engineering industries. The Federation of German Mechanical Engineering Industry found out in 1995 in this sector that about 22% of the companies with more than 20 employees were certified.

| 111 | Systems for automobile | 167 | certification | ISO |
| F R Germany | assembly | employees | < 2 years | 9001 |

111 is an independent company within a holding. The company has specialised in planning, installing and commissioning assembly lines for the automobile industry and in engineering special machines. It operates with a network of suppliers and it produces mainly unique products. The operations are controlled by project management.

The company is certified according to ISO 9001. In the quality philosophy of the company the ISO system is regarded to be an element of a systematic development of TQM. The benchmark for this development are quality standards of transnational motor vehicle groups, such as QS 9000 and Q1.

| 112 | Cramps and nails in | 90 | certification | ISO |
| F R Germany | magazine | employees | < 2 years | 9002 |

112 is a joint-venture company of a European group of firms and a US company operating as an independent profit centre. The company produces fastening material for industrial customers on the international market. The production technique is mechanical mass production, which is undergoing a modernisation process towards automation.

The company is certified according to ISO 9002. As a supplier of an international car maker, it obtained the Q1 award. The company utilises techniques of statistical process inspection.

| 113 | Equipment, | 20 | aspiring | ISO |
| F R Germany | transportation equipment for food industry | employees | certification | 9001 |

113 is an independent company conducted by an individual owner. The company operates in a co-operation of three SMEs. It makes, from conception to commissioning, equipment for the food industry, providing, in addition, customer service.

The company seeks certification according to ISO 9001 in a regional network of SMEs and is still at the beginning of this process.

114 F R Germany	Drive technology	22 employees	aspiring certification	ISO 9001

114 is an independent company conducted by an individual owner. It is a supplier of drive technology and produces mainly small batches and unique products in partially automated production. After a reorganisation, the company is structured as a cross-functional divisional organisation.

The company seeks certification according to ISO 9001, the main motives being the requirements of customers, to which it maintains a close relationship.

115 F R Germany	Ships, logistics	520 employees	certification > 2 years	ISO 9001

115 is a family-owned independent company. It operates in the military and civil shipbuilding and has diversified its programme by supplying state-of-the-art logistics technology. It also operates in international business co-operations.

The company was early certified in the military area according to AQUAP 1 and is certified according to ISO 9001 since 1992. It is working on the implementation of self-inspection by operatives and on the introduction of preventive quality techniques.

116 F R Germany	Fittings for industrial use	40 employees	certification > 2 years	ISO 9001

116 is an independent corporation. The company develops and produces special fittings, steam and float valves for industrial and large-scale industrial customers, in particular in the chemical industry, mainly as small batches and unique products.

The company is certified according to ISO 9001. The decisive motives were the requirements of customers.

Finland

The metal industry in Finland has become the largest industrial sector both in terms of exports and as an employer. It has five main divisions: metals, metal products, mechanical equipment, electrical equipment and vehicles. As a fraction of Finnish exports, the metal industry accounts for more than two fifths. More than a third of the manufacturing value of the gross national product is produced by companies in this field. Metal and engineering is clearly the largest of Finnish industrial sectors. It accounts for a good third of the total industrial value-added. From Finnish cross production the share is 35.3 % and the share of value-added is 37.6 %. Mechanical engineering is the largest subsector of metal and engineering, accounting for about half of the output value. It includes metal goods, machinery and transport equipment. In metal and engineering, approximately 40 % of the total output value is value-added, in the basic metal industry about 25 %.

The depression of the 1990s was harder in Finland than on the other OECD countries. The recession was very hard for SMEs. There were hundreds of bankrupt estates and quite deep reorganisation was happening in Finland during recession. Its deepest point was passed in 1994 when the GDP began to grow again. In 1995 even investment increased. In 1991 production volume declined on all subsectors of Finnish metal and engineering industry. The impact of the difficult years was especially severe on mechanical engineering which did not exceed its pre-recession level until 1995. The other subsectors recovered rapidly. The basic metal industry entered the path of steady growth after 1991 and electronics and electrotechnical industry has recorded output increases of about 25 % every year. This was seen also during the recession. SMEs working in this sector have their order books fully booked although the other sectors suffered from bankruptcy and there was lack of visions for the future. Home market has not recovered from recession as soon as the sector as a whole and that has been very heavy to SMEs. The recovery of firms that are suppliers for the companies having export has been much more rapid than the firms whose production is for the home market. Productivity of labour, i.e. production volume per hour worked has been growing intensively in the recent years. In metal and engineering, the productivity has been rising faster than in the rest of the industries, owning especially to the strong productivity increases of the electronics industry.

In Finland there are approx. 200 certified companies operating in the metal industry. All the large companies which have export have a certificate. Last two years the companies of the metal industry sector that are certified are mainly suppliers for these big companies. In Finland you can find three Awards: Malcolm Baldrige, European Award and also the Finnish one. All these differ a little from each other. The Finnish Award is quite similar with the Malcolm Baldrige one. The Finnish Award is very popular among the companies whose main market is same as home market. And there is really thousands of companies working with this development tool. Then Malcolm Baldrige Award is used for those firms which export goods, equipment, machines or services to USA or if they have co-operation with companies in that content. Similarly the companies which have co-operations or have interests in the European market choose the European Quality Award.

| 211 Finland | Coating machines, rolls, calendars, length cutters | 38 (1250) employees | certification > 2 years | ISO 9001 |

211 is an operating unit of a large firm. The unit produces rolls. The firm is divided into the production unit and three core business units. The latter are divided by product into coating machines and rolls, calendars and length cutters. These support the production unit, where in the immediate vicinity, is the planning, purchasing, calls, parts subcontracting, assembly, workshop, transport, dispatch and packing.

The company made the decision on quality certification in 1987; something had to be done about profitability if its operations were to continue. Certification was seen as a way to improve profitability and clarify functions. The quality system was certified in 1992 according to the ISO 9001. At present the firm is developing its organisation using Malcolm Baldridge´s self-assessment criteria.

| 212 Finland | Post-processing equipment to the graphic arts industry and components | 26 employees | aspiring certification | ISO 9002 |

212 is an independent company. It is a private company and was set up by the present owner. In this company, engineering and production are separate units although they are situated in same building. Production buys in services from the engineering company. The company produces post-processing equipment for the graphic arts industry and does subcontracting. The production techniques are for individual small series of products.

The company is not certified, but the ISO 9002 is implemented and forms the basis for the company's development. Yardsticks have been developed and adopted in connection with measuring product quality and to ensure consistent quality.

| 213 Finland | Gearwheels, special gear boxes, fine adjustment actuators, gear assembly | 55 employees | certification > 2 years | ISO 9002 |

213 is an independent company. The company was set up by the present owner and it has been in business for 17 years. It provides cog wheels and gears, gearwheels, special gear boxes, fine-adjustment actuators and gear assembly. Special gears are those where standard equipment is not suitable. The client gets in touch, and the product development is done together, striving to solve the customers problem. The main type of problem is power transfer; the equipment is used, for example in the paper industry. The products are used in vehicles: cars, trucks, tractors and cranes. Then there is the precision mechanics product line, where the precision 15 1/1000 mm. Such equipment is used in dentists' X-ray devices, laboratory equipment and the aircraft industry.

At the end of the 1980s, the firm was involved in a project led by Central Union of the Metal Industry aimed at developing quality in SMEs. The goal was to remove errors. The project ended in 1989. A consultant was engaged to plan a quality system, but it became evident that that was not a suitable way to operate and it was seen that active involvement in the development was necessary. All personnel take part in developing the system. The company was certified according to ISO 9002 in 1992 first time.

214 Finland	Open gear units and drives and segmented girth rings for industrial use	145 employees	certification > 2 years	ISO 9001

214 is a subsidiary of a holding company. The group supplies power transmission gear units to various industrial sectors and has a world-wide market. The group specialises in foundry products, mainly for Scandinavian manufacturers of heavy goods vehicles and engineering companies. The company runs its production operations on JIT principles. The group utilises the latest technology so that its order-driven manufacturing system can offer the cost benefits of several products. The company has gone through a comprehensive restructuring process at the start of the 90s to increase flexibility. The company has changed it's way of production to team organisation.

The group's operations are controlled by a comprehensive quality policy. A quality system is in use and it is the basis of further development. The factory was certified in 1992 according to ISO 9001. TQM is an essential part of management method.

Greece

The sector of metal products included in 1988 13,729 establishments with 47,081 employees, representing 9,5% and 6,7% of total industry. The sector of mechanical engineering included in 1988 5,290 establishments with 22,320 employees representing 3,7% and 3,2% of total industry. About 95% establishments of both sectors had less than 10 employees while only 0,5% had more than 50 employees (1% for total industry). According to the last available data (Industrial survey 1993) the number of establishments and employees in the large-scale (10 - 500 employees) industry are: metal products 379 establishments/11,401 employees, mechanical engineering 342 establishments/11,575 employees. The contribute to the Industrial Output Index is for metal products 6,3% and for mechanical engineering 1,9%.

The metalworking sector in Greece is in crisis working at about 50% of its overall capacity. The number of employees in the large scale industry decreased during the period 1980/91 by 28% in the sector of metal products and by 17% in the sector of mechanical engineering while the decrease in the number of employees in the total industry was 13%. A great decrease can be observed between the years 1980 and 1995 at the production level of most important products of the metalworking sector with the exception of boilers and secondly of wires.

In the middle of 1996 the total number of firms certified according to ISO 9000 in Greece was about 250, 200 (80%) of them belonging to the industrial sector. Among the industrial firms about 30 (15%) are metalworking firms, 8 having less than 50 employees and 22 employing 50-500 persons. The percentage of certified firms in the metalworking sector is slightly over the sector's overall percentage in the Greek manufacturing industry, although the two numbers are not directly comparable. National awards do not exist in Greece neither has a Greek company won any European award so far.

311 Greece	Accessories for military use	146 employees	certification > 2 years	ISO 9001

311 is an independent individually owned company. The company produces metallic accessories for military use as well as optics and electronics using mainly single-piece and mechanical production methods. The company's products are mainly absorbed by the Greek army.

The company has a long experience in quality management due to the AQAP system which existed already before the certification according to the ISO 9000 series. It has been certified since March 1994 with ISO 9001 covering all products and activities. The management philosophy is that assuring the quality of the product is of greatest importance for the company. The quality assurance concept was already implemented both in philosophy and practical experience before the certification according to ISO 9000 due to the existence of a system according to AQAP, the company's product being military material.

312 Greece	Metallic equipment for heating and water supply	47 employees	certification < 2 years	ISO 9002

312 is an independent individually owned company. The company produces metallic equipment for heating and water supply using mainly mass production methods, partially automated.

Quality Assurance has been implemented in the strategies of the company. The acceptance of the demands of the customer and the decrease in costs of defects is one of the company's main goals towards improvement. Quality is a part of life and the quality system has to be applied by people who believe in quality in order to be consistent for a long period of time which leads to continuous improvements.

313 Greece	Moulding pump products	260 employees	aspiring certification	ISO 9002

313 is an independent individually owned company. The company produces pumps using a great diversity of production methods.

The company's strength in quality assurance is considered to be the acceptance and use of the procedural instructions, which have been written by the personnel conducting each task. This enables the personnel to be familiar with the process and to feel that they only undertake the responsibility they can and not the one the management wants them to. Quality assurance has been considered as a restructuring tool focusing on customer satisfaction.

314 Greece	Air-conditioning machinery	170 employees	aspiring certification	ISO 9001

314 is an independent company. The company produces air conditioning machinery as single-piece product as well as serial product using production methods from manual production to fully automated production in different processes.

The company is seeking certification according to ISO 9001. The main reasons are competition, the company being sure to produce excellent and exportable products, and improvement of the internal organisation, in particular in the administration.

315 Greece	Mechanical engineering, metal construction, and machinery manufacturing	300 employees	certification > 2 years	ISO 9002

315 is an independent corporation. The company produces mechanical engineering metal constructions and machinery using mainly production methods of single-piece production, serial production and mechanical production.

The company has been certified since 1994 with ISO 9002. The company has a high technological and personnel level. In co-operation with international organisations a large training session takes place once a year and is followed by special sessions for each department.

316 Greece	Centrifugal power pumps	61 employees	certification < 2 years	ISO 9001

316 is an independent corporation. The company is producing centrifugal pumps using mainly single piece and serial production methods, partially automated.

The company was certified in September 1995 with ISO 9001, however an internal quality assurance system had already existed. Quality has always been a stable strategy for the company's management. A generally satisfactory quality system existed for many years before the ISO 9001 implementation. The potentials and capabilities in all fields were fully verified through the documentation.

Ireland

Metals and Engineering provides nearly 68,000 jobs and has the largest employment of any sector of manufacturing industry. At £6.5 billion it also has the largest gross output. The sector is extremely heterogeneous with over 1700 firms engaged in a wide range of activities ranging from Metal Processing through Component Manufacture and Aircraft Maintenance to Assembly and Manufacture of finished products.

In the 1970's and 80's Industrial Development Authority (IDA) promotion led to dramatic growth in Office and Data processing equipment, particularly computer assembly and testing, and Electrical Engineering. In the 1980's there was similar growth in Instrument Engineering, which tends to be more employment intensive. During the mid eighties there was a large drop in employment due to restructuring of the industry, following Ireland's joining of the EC. This led to the virtual disappearance of some sectors. During this time there were large declines in low-technology sectors as many indigenous companies went out of business. Structural Steel Fabrication and Tank and Vessel Manufacturing were severely affected. Some companies which still trade employ only fractions of their former workforces e.g. in Cars, Car Parts and Metal Production. There have been major changes in the business composition of Mechanical Engineering but output and employment have grown in the last two decades. The significant sectors today are Electrical Engineering with circa 32% of employment, Manufacture of Metal Articles 18.5% and Mechanical Engineering and Instrument Engineering which both have 12%. 75% of Engineering companies are Irish owned (Deloitte & Touche survey 1992). Although foreign-owned companies are in a minority they account for 80% of output and 60% of employment. Irish ownership is highest in Metal Production and Lowest in Instrument Engineering. Total average sales for the sector amounted to £ 4,048 million in 1991. Average sales for foreign firms based in Ireland was higher (£11,438 million) than for Irish firms (£1,647 million). Only 20% of sales were to the domestic market. Irish firms exported 56% of sales compared to 91% by foreign firms.

411 Ireland	Chassis, cover products for the computer and telecommunication markets	150 employees	certification > 2 years	ISO 9001/2

411 is a subsidiary of a holding company. The company produces Chassis / cover products for the Computer and Telecommunications markets. It deals mainly with large Multinational companies (MNCs).

The company has accreditation to ISO 9001 and 9002. The company philosophy is that quality management is not strictly about conformance to ISO standards but that it is the responsibility off all staff. The certification procedure was originally undertaken because of customer and competitive pressures. Other benefits however were enjoyed as a result of becoming quality assured i.e. customer orientation, reduction of wastage, improved efficiencies and the introduction of teamwork.

412 Ireland	Electronic enclosures, cables, harnesses especially for mainframe computers and data storage	130 employees	certification > 2 years	ISO 9002

412 is a subsidiary of a larger company. It has been in operation since the 1970s and continues to grow dramatically. Turnover doubled in 1993 and trebled in 1994. The company produces to order. The main products include Electronic

enclosures, Cables and Harnesses especially for mainframe computers and data storage. The firm relies on 3/4 very large customers to whom they provide a complete service. Some of the customers rely on this supplier to provide over 90% of their requirements. Hence the customer-supplier relationship is highly interdependent.

The company has accreditation to ISO 9002. Quality assurance is very much a part of strategic planning. It is ingrained in everything the company does. This approach is vital to organisational success as there is a strong mutual dependency between the company and its customers.

413 Ireland	Security cabinets	15 employees	aspiring certification	ISO 9002

413 is an independent company that has been two years in operation. It employs 15 staff at present but this will be expanding fourfold in the near future. The firm produces security cabinets to order.

The firm does not have accreditation to any quality standard. The company is very young and has had a quality orientation since the beginning. Consequently TQM has not induced change as such, because it originally underpinned all procedures and processes. Supplier verification systems, incoming inspections of materials, tracking of jobs and quality inspection procedures were set up from the outset. The drive towards quality assurance is deliberately slow as the General Manager introduced ISO into his previous employers firm and did not find it delivered all it promised. In this case most of the production is manual and it is very difficult to maintain quality standards.

414 Ireland	Injection moulded linear bushing components	49 employees	certification < 2 years	ISO 9002

414 is a subsidiary of a larger company and was set up twenty years ago to supply the German parent. The parent company is the firms only customer.

The company has received accreditation to ISO 9002 in the last two years. Quality assurance is very much part of the strategic planning of the firm. The quality manager was recruited two years ago for the purpose of obtaining ISO accreditation. The company already had a comprehensive quality inspection programme but it did not have the documentation to go with it. Also the approach at the time was that the quality manager alone took responsibility for quality. There was a need to introduce a cultural change that would make quality everyone's responsibility.

Portugal

In 1993 the Portuguese engineering industry represents approximately 20% of the employment and 21% of the number of companies of the whole industry. The sector includes 7,605 establishments with 185,154 employees, in the group of 10-499 employees 2,792 companies operate with 116,997 employees.

The metallic products industry (5,311 establishments, 76,119 employees) accounts for some 4% of the Portuguese industrial production. Characterised by an entrepreneurial structure with dominance of SMEs, the sector has been investing during the last years in the increase of production capacity, in marketing and vocational training and, in some segments, also in the introduction of new technologies with emphasis on the CAD/CAM system employed by some companies producing moulds for plastics. The mechanical engineering (1,258 establishments, 33,414 employees) has a relatively reduced weight in the context of the national manufacturing industry (2,6% of the industrial GVA) when compared with the situation in most of the EEC countries. The electrical engineering (602 establishments, 42,676 employees) is composed by a high number of small and medium-sized companies, essentially with national capital. The sector is considerably important in the context of the manufacturing industry, though the bulk of production is created by the larger companies, most of them associated with foreign capital. The electrical and electronic products have been enjoying a highly favourable conjuncture cycle during the recent years, and the actual growth of exports is very significant. Motor vehicles includes 434 establishments with 32,945 employees. The automobile industry, in spite of the 1988 liberalisation due to entrance in the EEC, has been growing increasingly both in production and exports. The industry has a vital position in the Community both in external trade and in technological innovation due to its impact on the sectors supplying components and parts.

1995 approximately 11% of the certified companies had origin in the engineering industry. In Portugal, a programme started in 1994 known as the "Excellence Prize". The Excellence Prize model is based on the structure of the European Quality Award, set up in 1992 at Western Europe level and supported by the European Communities Commission.

511 Portugal	Automobile radiators	181 employees	certification > 2 years	ISO 9001

511 is a subsidiary of a larger firm. It started in 1914, with the purpose of producing automobile copper radiators. Since 1991, there is a new production line able to produce aluminium radiators. In 1984, the company found itself in a serious crisis caused by the loss of its major customers in the first equipment market given the closing in Portugal of the assembly lines, the coming of a product technologically more up-to-date and the pressure exerted by an internal

competitor. As a question of survival, the company decided to try to penetrate the external market, realising then that that would not be possible without raising the quality level of its products.

The company was accredited to ISO 9002 in February 1994 and to ISO 9001 in August of the same year. In 1991 the company decided for certification to ISO 9002 as a question of survival. Five years later, and as a company philosophy, it is customer-oriented and struggles for space in an extremely competitive market.

512 Portugal	Vessels and tanks, heat exchangers, condensers, evaporators, reactors, columns, complete installations	85 employees	certification > 2 years	ISO 9001

512 is an independent company. The company is nowadays the dome of a universe of five SMEs, its presence in the Spanish and Moroccan markets being dominant in its nuclear business areas, that is to say, beyond those already mentioned, the production of metal structures and of facilities for alternative energy and the preservation and maintenance of gas and fuel vessels.

1990, and was accredited to ISO 9001 in February 1994. It was also awarded the TUV Certificate, the AENOR Certificate (in accordance with Spanish standards), the ASME Certificate, and the PME Prestígio Certificates in 1993, 1994, and 1995 (the Prestige Certificate is granted by IAPMEI, the Institute for the Support of Small and Medium-Sized Enterprises). It was also honoured with the First Honourable Mention of the Quality Prize in 1991 and with the Quality Prize in 1992. As an applicant to the "Excellence Prize - Portuguese System for Quality - PEX/SPQ 94", the company was one of the six finalists and the only Portuguese one. Since 1993, the company has implemented a total quality management system - TQM.

513 Portugal	Wood-working tools	130 employees	aspiring certification	ISO 9001

513 is an operating unit of a large firm. Set up in 1978, the company produces and commercialises cutting tools for wood, wood by-products, cork, plastics and aluminium working industries. In 1995, one modern and model factory unit started its activities culminating the merging and strategic reorientation processes begun in 1990. Recently, an associate company was set up in Brazil, and the process of acquisition of a Spanish company is about to be concluded, these first steps consubstantiating the internationalisation of the company.

The company was accredited to ISO 9002 in January 1994.

514 Portugal	Food industry equipment	431 employees	certification > 2 years	ISO 9002

514 is an independent company. The company was founded in 1953 for the main purpose of producing machines for the wood-working industry. Nowadays, the company centres its activity in the dairy, beverage and chemical industries.

The company was accredited to ISO 9002 in October 1992. The reason why the company decided for a quality management comes to aspects related to competitiveness in its business field. Its customers made it clear that greater pressures at the quality level - certified to international standards - would for the future be exerted. On the other hand, the company observed that some competitors were successfully working in projects aiming at the implementation of quality systems.

Sweden

The Swedish engineering industry has old traditions. The roots of the industry origins from several hundred years old mining sector as well as from some early very important inventions which in the early 20-century resulted in the birth of what later resulted in some very successful multi-international companies: AGA, Atlas Copco, ASEA, Electrolux, Ericsson, ESAB, Sandvik, Scania, SKF, Volvo, etc. Later other industries like Autoliv and Tetra Pac has expanded the number of Swedish multinationals.

The majority of the companies in the engineering industry are very small and more than 50% of the companies have less than 25 employees. In 1997 the industry consist of more than 3.000 companies with 370.000 employees which in 1996 represents 10.0% of the employment in the country. In 1996 53.5% of the total Swedish export came from engineering products.

In 1996 there are three approximately equally big industry sectors according to total engineering output in this industry: electrical machinery, telecommunication equipment 26.6%, machinery, equipment and computers 26.0%, transport equipment 25.3%. The two smaller sectors are fabricated metal products 14.9% and instruments 7.2%. The investments in the industry is very heavy and 72.7% of the total R&D costs and investments in the country is allocated to this industry.

The industry has gone thorough some major changes. In the sixties Sweden was the third largest ship producer in the world but after some major changes. The earlier very big shipyard industry has almost completed been closed down with only some very small shipyards still in business. Structural strategic merges, alliances and joint-ventures has also changed the scene e.g. the Cupertino between

ASEA and Brown Bovery, between Avesta and Sheffield, Scania and General Motors and the Electrolux buy of Sanussi.

In the late 1980 the industry met stiffening international competition and went through a very dramatically change process which resulted in several structural changes both in the macro as well s in the micro economical perspective. From the beginning of the late 80 most of the companies begun different change programs in order to make their processes more efficient and effective. Production, administration and development times were cut down with more than 50%. When the efficiency in the processes were improved the number of employees were dramatically reduces, in some companies with more than 50%. Still between 1994 and 1997 the number of employees has increased from 320.000 to 370.000 in total.

611 Sweden	Thermal printers, EAN code printers	110 employees	aspiring certification	ISO 9001

611 is a corporation that was founded in 1984. It is a subsidiary of a holding company. They recently created subsidiaries in Germany, Italy and the UK. The historical base are the markets of the Nordic countries and France. From that base they have expanded into other European countries. The company is a leading manufacturer of products for bar code systems.

During 1995 they launched a Total Quality Programme to improve quality standards. The programme involves all aspects of their business, such as product development, manuals, manufacturing, technical support, education, sales and service. The company is seeking ISO certification with the quality assurance according to ISO 9001. This is their second attempt, and their explanation to their failure the first time was that an external consultant was hired initially and he provided the company with a system they had to adjust to. This time the system is built upon the prerequisites of the company. Today they are participating in a national training programme run by the IVF - The Swedish Institute of Production Engineering Research - the aim of the programme is to support the SMEs in the metal working industry with their certification process.

612 Sweden	Heavy motor vehicle industry	125 employees	certification < 2 years	ISO 9002

612 is an independent corporation. The company mainly supplies a few customers especially with transmission components. The customer-supplier relationship is highly interdependent.

The company is certified according to ISO 9002. Main reason to invest in quality management has been customer demand. The company had used his own quality system but by reviewing it they found weaknesses. Currently the company is implementing a Total Productive Maintenance System.

613 Sweden	Spring units for furniture and Volvo Truck Co.	186 employees	aspiring certification	ISO 9002

613 is a corporation that was founded in 1972. It is owned by an individual owner, a family company where the succession will be from father to son. Today it is one of the largest companies within the production of spring units. The company develops, manufactures and markets spring units for the truck and furniture industries. Sales are conducted directly to industrial customers and via wholesalers and industrial retailers.

The company is seeking ISO certification with the quality assurance according to ISO 9002. A quality manager was recruited to the company some years ago to work with the quality management strategies.

614 Sweden	Espagnolettes	205 employees	certification > 2 years	ISO 9001

614 is a subsidiary of a holding company that is one of the world's largest lock groups. The company develops, manufactures and markets a broad range of building fixtures for windows, doors and entrances. Sales are conducted directly to industrial customers and via wholesalers and industrial retailers. The company strategy is organic growth in existing and new markets, notably in the Far East, Russia and the Baltic States, and in other parts of former Eastern Europe

The company has been ISO 9001 certified for more than 2 years. The product development manager was recruited to the company some years ago to work with the quality management strategies. A programme with high quality and good design is of major importance for new project sales and for attracting the attention of architects.

615 Sweden	Clips	110 employees	certification < 2 years	ISO 9001

615 is an independent corporation. The company has gone through major changes during the 1990s. The company's subsidiaries became one large unit. At the same time, in a high conjuncture they put a concentrated effort in implementing ISO 9001.

The company decided to employ a quality co-ordinator and to follow the Q4-project. Q4 is the name for a series of educational programmes which aims at helping SMEs in implementing quality control systems. The company today are saying that the quality handbook is standardised ISO 9001 (1-20) manual but shall from 1997 become a company based handbook. This handbook shall be used directly as education material.

616 Sweden	Plastic injection moulding	53 employees	certification < 2 years	ISO 9002

616 is an operating unit of a large firm. The company is certified according to ISO 9002. Their philosophy over the past fifty years has been to have a strong effort in quality and competence, and everything that is done within the company is a strive to higher efficiency and profitability and not higher volume.

United Kingdom

The engineering, automotive and metals industries together account for some 7 per cent of GDP and £40 billion of exports annually. In 1995 motor industry exports totalled £14.6 billion, greater than any other manufacturing sector.

The industries cover a wide range of materials, processes, components and finished products and together employ about 2 million people. While some parts of the industry have declined, others have increased. Steel production has increased and has seen a shrinkage in the number of companies involved, the emphasis moving towards fewer, larger companies. In metal forming and finishing there has been some contraction and the focus now is mainly on SMEs in this sector.

In the UK, the number of small firms and their share of output and employment has been steadily rising for at least 20 years. Some areas of the metal working industry, such as transport equipment, are dominated by a few large firms while other areas, such as precision tool manufacture, have seen strong growth in the number of SMEs over the last decade.

All parts of the sector have had problems with profitability and competition, environmental issues and training and education. Successful company strategies have been based on the introduction and creative use of new technology, training programmes for employees and the introduction and development of flexible working practices.

In 1996, there were 70,600 companies in the metalworking industries, an increase from 68,400 in 1987. This represented a declining share of the total number of manufacturing companies, from 44% to 39%, because of the overall increase in the number of manufacturing companies in this period (from 154,000 in 1987 to 180,000 in 1996).

Of these metalworking companies, 22,980 were SMEs (with employees in the range 10-499), a slight decrease from 23,320 in 1987. Overall, the position of SMEs in these industries changed little, from being 34% of companies in the metal industries in 1987 to 32.6% in 1996. A rise in the early 1990s (to 24,797 companies or 36% in 1992) has now dropped back, reflecting the volatility of business starts and closures over this period. This percentage is higher than the average for manufacturing in which nationally SMEs make up 30% of all manufacturing companies.

42% of manufacturing SMEs are in the metalworking sector, a decrease from 47% in 1987 and 48% in 1992 which reflects the rise in manufacturing SMEs over that period, from 49,000 to 54,000.

Globalisation and supply chain relationships are of particular importance in the metalworking sectors and maintaining competitiveness in these areas is seen as the next challenge after Quality. There is a growing movement towards system integration, and strategic sourcing is also becoming increasingly important.

711 United Kingdom	Fabricated machine parts	44 employees	certification > 2 years	ISO 9001

711 is an independent company. There is one owner (the company founder). There are five main production methods: single-piece production, serial production, manual production, mechanical production and partially-automated production. Current clients include the nuclear, gas-related, transport, pharmaceutical, and paper industries.

In 1986, the company was one of the first sub-contract engineers in the UK to have its quality system registered as complying with BS 5750: Part 2. In February 1995 the scope of Registration was extended to comply with ISO 9001. In May 1995, the company was recognised as an 'Investor in People'.

712 United Kingdom	Sheetmetal and painted components	120 employees	aspiring certification	ISO 9002

712 is a subsidiary of a holding company. In 1983 the company was sold to its employees and is now in the somewhat unusual position of being under Employee Ownership. The main production methods are single piece production, serial

production, mass production, manual production, mechanical production and partially automated production.

The company is currently BS EN ISO 9002 registered and committed to BS EN ISO 9001 compliance over the medium term. Quality management is considered to be the key to the future development of the business.

713 United Kingdom	Fabrication and pressure vessels	110 employees	certification > 2 years	ISO 9001

713 is an independent company as a subsidiary of a holding company. The company's heavy engineering division undertakes fabrication and pressure vessel manufacturing for multi-national customers whilst local businesses are served through the company's light engineering and car/commercial vehicle repair divisions. Their main customers are the oil, petro-chemical and nuclear industries.

The company is fully accredited by Lloyds Register Quality Assurance Limited to BS 5750 Part 1 (ISO 9001 - 1987 and EN 29001 - 1987). As the company provides components for the nuclear industry it is essential that high standards of quality are guaranteed.

714 United Kingdom	Aerospace, nuclear; special machine tool component manufacture	50 employees	certification > 2 years	ISO 9002

714 is an independent company owned by an individual owner. The main business of the company is the manufacture of special machine tool components, chiefly for the aerospace and nuclear industries.

The company has been ISO certified for more than 2 years and has ISO 9002. The company decided to invest in Quality management as this was seen as giving them a major competitive advantage. Because the company provides components for the aerospace and nuclear industries, 'quality is absolute'.

Quality concepts of metalworking SMEs

Quantitative findings

The interviewees were allowed to rate multiple criterions. The scale of 0 - 300 results from the rating scale of 0 - 3 and from the fact that the survey results based on different quantities of respondents have been extrapolated to a number of companies of 100 in order to obtain data that are comparable between the sectors.

Reasons for implementing quality management

In order to identify the motives and aims SMEs connect with the introduction of quality management, all interviewed experts have been asked the following question:

Question: Implementing a Quality Management system has cost implications - particularly for SMEs. What were the main reasons for your company deciding to invest in Quality Management? **Rate answers according to following key:** 0 = unimportant, 1 = plays a role, 2 = important, 3 = very important.

- Customer commitment (supplier duty)
- Competitive pressures (new competitive standard)
- Legal pressures (liability precaution)
- Impact of advertising
- Public promotion
- Costs of quality (reducing complaints; nonconformity costs/costs of its correction)
- Improvement of internal processes (clear working aims; co-operation of the departments)
- Shorter processing times
- Improving management procedures/systems
- Customer satisfaction
- Company philosophy
- Working atmosphere/employees motivation
- Changeover to team work

Reasons in the view of company experts

94 executives from 34 metalworking SMEs have been interviewed as company experts in the implementation of quality management.

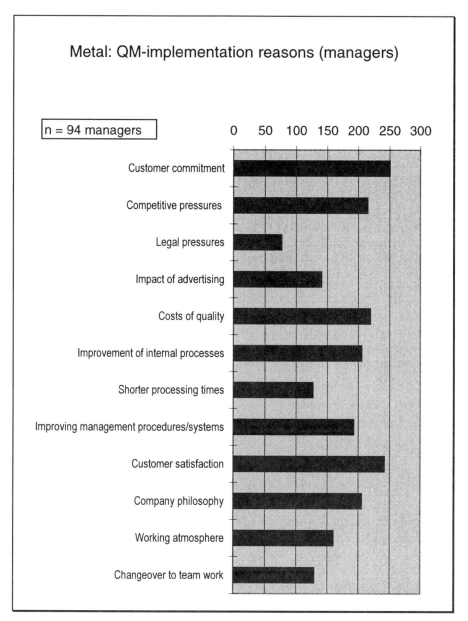

Figure 9: QM-implementation reasons in the metal industry (managers)

In the cumulative evaluation "customer commitment" reaches the highest rating. The introduction of quality management is preponderantly understood by the experts as being reactive, as an adaptation to external demands from customers for ISO-certified quality management. This interpretation is supported by the fact that "competitive pressure" reaches the fourth highest rating. This finding is relativised by the fact that "customer satisfaction" obtains the second highest and "company philosophy" the fifth highest rating. Yet this allows only partially to infer a proactive quality policy. These motives, too, are understood as being reactive, but they do not only include the formal fulfilment of standardised quality assurance procedures but also the fulfilment of concrete quality requirements of important customers.

It is striking that only a middle importance (rank 8) is attributed to the "impact of advertising" of a demonstrated quality system. This rating probably reflects the fact that quality management is meanwhile becoming common as a competitive standard also for SMEs in Europe, that an ISO certificate distinguishes a company less and less from others in the market. More striking, still, is that the interviewed experts attribute the lowest importance to "legal standards" when introducing quality management. Quality management is clearly considered essentially an internal economic and not a public-law standard.

Among the rather internal-company motives are the "costs of quality" on rank three in the foreground. Their identification is considered to be very difficult according to qualitative statements of the interviewed experts, and it is not, as a rule, pursued systematically in the respondent companies. A positive impact of the introduction of quality management on these costs is, thus, rather presumed instead of being based on an operationalised decision criterion.

The expectation of improvements in the operations - "improvement of internal processes" as well as "improving management procedures" - clearly play a role (rank 5 and 6) in the decision to introduce quality management. It is remarkable that this is scarcely connected with "shorter processing times" (rank 10). This coincides with statements that time-effective process improvements through quality management are compensated by the time expenditure for the quality assuring procedures and that the time expenditure for a quality system has represented a barrier for many of the respondent companies.

"Working atmosphere" (7) and "changeover to teamwork" (9) rank relatively low as motives for the implementation of quality management. The qualitative study shows, on the one hand, that especially the work organisation in the respondent companies is driven not primarily by aspects of quality management but much more by others such as economic and technological motives. On the other hand, it turned out in the expert interviews that establishing a quality system does not automatically improve the quality motivation.

Reasons from different functional views

The survey aimed at identifying whether the motivation of the experts for quality management differ according to their managerial function or whether there are significantly different views. Among the interviewed executives 32 were responsible for marketing, 34 for production and 28 for personnel management.

The deviation of the numbers of interviewed functional managers from the number of the surveyed companies (34) results from the fact that especially in some small companies the managerial functions are not very differentiated. The function-specific evaluation of the answers shows the following picture. The graph essentially shows a consonance in the assessment between the functional managers in the surveyed metalworking SMEs. The slightly higher rating of "impact of advertising" by the marketing managers and the "costs of quality" by the production managers hardly appear to be significant. Furthermore, a slightly higher rating of the connection of quality management with a "changeover to teamwork" and an improvement of the "working atmosphere" by the personnel experts compared with the production managers can be recognised.

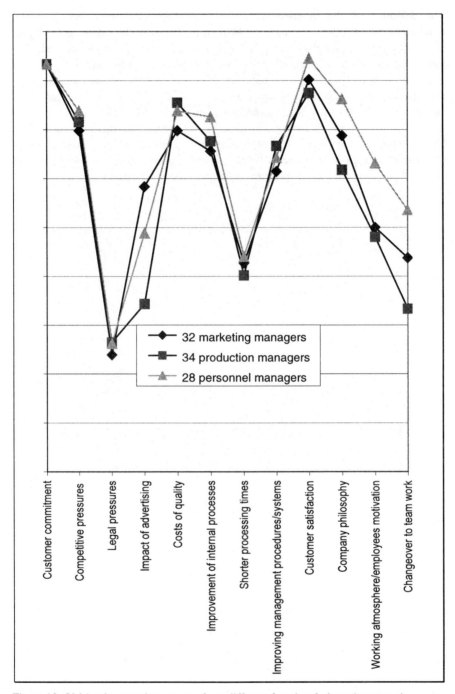

Figure 10: QM-implementation reasons from different functional views (managers)

Reasons at the level of companies

On the basis of averaged values the following picture is produced at a company level regarding the motives for introducing quality management:

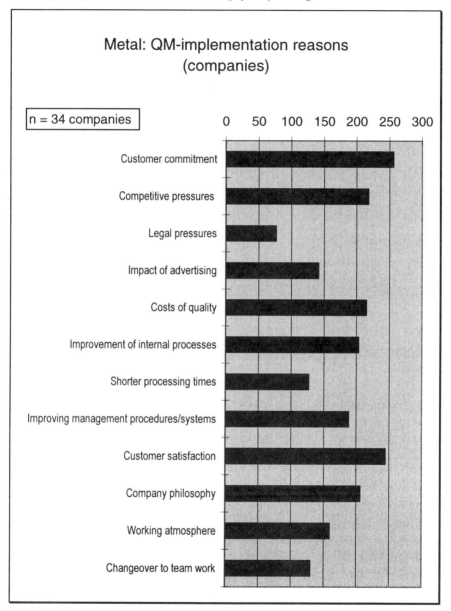

Figure 11: QM-implementation reasons in the metal industry (companies)

Extrapolating from these numbers a hierarchy of motives we obtain the following list:

1. Customer commitment (supplier duty)

2. Customer satisfaction

3. Competitive pressures (new competitive standard)

4. Costs of quality (reducing complaints; nonconformity costs/costs of its correction)

5. Company philosophy

6. Improvement of internal processes (clear working aims; co-operation of the departments)

7. Improving management procedures/systems

8. Working atmosphere/employees motivation

9. Impact of advertising

10. Changeover to team work

11. Shorter processing times

12. Legal pressures (liability precaution)

Qualitative findings: Barriers, critical points, examples of good practice

The following description of qualitative findings about quality concepts of the surveyed enterprises with regard to barriers, critical points and examples of good practice orientates itself to the aim of making practical company experiences and practical management know-how available concerning the implementation of quality management. This is to allow practical key actors to learn from the difficulties of others as well as to prevent them from having to re-invent transferable solutions. Therefore interviewed managers are directly quoted.

To come straight to a general finding: There is *one* ISO standard series for quality management but there is no *one* and only way for a company-specific implementation of quality management other companies only just have to follow. Particularly the introduction of quality-assuring and preventive quality engineering is subject in selection, "timetable" and design to product, procedure and other company specifics provided that the company can plan its quality policy free from external requirements.

A significant modification in the design of company-specific quality concepts of the organisational development results from a sector-specific differentiation of metalworking SMEs in Western Europe which, in addition, leads to country-specific differences in the European area. The - partly country-specific - specialisation strategies of SMEs (for example system development and services, suppliers, penetration of the own production, vertical and horizontal company co-operation) differentiate decisively the organisation and personnel structure of the companies. Also the ISO-certified quality management of SMEs does not coincide with the concrete quality aims and problems these companies need to master in their product, customer and European specialisation strategies. But the latter ones determine concretely the quality-oriented (re-)organisation.

In so far the presented successful individual solutions cannot simply be added up and made into an ideal "timetable". It remains to be the task of the companies to adjust the implementation and improvement of their quality system according to their specific problems and gear it to their specific needs. The survey, however, reveals examples of good practice predominantly in companies which make use of the certification process as a basis and take advantage of the audit cycle as a skeleton schedule for a gradual improvement strategy.

Quality: Traditional and new demands on the metalworking industry in the EU

Traditionally, in the metalworking industry high demands on quality are related to the *products* and defined by *technology*, technical standards, legal safety prescriptions and monitoring instances etc.. Special regulations and quality-assurance systems have long been in force for segments requiring a high level of safety like medicine, nuclear and military technology. The general liability law and the product liability law support these requirements.

Several tendencies have not only extended and sharpened these quality requirements in the metalworking sector, they also have suggested a redefinition of the task "quality" by the companies.

- The jurisdiction in Europe is not anymore content with the conformity of products with valid technical standards with respect to the responsibility of companies, but it requires the observation of the state-of-the-art technology, the expectations of the general public as well as the after-sale observation of the product. The European directive on the reform of the product liability points into the same direction.

- Accelerated technical innovation and shorter product life cycles suggest an increasingly preventive quality assurance to the companies themselves.

- The harmonised standards in Europe require extensive documentation and expressively connect methods for the assessment of product conformity to standardised quality systems of the ISO 9000 series

- The mainly industrial customers of the metalworking sector require more economical and customised products and services, and they increasingly expect their suppliers to have a quality system. Here, the large carmakers are trail blazers.

- At the international level, West-European metalworking enterprises must compete with the quality of technologically highly developed products and with the quality of services, while the market for standardised products is increasingly covered by suppliers from the newly industrialised countries. Also small and medium-sized enterprises increasingly operate in new, also transnational forms of work division and company co-operation, and therefore need reliable forms of quality co-operation.

Due to these tendencies small and medium-sized enterprises increasingly try to manage the task "quality" in a comprehensive quality system.

ISO 9000 and metalworking SMEs

The interviewed managers *all* agreed that the decisive motive for the *introduction* of the ISO system is the fact that the certificate is an *external business prerequisite* of their company, either as a direct customer demand or a competition standard. This assessment was declared to have superseded the expectation of a direct competitive advantage.

Naturally the ISO standards put the same requirements on all companies. Therefore the barriers and critical points which occur in the companies when fulfilling these requirements can still easily be generalised. But as soon as it comes to using the certification process as a basis for their own quality policy, the investigated companies take different ways the less they merely aim at the external effect of the certificate.

Barriers

Expenditure of time or: "paperwork"

For many surveyed companies the expenditure of time for the systematisation and documentation of operational processes according to ISO elements creates a considerable barrier. This is true for both the preparation of the initial certification as well as for the maintenance and actualisation of the documentation with regard to re-audits. This problem particularly increases in the following cases:

- Simultaneously the competitive pressure requires of the company and of its management measures and/or programmes for the improvement of the cost situation and/or the shortening the process time.

- Simultaneously the company has to master fast growth processes, market-induced re-assessments and other re-structuring processes.

- The company handles a very large range of products, has to master a rapid product change, has to up-date its technology.

With a view of management on the company structures concerned, the barrier "expenditure of time" often means

- additional or too much work load for the management staff
- additional or too much work load for the employees.

Statements

"The main difficulty was the increased bureaucracy and the continuous strive of the personnel to adjust to this. All employees as well as executives have several duties caused by a cost reduction program and resulting to a lack of time for conforming with the QAS requirements. (316/Greece/61 employees/certification < 2 years/ISO 9001)"

"The company is small enough to survive without formal work scheduling. There is constant interaction between functions. However this will become a problem as the company expands and to overcome this a process planning programme is currently being designed." (413/Ireland/15 employees/aspiring certification/ISO 9002)

"Shorter processing and delivery times were and still remain one of the principal goals of the company, but they were not a reason for deciding the implementation of the Quality Assurance system." (311/Greece/146 employees/certification > 2 years/ISO 9001)

"The standardisation inadequacy in the heating and water supply market causes a wide range of accessories that we produce. This way most often it is difficult even for the customer to tell us exactly what he/she wants. For special orders, unlike the standard product, particular attention is given and information is needed, about the operability of the accessory, the surroundings and the planning of the production process takes place in accordance with the samples and the plans." (312/Greece/47 employees/certification < 2 years/ISO 9002)

"In the beginning you make enemies in the company, both at the top and at the bottom. You "meddle" with management responsibilities." (114/F R Germany/22 employees/aspiring certification/ISO 9001)

Quite often it becomes obvious that the *same weaknesses* of the company structures are responsible for difficulties in tackling competition requirements and internal alterations, on the one hand, as well as in quality management, on the other hand, and that there only seems to be a "double pressure", for example:

- In small enterprises too much work load on management staff results from a lack of structuring and systematisation of management tasks which are performed by only one or a few persons. This leads to an accumulation of case-to-case decisions and prevents delegation of tasks relieving management. In bigger companies frictional loss and clumsiness of rigid hierarchies and/or unclear function responsibilities cause too much work load on managers.

- Too much work load on employees is due to "bit-by-bit" and/or *unsystematic* instructions. In bigger companies *too narrow* work requirement profiles, when e.g. work is divided into very small steps, prevent the integration of new tasks which then only appear to be additional work.

- There is no underlying systematic evaluation of company strengths in product and technology policy, no consolidation and standardisation of reliable components, no strategy.

In cases like these, elements of quality systems do not occur as *contributions* to a solution of company tasks, which they could be by nature: e.g. clear task assignment, reliable information and steering channels, quality-oriented product, technology and process strategies. But the assurance of a quality system is seen as an *additional* task induced externally which is to be mastered *formally*.

Other companies show opposite experiences in that setting up a quality system supports restructuring necessary in other areas of the company.

Statements

> *"The good thing about the ISO standards is that order processing and work tasks are to be documented. This saves time because you do not have to personally give instructions all over again for every single case. And it makes replacement of an absent employee easier." (113/F R Germany/20 employees/aspiring certification/ISO 9001)*

> *"We decided to build the new factory unit at the same time that we introduced the new quality system according to ISO 9002. People can say that both projects were planned together and at the same time. We achieved Quality Management and simultaneously we also achieved production efficiency." (513/Portugal/130 employees/aspiring certification/ISO 9001)*

Cost expenditure or: "uneconomic"

The costs for obtaining the certificate and for maintaining the quality system meet with structurally thin capital resources in SMEs. The surveyed companies draw different, even contrary conclusions from this:

- dissatisfaction with the direct costs and marketing effects

- acceptance as "the price for the entry into the market"

- treatment as a strategic investment

Dissatisfaction with direct costs and marketing effects often fails to see that only the implementation of quality systems allow a more exact recording of cost sources and particularly the identification of nonconformity costs which of course do not disappear with identification. Other objections insist on closely counterbalancing nonconformity costs and costs of nonconformity prevention which is only possible with strictly standardised processes or process elements. Especially with highly complex and necessarily flexible processes in the metalworking industry and particularly in mechanical engineering this is not always possible.

Acceptance of the costs of the quality system as "the price for the market entry" points into the direction of a strategic calculation; it does, however, limit itself to a strategy of preventing the loss of customers and exclusion from the market.

The pro-active treatment of quality system costs as a strategic investment complements direct cost savings with long-term advantages which cannot be measured as easily:

- the prevention of direct nonconformity costs with the effects of company know-how which has developed over the years, improved customer satisfaction and a better market standing

- the direct reduction of control costs with the effects of a higher job satisfaction and motivation, more effective work and reliable supplier relationships

- the reduction of administrative costs in the narrow sense with the effects of clear and solid organisation and process structures.

Statements

"Quality is everything - where is economy in ISO?" (611/Sweden/110 employees/aspiring certification/ISO 9001)

"We do not believe that reasons of administration or responsibilities allocation are very important. We do not believe that without the ISO 9001

we would lose customers." (314/Greece/170 employees/aspiring certification/ISO 9001)

"We weren't going to get business otherwise." (711/United Kingdom/44 employees/certification > 2 years/ISO 9001)

"With quality management the marketing manager needs no longer justify to the customer. For this reason the certificate is crucial. But this does not cover the expenditure of time and costs for the certificate. In order to get a 'return on invest' we have decided to develop the "means" quality management at all levels towards TQM." (111/F R Germany/167 employees/certification < 2 years/ISO 9001)

"In this business the important factors to the customer are supply continuity and process capability. Good QM systems support this at a price worth paying." (712/United Kingdom/120 employees/aspiring certification/ISO 9002)

"Changing over from quality control to quality management is a question of economy but it is not only a question of economy. Not only was there a big department which constantly checked and controlled. It also gave rise to anger among staff: They grumble and grumble." (115/F R Germany/520 employees/certification > 2 years/ISO 9001)

"Implementing quality management systems will automatically instigate a review as to how business is currently performed and stimulate the thought process as to how it can be performed better in the future. Hence as well as the customer benefits, proactively the implementation of a structured Quality System should simplify processes, increase focus and ultimately reduce cost in the long term." (712/United Kingdom/120 employees/aspiring certification/ISO 9002)

Critical analysis of the ISO standards

At the beginning of the certification process, ISO standards were or are treated with scepticism in many surveyed companies. But also experienced companies control the maintenance and development of their quality system in a critical analysis of the ISO specifications in relation to the company-specific quality objectives and quality conditions.

There are three critical points in the ISO system or in the weighting of its elements from the point of view of the interviewed metalworking SMEs:

- orientation towards the internal problems of organisation and information flow in the large-scale industry - particularly from the point of view of small enterprises
  In this view, the formalisation secures multi-grade operations in big industries, but it is less suitable to improve the short, often informal paths in SMEs.

- a lack of flexibility - particularly from the point of view of enterprises with made-to-order production and complex project operations
  The department-oriented degrees of demonstration ISO 9001, 9002, 9003 do not correspond with the specialisation profiles and co-operative relations of SMEs. Quality strengths of SMEs in the metal industry such as customer-oriented flexibility and rapid product innovation can even be constrained.

- insufficient relation to the sector

The criticism from the metalworking companies of "insufficient relation to the sector" seems slightly unfair in a sector comparison since the metal-related vehicles construction has substantial influence in the development of ISO standards, in the certification practice and in the design of external consulting and training issues. The criticism on the "rigidity" and "lack of flexibility" of the ISO system mentioned in some - mainly small - companies can be contrasted with the experience of other - partly also small companies - that the - frequently first - standardisation of company processes opens up planning reliability and scheduling freedom and leads to a clear delimitation of those functional areas in the company where it has to secure flexibility potentials.

But basically this criticism is a productive scepticism as long as it does not reduce the quality system to a sort of small version for small enterprises but leads to a concrete adaptation to quality-decisive interfaces and processes of the company. It is striking, however, that some interviewed managers emphasise in their answers that standards for ISO procedures have nothing to do with technical standards. Hence it is highly probable that this incorrect differentiation is maintained in company practice.

Statements

"In big companies they have to go through umpteen floors for every trifle."
(113/F R Germany/20 employees/aspiring certification/ISO 9001)

"Since 10 or 15 years ago our customers became more and more rigorous as for quality standards, so I have to say that the search for quality did not start with the certification process according to ISO 9000. A company that

produces, for instance, pressure reservoirs must have high quality standards ... In my opinion, perhaps one of the main reasons to implement quality management according to ISO 9002 was that it was a fashionable management idea." (514/Portugal/431 employees/certification > 2 years/ISO 9002)

"Quality management system has not brought anything special concerning reorganisation. But we have bought some new machines. We are collecting our mistakes and flows from here and there. If we notice that something is missing that is possible to correct with new machines we are ready to invest." (213/Finland/55 employees/certification > 2 years/ISO 9002)

"The German technical standards, especially DIN and the German legal regulations are much more precise and stricter than the CE standards, which compared to those are elastic clauses, let alone the ISO standards" (113/F R Germany/20 employees/aspiring certification/ISO 9001)

"There are of course special cases where you have to deviate from existing procedures in order to avoid unnecessary obstacles because practice orientation is priority. Procedure instructions have not been devised for every conceivable process." (111/F R Germany/167 employees/certification < 2 years/ISO 9001)

ISO process as a basis for tailor-made quality systems

The least problems with certification requirements and the highest satisfaction with the practical benefits of the ISO standards have been voiced by those questioned companies which follow one or several of the following guidelines for the certification and in the ISO process under way:

- using the preparation for the initial or for the re-audits as an internal check-up

- using the audit cycle or the standardised size of demonstration of the ISO 9000 series as steps towards the realisation of company-specific quality objectives or a continuous improvement strategy of the quality system

- handle the tasks for the implementation and development of the quality system by a cross-departmental project team with increasing participation of employees.

Examples of good practice are found especially in companies where implementation of quality management was part of a strategy of innovation and new entry in new markets.

Statements

"ISO standards are useful as a checklist." (113/F R Germany/20 employees/aspiring certification/ISO 9001)

"Our certification process did not result from acquiring and implementing a package of guidelines delivered by any consultant company. It was a years long, slowly but assuredly evolving process. Actually, a great number of organisational changes occurred as a result of several years of practical experience. Certification according to the system consubstantiated in ISO 9000 series of standards was just the formalisation of a seven years long process, during which the necessary changes were being made. There were no problems in implementing the system of rules and written procedures, since the company hitherto had a formal system in force. Our first quality handbook dates from 1983. Since then, every effort was made in training development, that, in association with the progressive steadiness of the company culture, afforded favourable conditions for the implementation of ISO standards and no difficulties arouse that must be pointed out." (512/Portugal/85 employees/certification > 2 years/ISO 9001)

"Setting up the DIN ISO 9001 the company decided to examine all quality-related areas very carefully. Because high expenditure on quality assurance is part of the corporate strategy. Therefore, a specific team with external consultants was established. The method we used was value engineering. Apart from the department of quality assurance, all departments and areas were reviewed. The team was composed of managers: the production manager, the administrative manager, the project manager, the quality manager, computing/organisation. This team found out that the company needed restructuring if it was to stay in the market." (115/F R Germany/520 employees/certification > 2 years/ISO 9001)

"Certification is considered as a precondition of good practices and it is not emphasised separately. Today we consider quality system as an essential part of the processes and functions and the work processes include the quality system requirements." (211/Finland/38 (1250) employees/certification > 2 years/ISO 9001)

"Our targets evolved according to the implementation phases of our Quality Management System. Our first target was to improve products and services quality and to be certified according to the ISO 9002 standard. Our second target was to be certified according to ISO 9001 standard and supply EU markets. Our present commitment is to monitor improvement programs in order to obtain TQM accreditation." (511/Portugal/181 employees/certification > 2 years/ISO 9001)

"ISO cannot deliver many of the proposed benefits of quality assurance. This is because a company could be quality assured merely by hiring a few quality inspectors and by managing the quality function separately from the rest of the company. In this instance benefits such as improvement of internal processes and new corporate culture, would not materialise. ISO can only deliver substantial benefits if it is introduced in conjunction with WCM and CIP." (411/Ireland/150 employees/certification > 2 years/ISO 9001/2)

"The basic goal of the company is towards total quality. The first step happened with the ISO 9002 certification and now we are trying to establish the ISO 9001 standardisation. After the certification the main concern was focused on cross-departmental processing in order to achieve the best co-operation among personnel of all departments. We think that setting a quality award for the best department could be helpful for improving teamwork." (312/Greece/47 employees/certification < 2 years/ISO 9002)

"First when we started to build a quality system we took a man from outside the company who was unfamiliar with our processes. So it was a mistake. We had a wrong method. The process was not implemented in the organisation. After that experience we started to think among us what to do. The employees know the work of their own. But to put it on the paper is more difficult. So we took our employees with us and made work instructions together. Similarly this concerns clerical workers. This job took a long time but it was worth to do. Quality management system has influenced positively the working atmosphere and motivation. We have done working instructions together, all the staff." (213/Finland/55 employees/certification > 2 years/ISO 9002)

"One of our strengths in quality assurance is the acceptance and use of the procedural instructions. The reason for this is that they have been written by the personnel conducting each task so that they are familiar with the process and feel that they only undertake the responsibility they can and not the one that the management want them to." (313/Greece/260 employees/aspiring certification/ISO 9002)

"In order to face the European Common Market in 1993 and all the challenges connected with it, in 1990 the company decided to adopt a strategic development plan, which meant an aggressive and innovative policy. With the facilities afforded by PEDIP - a EU structural fund meant for the development and updating of the Portuguese industry -, we decided to implement a quality system that could reduce complaints and product returns, increasing at the same time clients satisfaction. Concerned about the Common Market, we decided to invest in quality before all companies in this sector." (513/Portugal/130 employees/aspiring certification/ISO 9001)

Metalworking SMEs and the implementation of quality management

None of the surveyed companies refereed to the introduction of a quality system for the certification according to ISO 9000 as the *decisive* impetus for extensive alterations in the organisation and process structure. ISO 9000 was conceded to have had at least an essential impetus by an exceptional two suppliers of security-related products who have changed their quality system which was previously based on military standards. In all the other cases the quality system according to ISO 9000 was made use of as systematisation and standardisation, a merely selective improvement and, above all, documentation of

- existing and successful organisation and operations structures of companies

- organisation and process structures updated for other reasons.

Various and partly extensive steps towards restructuring the company organisation and processes and those forms of work which are related to product and process quality were however identified in all of the surveyed companies. However, they do not represent a mere translation of quality objectives or requirements of the quality system. It therefore does not seem to be appropriate to interpret and assess them as development steps in a development continuum to use it as a basis for a one-dimensional company comparison. Companies exercise e.g. TQM-oriented teamwork, yet at the same time they have great difficulties in documenting the processes for the certification. Other companies, which have long been certified, are only now starting to review their organisation structure.

In most surveyed enterprises there is a correlation between reorganisation and quality management where, depending on the company structure, technical and necessary economic alterations of processes and work forms are adjusted to quality demands and quality objectives and, conversely, quality-induced optimisation possibilities for processes and work forms are examined from the point of view of their economic justifiability. In some cases it has to be said, however, that management staff do not realise or systematically identify these connections between process and work organisation and quality management.

From the interviews with the managers some aspects can be generalised influencing the complex decision-making process for the company-specific design of the process and work organisation, on the one hand, and quality management, on the other.

• A considerable number of interviewed managers are sceptical against the monocausal reorganisation imperatives of the "ISO and TQM gurus". However, the degree of information and the subjective approach of the managers play an important role here.

• Especially small enterprises try first of all to consolidate and advance their structures, which have developed over the years, with the requirements to build up and document their quality management.

• Cross-departmental management (e.g. project management) and teamwork at the operating level of plant engineering or with products which can only be handled as projects is more likely induced by production methods than by the imperative of quality management.

• Below these sectoral specifics the product orientation is an important reason for the technical and organisational development of processes and work forms and for the decision on what kind of new quality engineering is implemented in these structures and what kind of quality-promoting reorganisations of work are carried out. Product specifics induce company-specific weighing of quality-related interfaces and their design. On the other hand, market or customer-induced product change and shorter product life cycles in general are given as decisive reasons for the implementation of quality management and preventive quality methods.

A significant modification in the design of company-specific quality concepts of the organisation development results from different performing or manufacturing penetration, from the status of the company within the value-added chain and from the nature of the supplier relationships and company co-operations. This point deserves special attention because it concerns a sector-specific differentiation of SMEs which, in addition, leads to country-specific differences in the European area. As relevant differentiations of these operating conditions for quality-related organisational tasks the following can be indicated for this sample of surveyed companies:

- Producers of complex final products with a high performance penetration are facing the most extensive internal organisational tasks of quality-related co-operation among functional areas and hierarchy levels in the company.

- System producers in a vertical division of labour and/or with a network of suppliers need to co-ordinate internally mainly directive functions in a quality-related way and externally comprehensive customer and supplier relationships.

- SMEs in horizontal company co-operations are facing organisational tasks of quality-related external allocation and co-operation of company functions - e.g. joint distribution - and the appropriate internal auxiliary work.

- Supplying companies concentrate mainly on functions of manufacturing and they predominantly have to implement externally defined quality requirements.

Effects of quality management on the organisation and process structure

The complexity of motives for the company-specific design of the organisation and process structure under quality imperatives advises caution with the extrapolation of generalised tendencies. However, with this reservation the following qualitative findings of the survey on quality-related (re)organisation tendencies emerge:

1. The implementation of quality management normally alters the tasks, the structure and routine of company management.

2. At the middle and operative level quality-induced cross-departmental work and teamwork within the departments can mainly be found in rather dispositional functions up- and downstream the production. In these functional areas an integration of different hierarchy levels also takes place.

3. Production itself appears to be the critical point in the implementation of cross-departmental responsibility for quality. The reason most frequently given is the difference in technical quality requirements with regard to product and manufacturing. The changes at the production level focus on the relocation of quality control to a previous stage, partly by means of modern test and control technologies, and on the reorganisation of the material flow and of maintenance. The extension of job profiles refers above all to the integration of operator self-inspection and is predominantly considered as a difficult and lengthy process.

4. The implementation of customer-related quality concepts at the production level still appears to be hard to operationalise.

5. Whereas the imperatives of quality management - as guidelines for the design of the internal-company relationships - are implemented with scepticism and

above all in a balanced conjunction with other company guidelines, the surveyed companies show a stronger orientation of the organisation of the external relationships to aspects of quality management.

Management

Modern quality management is a top-down task. The ISO standards face all surveyed enterprises with the tasks to define the quality responsibilities and tasks in a company-specific way, to co-ordinate them with other management tasks, to define and organise managing-delegating relationships, determine personnel responsibilities and implement them into the management structures or re-structure them and add managerial staff if necessary. From the point of view of the interviewed managers all of these tasks have been solved satisfactorily in almost all of the surveyed companies. Criticism about lacking support of quality management by or in the company management was an exception. Also co-operation problems of the quality management with other management functions were seldom mentioned. A specific research interest of the survey as to identify by interviewing managers of different functions whether there are function-specific diverging views of the tasks of quality management in the company can be considered to be answered essentially in the negative. Within the respondent companies there was no significant difference in how the executives viewed the company-specific tasks and role of quality management.

There are, however, significant differences between the companies. In the institutionalisation of quality management as a management task the surveyed companies have made quite different *organisational decisions*. These decisions are based on different and differently combined decisive factors. The differences in the organisation of the management task "quality" can be seen at the following levels:

- the design and weighting of the tasks of quality representatives between tasks of classical quality control and total quality management

- the position and role of the quality representative within the management structure of the company

- organisation and institutions of information flow and decision making within the management as regards the integration of quality management

- person-related influencing factors

In *weighting the tasks* of the quality representatives between classical quality control and total quality management, not only the development state of quality management in the different companies play a role but also particularly the product and production type and the resulting quality methods (e.g. rather statistical inspection techniques in mass/serial production - rather preventive methods in plant engineering/single-piece production).

The *position and role* of the quality in the management of the surveyed companies varies basically in the following types:

- full-time quality manager versus quality manager with other management functions (general manager, marketing function, design function, personnel-related function),

- cross-occupational, equal or subordinate function of the quality representative in the management hierarchy.

Not only the development state of quality management in the company plays a role here but also the size of the company and the existing management structure. For example, particularly in small enterprises the quality tasks can be found in personal union with general management functions. The specific role of the quality manager is more narrowly defined if quality tasks are integrated into existing team structures of business management than if they are integrated into departmental structures (overhead). Finally, the importance of the formal organisational role of the person responsible for quality is strongly relativised in company practice by the institutions of the information flow in the management, the decision-making and the integration of quality management into the general business management.

Person-related influencing factors were identified particularly in companies which have hired a new person for the new task of quality management. The quality approach of the new manager induces a redefinition also of other management functions. Another observation during the interviews suggests that the previous management function of the quality manager has an influence on his/her definition of the task: many quality managers in the surveyed companies come from the departments "development & design" and "production planning"; relatively often the main tasks and/or the best implementation conditions were seen in these departments. This can only to a certain extent be interpreted as a person-induced influencing factor because a strong technical orientation can always be found in metalworking small and mediums sized enterprises.

As regards quality-related *reorganisation processes* of management structures in the surveyed companies, scepticism can be found against abstract requirements for "flat hierarchies". In terms of the reasons for reorganisation measures at the management level the company weighs, in correlation,

- quality management-related decisive factors against

- factors which relate to company growth, costs, products, manufacturing penetration.

There is a growing influence of new co-operation forms especially with suppliers or customers on the company-specific management structure in metalworking SMEs. In these cases management functions are executed by the companies in a division of labour so that also tasks of the quality management need to be co-ordinated at a cross-company level. Some supplier companies in the sample represent another type. Here the customer determines not only essential specifications for the product development, the distribution etc. but develops also the basic features of the quality concept, so that quality management in the supplier companies is predominantly an operating task.

Quality manager

One quarter of the interviewed companies, at the most, still defines the tasks and the role of the quality manager traditionally as executive of the department "quality control". The analysis also shows that a lot of these companies give cross-departmental responsibility to the quality manager. Because cost pressure and competition demand a fast elimination of identified nonconformity sources and, therefore, require an efficiently organised influence of the quality manager on other company functions.

Examples of good practice occur mostly in companies where there is a cross-departmental definition and organisation of the task of the quality manager. However, in most cases this did not base on the fact that the implementation of quality management lead to such a management organisation. More frequently it was the reverse way: the new managerial function of quality management was implemented into already networked management structures.

Particularly relevant to the perspective of this survey is the finding that the new quality management task stimulates in some companies the reorganisation of the personnel management task. The quality manager gives impetus particularly for personnel development more often than the more administrative personnel department, in some companies personnel development is entirely the responsibility of the quality manager.

Statements

"Quality management is involved in every innovation. This applies to new design, new procedures, new materials. Product-related technical innovations for cost reduction or shortening of production times are surveyed in terms of quality demands before they are entered into offers to customers. So: quality management is involved in every innovation. Whether this works also the other way round is a question which also depends on cost considerations." (115/F R Germany/520 employees/certification > 2 years/ISO 9001)

"The implementation of Quality Management induces organisational change. The Quality Procedures were made with the collaboration of all departments and interfunctional responsibilities were written in those

procedures. We used teamwork for the Contract Acceptance and to solve Quality problems of the products and to improve our organisation whenever weak points were found. In the scope of the Quality Project, interdepartmental commissions were set up for the different areas, as, for instance, the Marketing and Production Departments or the Department for Human Resources/Training Activities. These commissions meet regularly." (511/Portugal/181 employees/certification > 2 years/ISO 9001)

"All the members of the management of the company belong to the Quality Commissions. All the members of the management of the company attended the Internal Audit course. I think Internal Audits are very important to improve the procedures and increase quality." (511/Portugal/181 employees/certification > 2 years/ISO 9001)

"There used to be big meetings every month where everything about customers and markets was discussed, but that didn't really lead anywhere. Now, there is a weekly meeting of all product-line managers. And it works." (114/F R Germany/22 employees/aspiring certification/ISO 9001)

"The close relation between marketing management and customers is very important because it allows us to get "feed back" that is very important to improve product quality. Participation in the weekly meetings of the Board of Directors dedicated to "Product Quality" is a very important way of personal involvement." (513/Portugal/130 employees/aspiring certification/ISO 9001)

"Normally, demand for new technology comes up in the respective departments and then it is a question of funds. Settling the priorities between the departments and the cross-departmental benefit and effects could well be done by departmental meeting. This is also true for EDP-solutions for data registration and administration. But sometimes the quality management is at least a catalyst. For example purchasing/material management: 100% control of all externally manufactured components. The data registration of nonconformity and the nonconformity rate has so far been written by hand. The task of the quality management for supplier inspection instigated the necessary changing over to EDP. This requirement already resulted from the strong outsourcing of the company. The quality system only absorbs the information from all other departments. It monitors and moderates the problem solutions in the

various areas together with the responsible staff." (111/F R Germany/167 employees/certification < 2 years/ISO 9001)

Management teams

Particularly in mechanical engineering companies, the implementation of the quality management task met with already existing cross-departmental management structures either in the company organisation structure or as a method in the process organisation. The sample of surveyed companies includes cases of product-line or divisional management structures, matrix organisation and project management structures. Crucial reorganisation imperatives for the quality-oriented company management had already been fulfilled here so that the quality manager has again a certain special responsibility.

Statements

"Reorganisation has changed the way of management and the way to organise projects. Sales and marketing have became more close to each other. The company is aiming to integrate functions in different units. For ex. to integrate design and product development so that it would be similar in different units. Work scheduling has changed. Before there were many different schedules for one project. Now schedules are integrated and it is much easier to manage. Also scheduling has improved." (211/Finland/38 (1250) employees/certification > 2 years/ISO 9001)

"Since we produce predominantly single pieces cross-departmental project handling has long been common practice. The project manager usually belongs to the design/development department. Once the order is worked out, it is passed on to the project team set up by responsible staff from all the departments involved. The project teams are not so much composed of heads of departments but rather of staff responsible at the operative level, i.e. designing engineers, supervisors from production and assembly. This project team has the overhead function up to the starting up at the customer's. This has become more regular with quality management but actually we have always worked like this because in plant engineering common sense dictates project management. The project team does not only consist of bosses." (111/F R Germany/167 employees/certification < 2 years/ISO 9001)

"Purchasing, order handling and sales used to be separated. In connection with quality management, an organisation structure was developed according to product-line groups headed by 2 responsible people each.

Design remains an extra department supervising a project team where most of the designs come in. The responsible staff for the other product-line groups have also design know-how so that interface problems have not occurred so far. Purchasing and material management/inventory have been systematised. Based on systematic incoming-lot control a supplier inspection is worked out. This teamwork combines ideally with quality management. And we have become faster. With teamwork many problems do not occur in the first place. You push each other." (114/F R Germany/22 employees/aspiring certification/ISO 9001)

"For virtually every order there is a technical contract with the customer including detailed construction requirements and construction drawings. Before the contract is made, the project team knows virtually everything including the dates. There is no other way to handle such a complex technical project. A cross-departmental project team is established for every order involving a responsible person for quality. Involving employees of the different departments in different project pools puts a high demand on co-operation. This is a pool which is created for every project. It can happen that a head of department is sitting all by himself in his office because his staff are involved in the different pools." (115/F R Germany/520 employees/certification > 2 years/ISO 9001)

Middle management

In accordance with the theoretical imperatives of quality management several respondents emphasised the key position of middle management for the implementation of the quality system. Others reported that in middle management the implementation of quality management meets with biggest barriers at least temporarily.

Before trying to generalise quality management-induced tendencies to change the role of the middle management in the surveyed companies, one finding of the survey is to be retained that the category "middle management" particularly in this company segment - according to sector specifics and size - comprises extremely different task profiles and hierarchy levels. In small enterprises the middle management, traditionally the "supervisors", carry out leading functions especially in directing and technical functions. Similar characteristics can be found in some sub-supplying companies concentrating on manufacturing. In these cases the findings about new quality-induced management tasks cover to some extend the changes in the task profiles of this group of staff. In bigger companies, particularly those with large design and process planning departments, the operating element within the job profile of this group of staff increase.

Despite the blurred outlines of this "middle level" the statements of the interviewed managers of the companies prove its key position for a successful implementation of modern quality management. A movement running into the opposite direction has to be mastered in the companies:

1. The formalisation and documentation of quality-assuring procedures concerns particularly this group of staff. Some responding companies set written work instructions only up to this level. The formalisation of tasks is considered in some cases at least temporarily as a restriction of decision making and authority in work scheduling and as a devaluation of specialist knowledge and professional experience. Very often this view of the "effects" of quality management meets with even more drastic changes of the task profile resulting from the introduction of computer-aided cross-company or department-specific control systems. The quality management key word "flatter hierarchies" is perceived as a threat to status.

2. On the other hand, the interviewed executives emphasise that quality management requires new and extended skills from the "middle level":

   • imparting quality aims of the company, customer demands and product requirements to staff as a guideline for workplace-specific quality requirements

   • motivating a proactive quality consciousness of staff to identify the causes of nonconformities and process weaknesses

   • representing quality requirements of the own work areas dowards related departments and for the improvement of the quality system

   • identifying skill needs of staff, ensuring in-service training and supporting the practical use of skills of staff.

About half of the interviewed experts were aware of the necessity to transform traditional authority into co-operative competency. The implementation is still in its infancy in the interviewed companies.

Statements

"The actual state is as follows: There is no job description for employees below supervisors. Wherever a possibility of failure in conformity exists there is a job description." (316/Greece/61 employees/certification < 2 years/ISO 9001)

"For the preventive maintenance, which is controlled by the results of the statistical process control, it was not only necessary to train staff but old supervisor structures ("secret experience-based knowledge") and

competition structures had to be overcome. There were 5 to 6 people who were put on a pedestal. This triggered the motivation of capable young specialists to advance in their career. The practical use of new specialist knowledge requires new co-operation techniques. The new people do pass on the new knowledge." (112/F R Germany/90 employees/certification < 2 years/ISO 9002)

"Only the big companies have problems with hierarchies and official channels. But sometimes we small companies make our experiences. When a supervisor was absent due to illness I myself discussed the whole project with the people and I said: 'Now you have to manage it yourselves'. And that revealed the difference: Normally they got their instruction only bit by bit." (113/F R Germany/20 employees/aspiring certification/ISO 9001)

"I go to the manufacturing supervisor to ensure the manufacturability of the design." (114/F R Germany/22 employees/aspiring certification/ISO 9001)

"The superiors have to motivate the quality consciousness of staff. The employees have a treasure of experiences which we have to dig up. At the production level we have established small groups to make up teams." (115/F R Germany/520 employees/certification > 2 years/ISO 9001)

Work organisation

The following details focus on the organisation of the direct production of goods and services in the surveyed companies. They deliberately leave out special internal organisation forms of implementing quality management such as quality circles.

In terms of quality management-related reorganisation of the process organisation, work forms and job profiles the following points can be retained:

1. At the middle and operative levels quality-induced cross-departmental work or departmental teamwork can mainly be found in rather dispositional functions up- and downstream the production. The focus of the critical examination of processes and work organisation and of reorganisation measures is on the interfaces between external- and internal-company processes: contract inspection in terms of specific customer requirements and the internal capability to fulfil them offer-oriented as well as manufacturable design,

purchasing (supplier relationship) and material management, distribution and service.

2. Production itself appears to be the critical point in the implementation of cross-departmental responsibility for quality. The reason most frequently given is the difference in technical quality requirements with regard to product and manufacturing.

3. The changes at the production level focus on the relocation of quality control to a previous stage, partly by means of modern testing and control technologies, and on the reorganisation of the material flow and of maintenance. These changes in work organisation and job profiles go frequently along with the implementation of (computer-aided) production technologies and are therefore not only quality- but also at least to the same extend technology-induced. As a critical point in the implementation of modern, also preventive quality assurance methods as well as the appropriate work instructions and documenting tasks for the operators it was indicated that, for the time being, quality management moves away from existing specialist and experience-based knowledge of the operators. According to the interviewed managers it is therefore crucial to impart to operators the effects and the benefits of these methods.

4. The extension of job profiles refers above all to the introduction of operator self-inspection and is predominantly considered as a difficult and lengthy process. Decisive for the success is the work organisational and mental mastering of the tension between traditional and partly remaining external inspection and self-inspection.

5. The implementation of customer-oriented quality concepts at the production level still appears to be hard to operationalise. The sector-specific technological complexity of the demands of industrial customers was the reason given by interviewed managers. At the production level this leads to abstract technical specifications as quality requirements which can hardly be related to customer benefits and the requirements for the use of the final product. It is worth mentioning, however, that many of the surveyed companies - suppliers of the final product as well as suppliers - cited the consciousness of staff about the decisive value of their work contribution to customer satisfaction as a critical point in the implementation of quality management at the operative production level.

Inter-departmental work organisation and departmental teamwork

In the qualitative analysis of the practice of metalworking SMEs, work-organisational imperatives of the theory of quality management turn out to be problematic terms. This is particularly true for the term "teamwork".

- Many interviewed managers share the scepticism against a normative deduction of teamwork in the process organisation from quality management.

- In many cases "teamwork" is only a new name for the unchanged work division in the company.

- Many managers associate with "teamwork" not so much the practical work organisation but the social interrelation of the hierarchy levels and the social behaviour of the status groups.

More closely related to the issue of quality-oriented reorganisation measures of the work organisation are the following findings:

- Especially small enterprises see no need for changing their clear processes and department structures. Quality management does not introduce but systemise co-operation that was informal before.

- Only in exceptional cases "structural conservatism" is the reason for the prudence in introducing teamwork, in most cases cost and time aims are taken into account.

- While cross-departmental teamwork exists mainly at the managerial level, at the operative level teamwork structures are predominantly departmental. This is rarely an impact of quality management but based on technical requirements of the metalworking industry. Traditionally, teamwork among specialists within departments and multi-functional job profiles can be found.

- Several managers denied a monocausal deduction of departmental and cross-departmental co-operation from quality management. They saw predominantly product-related reasons, the innovation of internal information, control and production technologies as well as customer orientation.

Customer orientation or the improvement of the company's capability to fulfil specified customer demands flexibly at the same time keeping quality demands was clearly the main drive for companies to introduce teamwork. Therefore this restructuring process comprises first of all the up- and down steam departments of production.

Statements

"Teamwork does not exist. We do have flat structures at the management level but we still implement vertical structures in the production in order to save money." (313/Greece/260 employees/aspiring certification/ISO 9002)

"We already have teamwork, it's nothing new. In plant engineering you have to work hand in hand anyway, and here you can keep track of everything." (113/F R Germany/20 employees/aspiring certification/ISO 9001)

"Teamwork exists in our company amongst different departments but not for each person individually. All departments begin the job simultaneously which leads to one total assembling machine. There has to be a physical flow related to the above procedure. There is no close workmanship amongst the workers. The department is structured in such a manner that no one can feel that he is working harder than another. The different departments have a job to do and it will be done." (315/Greece/300 employees/certification > 2 years/ISO 9002)

"We have no teamwork in the sense it is determined in books. We have taken ideas and try to apply them to our functions." (213/Finland/55 employees/certification > 2 years/ISO 9002)

"The introduction of top-of-the-line technologies facilitates flatter hierarchies, at least at the production level, seeing that a machine possibly demands more skills from the worker but releases from previous needs of co-ordination and organisation of small teams of workers usually joined by exclusively functional reasons." (513/Portugal/130 employees/aspiring certification/ISO 9001)

"While teamwork, especially cross functional, is important, it is only possible to have a limited number of teams operational at any one time. The ideal number is 6-8 teams as each team requires approximately two hours per week for discussion groups etc. This is the maximum disruption the production department can sustain without falling behind schedule. As a result the change process takes a little longer to implement." (411/Ireland/150 employees/certification > 2 years/ISO 9001/2)

"The company is only two years old and quality standards/procedures were established from the beginning along with a strong customer focus. Many of the TQM concepts such as teamwork were operational from the outset. As the company expands in the near future it will become important to document these procedures to maintain consistency of output." (413/Ireland/15 employees/aspiring certification/ISO 9002)

"The marketing staff handling the customer inquiry up to the implementation stage of the project they understand everything, customer requirements are their job. But these are not the people who work at the

project. This is the reason we have inter--departmental work." (111/F R Germany/167 employees/certification < 2 years/ISO 9001)

"In our plant we have no experience of flat organisation because our structure has stayed the same for a long time. In most departments there are 5 layers, which are much more than needed: Production Manager, Head of Production, General Supervisor, Department Head, Shop-Floor Workers." (514/Portugal/431 employees/certification > 2 years/ISO 9002)

"1. Multi functional project teams who deal directly with the customer.

2. Secondment of staff members to customers plants and vice versa. This has led to a sound understanding of customer requirements.

3. Sales people have technical training and therefore do not write specifications that manufacturing cannot produce.

4. The customers orders are never accepted at face value. The company have a list of questions that have to be addressed before an order reaches the factory floor. Then a quality plan is drawn up by a multifunctional team and agreed between the client and the company. This overcomes problems where the customer is not sure what they want. Often the company is in a better position to know what exactly the customer wants. This is especially the case in recent years as many MNC's no longer employ design engineers in their subsidiaries. The supplier increasingly has to take on the role of technical advisor. (411/Ireland/150 employees/certification > 2 years/ISO 9001/2)"

"At production level small groups have been established to make up teams." (115/F R Germany/520 employees/certification > 2 years/ISO 9001)

Production

The production department itself appears to be a critical point in the implementation of new work forms for the organisational assurance of cross-departmental responsibility for quality.

The expert interviews reveal reasons.

• It is typical for the sector that administrative and engineering expert knowledge determines customer demands, the requirements of use of the products at the customer's premises, the product-related quality demands. Production staff do not have this kind of expert knowledge.

- The production-specific quality requirements are different and extensive: mastering the production technology and the work and inspection steps, product handling, understanding the related processes such as materials flow etc.

- Productivity targets and production-technological equipment still require division of labour and specialisation. Despite an existing problem awareness regarding the demands of quality co-operation, metalworking small and medium-sized enterprises insist on the unsurpassable necessities of a department-specific work division also regarding quality tasks.

- The aim of short processing time limits the time for departmental and cross-departmental co-ordinative work.

The expert interviews also reveal the risks.

- Rigid production systems restrict the market and customer flexibility of the companies.

- Department boundaries lead to conflicts between product or design and manufacturing requirements.

- In production quality tasks are executed formally as a secondary "duty".

Statements

"So I wouldn't say that the 9001 brings production closer to the customer, there is a separation. This is more important to the consumer goods industry not so much to us. We produce on order. The questions of process and product engineering, which have to be confirmed with the customer, are completely different from those of production engineering. If it is not clear whether something is practicable for production, it has to be settled before contract acceptance." (116/F R Germany/40 employees/certification > 2 years/ISO 9001)

"The biggest problem that occurs is always with production and some problems with the engineering department. There is a different philosophy generally in manufacturing." (315/Greece/300 employees/certification > 2 years/ISO 9002)

"In our strategic plan, established five years ago, we found the implementation of quality management was essential to assure our customers' satisfaction, especially the foreign ones. The separation till then existing between production and customers' needs, that is to say an

obvious supremacy of production over marketing, almost led the company to a very difficult situation, since it endangered most of its markets, especially the export trade." (513/Portugal/130 employees/aspiring certification/ISO 9001)

"There is very much interaction between marketing, product development and design. There is close co-operation between departments. Less with production." (211/Finland/38 (1250) employees/certification > 2 years/ISO 9001)

"Easier to implement the process into construction than manufacturing." (611/Sweden/110 employees/aspiring certification/ISO 9001)

"The main difficulties are concerned with the translation of customer requirements into consistently manufacturable items. There is a fine balance between product functionality and manufacturability. The secret to success is getting that balance right." (712/United Kingdom/120 employees/aspiring certification/ISO 9002)

"The production supervisors have to know the projects which determine the capacity planning. The production operative has to know his work documents with the specifications, measures and tolerances, he is supposed to be quality-conscious in his work, no matter for what customer; after all he is not to perform better work for one customer than for the other." (111/F R Germany/167 employees/certification < 2 years/ISO 9001)

Quality control and steps towards operator self-inspection

A crucial change of the work processes in production resulting from the introduction of modern quality management is that quality control is shifted to the production process. This seems to be a sector-specific ambitious issue especially in mechanical engineering companies with mainly unique products, less in mass production with "friendly" production technology. The precondition is always a systematisation and documentation of the work steps for a clear definition of where the inspection takes place.

The survey shows that this reorganisation of quality control has to be differentiated from a reintegration of responsibility for quality into the work of operatives and the resulting extension of their job profiles. Some interviewed managers indicated a tension.

- Normally the surveyed companies do not replace final inspection by production-integrated quality inspections but organise them as complementary jobs.

- Quality demands, particularly external ones, by legal regulations and customers make it necessary that also production-integrated quality inspections are carried out by specialists - partly with certified special qualification - and not by the operatives themselves.

The extension of job profiles induces the implementation of self-inspection (operator inspection). This transition was described by most of the interviewed managers as a difficult and lengthy process. Tensions between traditional and partly remaining external inspection and responsibility of operatives occur in this process, but their solution is crucial to the success of the company.

The responsibility for the maintenance and checking for 'standard' was often with the operative. The issue is whether or not this responsibility is becoming embedded as part of the value system of the operative or whether it depends on vigorous managerial intervention and sanctions. Examples of good practice are found in companies where the management was conscious of the following:

- High quality consciousness as a traditional element of the corporate culture proves to be a favourable implementation condition, on the one hand. On the other hand, to overcome the well-established understanding of quality control as a management function with the right to sanction operators turns out to be a critical point in achieving a higher degree of individual responsibility.

- One task of quality management is the organisation of an objective co-operation between specialised inspection staff and "self-inspectors".

- In two cases the compensation for production activities, extended by activities which where formerly activities of a higher level in the hierarchy, was indicated as a task to be solved.

Statements

"There are procedures in production that are carefully followed step by step analytically by every worker. Control is always followed and the quality checker can intervene in whatever stage he wishes. Secondly he can do a destructive or/and non-destructive check. When the quality manager comes here every 15 days there is always something new that has to be corrected." (315/Greece/300 employees/certification > 2 years/ISO 9002)

"QM affects all the company - it's 'fundamental'. The procedures are regarded as "bringing people together". Operators are, for the most part, expected to carry out their own quality inspections (90+% of the time).

Quality Controller inspects work, 1. if client requests it, 2. if it's the first of a batch, 3. if a job requires it (e.g. a complex one)." (711/United Kingdom/44 employees/certification > 2 years/ISO 9001)

"We have 80 % operator self-inspection, only the final inspection is done by the responsible person for quality assurance. Each manual part is measured individually, CNC parts are measured in sampling inspection in order to carry out programme changes if necessary." (116/F R Germany/40 employees/certification > 2 years/ISO 9001)

"Self-control on the shop floor is very difficult to achieve, because employees do not yet understand its importance." (511/Portugal/181 employees/certification > 2 years/ISO 9001)

"Certainly drives responsibility down to direct employee level. However, not easy to achieve. Ownership of problems need a lot of management effort so that the 'owners' take the responsibility." (713/United Kingdom/110 employees/certification > 2 years/ISO 9001)

"We stopped these senseless inspections by a large extra department. The employees sat back and waited what the inspector had to say. We left this philosophy behind. We rely more on individual responsibility and operator inspection. This has been introduced with changing over to ISO 9000 but it is a long-term process" (115/F R Germany/520 employees/certification > 2 years/ISO 9001)

"The company has been on the way to operator self-inspection for years. Based on standardised and documented work and process instructions the individual inspection instruction and its specifications plus the inspection report is integrated in the work documents ("work packages"). In co-operation quality management and production planning make sure that there are no gaps." (115/F R Germany/520 employees/certification > 2 years/ISO 9001)

"This is a process which will go on for 8 - 9 years until the attitude changes. I think, we will still be talking about this in the year 2000. We have also gone through this change. Here is a man who made a component for 20 years, and somebody else told him whether it is okay or not, and

now he has to inspect his work himself, this is difficult. We used to have more staff and a supervisor squad of the old school. They said: Do your work, you do not get paid for thinking. Do what you are told to do and what is in the drawings. And now comes some quality manager and turns everything upside down: Now the employee has also to decide and point out if something is wrong. This is difficult particularly for old employees. They say: "For 20 years they told us differently and now we have to turn 180 degrees." Taking over the responsibility for one's own component is difficult. There is this worry: If something ever happens during warranty, they will pull out the old piece of paper and say: "But you signed it." The employee knows that the notification of nonconformity, the re-working costs the company a lot of time and money." (115/F R Germany/520 employees/certification > 2 years/ISO 9001)

"The main problems with implementation are (...) staff not wishing to 'sign-off' their work because it implicates them if something goes wrong. This has been overcome by placing emphasis on problem solving rather than on apportioning blame. Second: Disagreement over payrates. In theory every employee acts as a 'quality inspector' but not every employee gets paid the same rate as an official quality inspector." (411/Ireland/150 employees/certification > 2 years/ISO 9001/2)

"In Germany staff asks with every innovation: "We have to learn something new, how much more will we earn?"" (112/F R Germany/90 employees/certification < 2 years/ISO 9002)

Quality documents and statistical methods

The strong emphasis on documentation and statistical evaluation of all company operations as the basic element of quality management is contested by many experts in the metalworking SMEs. Some respondents shared the dislike of their staff for the "red tape". Examples of good practice can be found in companies which

- limit these procedures strictly to operations where they improve decision and control processes
- set a high value on the fact that these procedures are comprehensible for staff and that they understand their benefits
- make evident that documentation leads straight to improvement.

Statements

"Intention is to keep procedures as simple and understandable as possible in order to ensure that there is a good chance of them being adhered to. People have to understand why things have to be done in certain ways. Paperwork is kept to a minimum." (711/United Kingdom/44 employees/certification > 2 years/ISO 9001)

"There was originally a problem as staff could not read engineering drawings. All staff were given training to overcome this problem. Now, work instructions are incorporated into pictorial representations of the product part/ process in question and these are placed at the appropriate work centre. There is a person employed full time to design and output these work instructions. This has worked extremely well as it is far easier than reading complex sets of instructions/ engineering drawings." (411/Ireland/150 employees/certification > 2 years/ISO 9001/2)

"Very often the statistics paperwork is not evaluated at all, the customer is impressed, the managing director and the plant manager are satisfied. But this does not help the man who wants to make a good product. "Here they are, employing another person taking away our money." The people have to see that the quality of the work gets better. An important point was here the preventive maintenance which is steered by the results of statistic process control. Before supervisors used to do this from experience." (112/F R Germany/90 employees/certification < 2 years/ISO 9002)

First signs of comprehensive quality politics

If the development tendency of quality management in the surveyed metalworking SMEs were to be measured against the introduction of current preventive quality methods and advanced quality technologies, the picture would be quite clear: The large majority of the surveyed companies still adheres to the ISO system.

The statements of the interviewed managers and the analysis of the individual company modifies the picture. The number of companies which do not believe that the ISO system ensures their quality aims is considerably higher than the number of those companies which apply the current procedures of comprehensive quality management. The following reasons can be identified for this divergence:

- Companies are oriented to the comprehensive quality *aims* of advanced quality management procedures such as market- and customer-oriented quality planning, proactive nonconformity prevention, process quality, but they do not consider the current procedures as being applicable in SMEs.

- Companies are focusing on their "own in-house strengths" and are looking for technical solutions.

Statements

"CAD is very good, but there is one problem. The designs and calculations work but they do not take into account the interest of the production which is to work with proved standard components. Why cannot all threaded joints be unscrewed with the 9-screwdriver?" (113/F R Germany/20 employees/aspiring certification/ISO 9001)

"Yes quality management does influence technical change e.g. the firm conduct process capability analyses to establish whether the process can deliver the required quality standard. If not then changes are made to the process. In this way quality drives technical change." (411/Ireland/150 employees/certification > 2 years/ISO 9001/2)

"Shorter processing and delivery times were and still remain one of the principal goals of the company, but they were not a reason for deciding the implementation of the Quality Assurance system. We tried to use MRP for this purpose but it was too complicated.

Pro-engineering is a serious attempt towards creating technical infrastructure for QM. This program has a lot of similarities with CAD. It has an advantage in implementing planning changes to all related departments." (311/Greece/146 employees/certification > 2 years/ISO 9001)

"New customer demands require R&D work. This leads to new ways in design, the use of new materials and a new production engineering. This is why we decided to have a first group of employees trained in FMEA." (115/F R Germany/520 employees/certification > 2 years/ISO 9001)

"ISO cannot deliver many of the proposed benefits of quality assurance. This is because a company could be quality assured merely by hiring a few quality inspectors and by managing the quality function separately from the rest of the company. In this instance benefits such as improvement of internal processes and new corporate culture, would not materialise. ISO can only deliver substantial benefits if it is introduced in conjunction with

WCM and CIP." (411/Ireland/150 employees/certification > 2 years/ISO 9001/2)

Customer-supplier, company co-operation

Whereas the imperatives of quality management as guidelines for the design of the *internal*-company relationships are implemented with scepticism and above all in a balanced conjunction with other company guidelines, the surveyed enterprises show a strong orientation of *external*-company relationships to the aspects of quality management. Quality-related changes were evident in the relationship with customers and suppliers and in co-operation structures of companies.

This general tendency varies according to the types of companies. For the suppliers the customer relationship particularly at the management level is the most important task. For producers of final products this is true also at the operating level, particularly if there are customer services like the areas of assembly, starting up, maintenance and other extensive customer services. Here companies develop new organisational forms of cross-departmental involvement of employees of those areas as well as extensive job profiles for these employees.

In summary, the following findings from the expert interviews can be retained:

- In the **customer relationships** of the surveyed enterprises the product- and technology-oriented notion of quality made, for the most part, way for customer satisfaction as the company objective. Some companies show in an exemplary way that they do not rely on the dangerous motto: "Quality is what pleases the customer." They consider it as their service task to give the customer critical advice based on their know-how. Of course, the fact plays a role that it is typical for this sector that the customers have mostly other companies as customers and that these are of the same sector or related to the sector.

- In the **supplier relationships** many companies are trying to advance from a systematic incoming-lot control - partly through supplier inspection - to a relationship of trust based on a mutual quality system.

- From mutual information between customers and suppliers about the company's quality system and its development and from practical quality agreements some surveyed enterprises develop permanent **interaction and co-operation relationships** with regard to quality targets, quality management experiences and efforts to extend or improve the quality systems. A special case are companies having a very close long-term supplier relationship with one or few customer companies. Crucial elements of the quality system of the suppliers are developed in direct co-operation with the customers.

- In some cases network-like structures for the tackling of new quality management tasks have emerged from consulting networks for the preparation of the ISO certification. Some companies wish for those structures which they consider to be best suited for the adaptation of quality management to the specific conditions of SMEs.

Statements

"The process of collection of the customers demands itself seems to create the most serious doubt. This could partially be explained by the fact that usually our customers have a low educational level (farmers). In the Greek Public Sector the main difficulty is that in order to reach the prices asked we have to lower our product quality with the consensus of the buyers." (313/Greece/260 employees/aspiring certification/ISO 9002)

"There are very few problems achieving quality standards. The customer draws up a quality/production plan for each product and visits the factory to ensure the procedures are being correctly implemented. The customer/parent also provides training in any new procedures or production methods. There is an excellent relationship between the company and our customer. Initially when ISO was being introduced there was a somewhat impatient attitude toward the increased bureaucracy and also toward the customer but this has been overcome." (414/Ireland/49 employees/certification < 2 years/ISO 9002)

"Sometimes customers do not understand the production process and make unrealistic quality demands. This is usually resolved by inviting the customer to the plant to explain the entire process and its capabilities." (412/Ireland/130 employees/certification > 2 years/ISO 9002)

"The customers orders are never accepted at face value. The company have a list of questions that have to be addressed before an order reaches the factory floor. Then a quality plan is drawn up by a multifunctional team and agreed between the client and the company. This overcomes problems where the customer is not sure what they want. Often the company is in a better position to know what exactly the customer wants. This is especially the case in recent years as many MNC's no longer employ design engineers in their subsidiaries. The supplier increasingly has to take on the role of technical advisor." (411/Ireland/150 employees/certification > 2 years/ISO 9001/2)

"There is a particularly high degree of individual responsibility in the activities of assemblers or assembling supervisors consulting with design. For when starting up on-site, deviations of the practical production requirements of the customer from the specifications or the samples in his inquiry often come up - e.g. offsize of parts or components. At the customer's the assembler is our company!" (111/F R Germany/167 employees/certification < 2 years/ISO 9001)

"The management of suppliers has distributed to those units that are working with them even before there have been meetings with suppliers, during which the quality of their products are monitored and also discussed about the delivery times of suppliers. There is also discussed about the terms and conditions, when the contract is terminated with a supplier. Purchasing has been distributed to different units. The arrangement guarantees development and scheduling. There is no special quality inspection." (211/Finland/38 (1250) employees/certification > 2 years/ISO 9001)

"We have business relations with a large-scale company. This is where we get the most reliable and practice-oriented information about the development of quality-related legal standards." (113/F R Germany/20 employees/aspiring certification/ISO 9001)

"With the traceability we effaced the mistakes. There is written procedure and new forms that promote our working manner. In this way, if there is a complaint by phone, it will be registered, the quality control department will be informed, and we will take the specified improvement measures in the production process. Until now this was not done." (312/Greece/47 employees/certification < 2 years/ISO 9002)

"Information has to flow! We use the explanation of our measures for quality assurance but also complaint statistics as a basis for talks with customers where problems of wrong application of company products are identified. The other way round, information about the conditions of the application at the customer's flow back to the company." (112/F R Germany/90 employees/certification < 2 years/ISO 9002)

"In the "After Sales Service" we have a good support from the "Quality Department". An example of that is the inquiry that we send on a yearly basis to our customers in order to check their satisfaction level." (511/Portugal/181 employees/certification > 2 years/ISO 9001)

"There is a network of SM companies, where management can meet one another and discuss about quality management and developmental questions of the companies. 17 companies take part in this network and it is considered as developmental work." (212/Finland/26 employees/aspiring certification/ISO 9002)

"We organise a round table for the quality managers of the region where not the theory but concrete issues of quality management in the companies are discussed." (111/F R Germany/167 employees/certification < 2 years/ISO 9001)

Corporate culture

Many of the interviewed companies comprise the changes going along with the implementation of quality management under the heading "cultural change".

One aspect of this term calls for scepticism. It embraces in a strikingly undifferentiated way changes of the external and internal relationships, preconditions and requirements, on the one hand, and results of quality management, on the other, objective changes in the company organisation and subjective motivational changes.

At the same time, this term puts the social and subject-related dimension of quality management into focus: the role of the employee in the company.

Statements

"The amount of internal complaints has increased, which is positive. Then we can make the corrections instead of having external complaints." (614/Sweden/205 employees/certification >2 years/ISO 9001)

"Now we have to take the step that everybody at his workplace says: It depends on me, I produce quality. There are still reservations to write down the problems and hand them in to the quality department, then you have to go and talk to them - not in form of questions and answers , there you are two levels below. If they do not see it, who else does? This is our

potential."(111/F R Germany/167 employees/certification < 2 years/ISO 9001)

"Today we think here it is the most important tool of competitiveness through quality in association with a culture of people valuation, where all collaborators feel moved and conscious of the importance of their participation in the achievement of the results of the company. Today, self-responsibility is an absolute priority of the company. Non-quality detected day-by-day is felt by everybody, so that everybody can take part on the solutions and on the results." (513/Portugal/130 employees/aspiring certification/ISO 9001)

Personnel-related concepts of metalworking SMEs

Quantitative findings

The interviewees were allowed to rate multiple criterions. The scale of 0 - 300 results from the rating scale of 0 - 3 and from the fact that the survey results based on different quantities of respondents have been extrapolated to a number of companies of 100 in order to obtain data that are comparable between the staff groups and between the sectors.

Different universes of companies in evaluated occupational groups are based on the fact that the corresponding departments or hierarchical groups of employees are not represented in all the companies in the sample. A quantitative evaluation of the assembly and service department as well as of the hierarchical level semi-/unskilled staff in the purchasing and development departments has been avoided because too little of the respondent companies have an independent assembly and service department and in the other departments there are hardly semi-/unskilled employees.

Quality-related demands on the staff and staff groups

An essential aim of the survey was to gain insight into the practical implementation of quality management in the quality loop of the departments and, more specifically, in the job of different employee groups. The surveyed companies were asked to state quality-related job demands (work requirements) for the following departments and staff groups:

Development (R&D):	Supervisors	Skilled staff	Semi/unskilled staff
Purchasing:	Supervisors	Skilled staff	Semi/unskilled staff
Production:	Supervisors	Skilled staff	Semi/unskilled staff
Assembly/service:	Supervisors	Skilled staff	Semi/unskilled staff

Therefore, they were asked the following standardised question whose criteria follow terms of the ISO standards or on internationally accepted terms of quality management:

Question: In order to achieve the quality demands of the company, to what extent do you consider it necessary to know, understand, master or ignore the following **(Rating according to following key:** 0 = ignore (unimportant), 1 = know (be informed), 2 = understand (skilfully follow), 3 = master (plan, carry out)):

- Proper handling of means of production
- Handling of products
- Document use (work, procedures instructions)
- Workplace safety
- Nonconformity identification and documentation
- Test equipment
- Quality inspections
- Document control
- Control of nonconforming products
- Quality demands of related departments
- Inspection planning
- Nonconformity analysis and assessment
- Corrective action
- Composition of the company products
- Quality aims of the company
- Quality-related costs
- Legal standards
- Data collection & statistical methods e.g. 7 QC tools, SPC (statistical process control) etc.
- Preventive QM methods e.g. QFD (quality function deployment), FMEA (failure mode and effects analysis) etc.
- Team work
- Structuring of operations of the company
- External customer-supplier relations
- Internal customer-supplier relations
- Co-operation techniques e.g. communication tools, problem analysis techniques, creativity techniques, team building, conflict settlement etc.

Quality-related demands on development supervisors

The following profile was identified for this staff group:

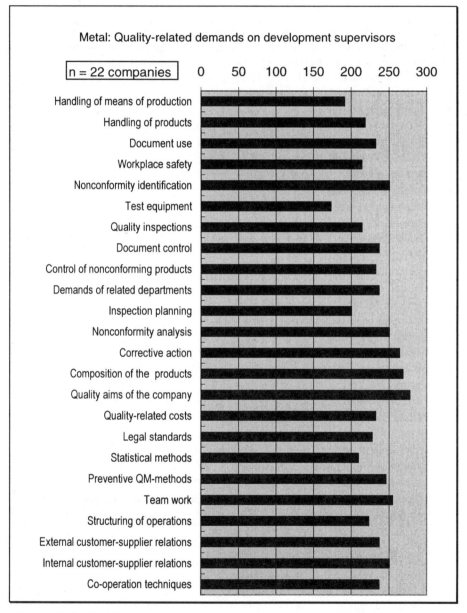

Figure 12: Quality-related demands on development supervisors in the metal industry

The respondent companies expect supervisors of the development department preponderantly that they master the "quality aims of the company" and the "composition of the company products". This corresponds to functional job profile of the development department. But already the next highest rated requirements - "corrective action" and "team work" - characterise a cross-departmental profile of responsibilities in relation to the quality aims in the entire company. With an equally high rating of the responsibility for "nonconformity identification and documentation", "nonconformity analysis and assessment" and "internal customer-supplier relations", which obtain similar ratings, this staff group is obviously assigned a strategic role in the implementation of quality management in the internal operations. This corresponds to the finding from the qualitative expert interviews, that many quality managers or staff responsible for quality in the surveyed companies are recruited from the employee group of development engineers. The relatively high rating of "preventive QM methods" (6) as a demand on the supervisors of the development department is also striking, namely diverging from the findings in the other occupational groups. Apparently this occupational group is attributed a trail blazing role in the implementation of preventive quality management.

Low ratings attain particularly requirements which are rather considered as production-specific such as "proper handling of means of production". But it is also striking that "data collection & statistical methods" attain a low rating. This suggests the interpretation that metalworking SMEs regard these requirements as a less suitable quality instrument for their little standardised operations often producing small series or unique products, which are often oriented towards individual customer requirements.

Quality-related demands on development skilled staff

Skilled staff is mainly expected to work in teams. With the next best ratings for the requirements "document use", "nonconformity identification and documentation" and "corrective action", which attain similarly high ratings, as well as "quality inspections" the job profile of company-wide quality assurance at an operative level crystallises for this staff group.

The low-rated requirements correspond essentially to those with the supervisors of the development department.

The following profile was identified for this group of employees:

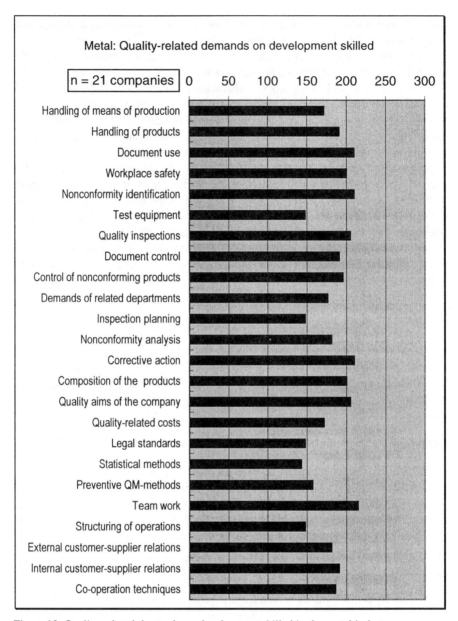

Figure 13: Quality-related demands on development skilled in the metal industry

Comparison: development

Extrapolating a hierarchy of the five best rated quality-related job requirements from the occupational group-specific ratings, the following picture is obtained:

Table 2: Best rated quality-related job requirements in the development department (Metal industry)

Development supervisors	Development skilled staff
1. Quality aims of the company	1. Team work
2. Composition of the company products	2. Document use (work, procedures instructions)
3. Corrective action	3. Nonconformity identification and documentation
4. Team work	4. Corrective action
5. Nonconformity identification and documentation, Nonconformity analysis and assessment, Internal customer-supplier relations	5. Quality inspections
6. Preventive QM methods	

Some department-specific as well as hierarchy-specific statements can be deduced from this picture:

The development department in metalworking SMEs is obviously attributed a cross-departmental responsibility for the quality aims in the entire company. This corresponds to a quality concept of the sector, which is essentially oriented towards product innovation and product quality. This employee group is ascribed a strategic role in the practical implementation of quality management in the internal operations of the company. Furthermore, it is obviously presupposed that essential impulses come from the development department for the extension of the quality system through the introduction of more developed quality methods.

From a hierarchy-specific point of view a certain maintenance of the pattern "target definition versus execution" can be observed, but, at the same time, it is striking that the requirement "teamwork" is attributed an approximately equally high rating for supervisors and skilled staff.

Extrapolating a hierarchy of the five lowest rated quality-related job requirements from the occupational group-specific ratings, the following picture is obtained:

Table 3: Lowest rated quality-related job requirements in the development department (Metal industry)

Development supervisors	Development skilled staff
• Quality inspections	• Test equipment
• Data collection & statistical methods	• Inspection planning
• Inspection planning	• Legal standards
• Proper handling of means of production	• Structuring of operations of the company
• Test equipment	• Data collection & statistical methods

The low rating of "data collection & statistical methods" is striking. This suggests the interpretation that metalworking companies consider these quality methods as comparatively little suitable for their flexible processes. Given the outstanding role of the development department for the company-wide quality assurance, the low rating of the task "inspection planning" appears a bit contradictory just like low demands on development skilled staff with regard to "structuring of operations of the company".

Quality-related demands on purchasing supervisors

The following profile was obtained for this group of employees:

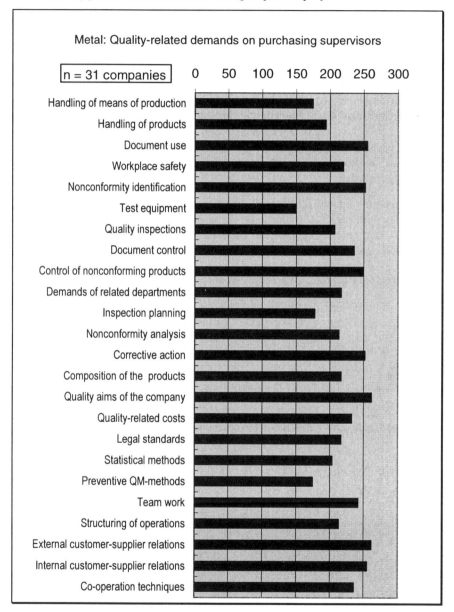

Figure 14: Quality-related demands on purchasing supervisors in the metal industry

Supervisors in the purchasing department are expected to equally master "quality aims of the company" and "external customer-supplier relations". Here the traditional functional tasks and new requirements of the quality system coincide. In the external relationship to the suppliers the purchasing supervisors represent the quality demands of the company on intermediate products and materials. This corresponds to the finding from the qualitative expert interviews, that quality assurance in the supplier relationship is being increasingly systematised. But the requirements "document use", "internal customer-supplier relations", "nonconformity identification and documentation" and "corrective action" also obtain strikingly high ratings. In the quality system most respondent companies obviously attribute a cross-functional interface task to the purchasing supervisors. Having know-how about the downstream internal production processes, the purchasing supervisors are expected to provide a secured material flow as well as to prevent nonconforming intermediate products and materials from entering the production process.

Low demands on the purchasing supervisors are made by the respondent companies with regard to rather production-specific criteria such as "handling of products" and "proper handling of means of production". The same applies to specialised quality assurance methods.

Quality-related demands on purchasing skilled staff

The job requirement "document use (work, procedures instructions)" attains the highest rating in relation to skilled staff of the purchasing department. This seems to reflect the fact that this staff group works being bound to directives. The high ratings for "control of nonconforming products", "external customer-supplier relations", "internal customer-supplier relations" and "corrective action" also characterise the job profile of the purchasing skilled staff as an interface within the quality system.

The following profile was obtained for this employee group:

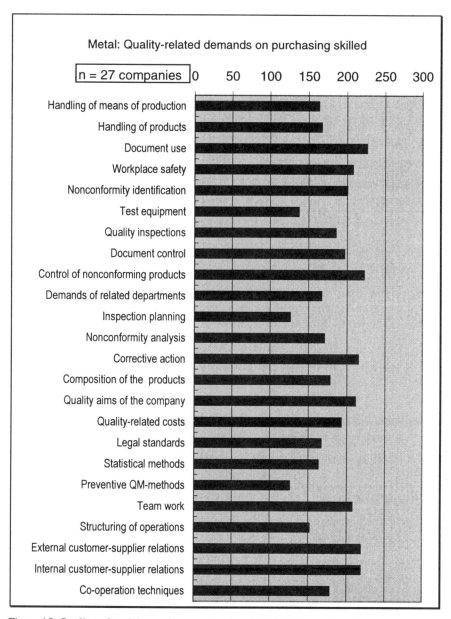

Figure 15: Quality-related demands on purchasing skilled in the metal industry

Comparison: Purchasing

Extrapolating a hierarchy of the five best rated quality-related job requirements from the occupational group-specific ratings, the following picture is obtained

Table 4: Best rated quality-related job requirements in the purchasing department (Metal industry)

Purchasing supervisors	Purchasing skilled staff
1. Quality aims of the company	1. Document use (work, procedures instructions)
2. External customer-supplier relations	
3. Document use (work, procedures instructions)	2. Control of nonconforming products
	3. External customer-supplier relations
4. Internal customer-supplier relations	4. Internal customer-supplier relations
5. Nonconformity identification and documentation	5. Corrective action

Some department-specific as well as hierarchy-specific statements can be deduced from this picture:

The surveyed companies ascribe an interface function between external and internal customer-supplier relationships to the purchasing department. Across the hierarchies the job profiles in this department comprise cross-departmental quality tasks and elements of preventive quality assurance.

The fact that the "quality aims of the company" are left to the purchasing supervisors as a decisive orientation of their job can be interpreted, above all, as a hierarchical division of responsibilities.

Extrapolating a hierarchy of the five lowest rated quality-related job requirements from the occupational group-specific ratings, the following picture is obtained:

Table 5: Lowest rated quality-related job requirements in the purchasing department (Metal industry)

Purchasing supervisors	Purchasing skilled staff
• Handling of products	• Data collection & statistical methods
• Inspection planning	• Structuring of operations of the company
• Proper handling of means of production	
	• Test equipment
• Preventive QM methods	• Inspection planning
• Test equipment	• Preventive QM methods

Low demands are made on purchasing skilled staff with regard to rather production-specific criteria and specialised quality assurance methods

Quality-related demands on production supervisors

For this staff group the following profile was identified:

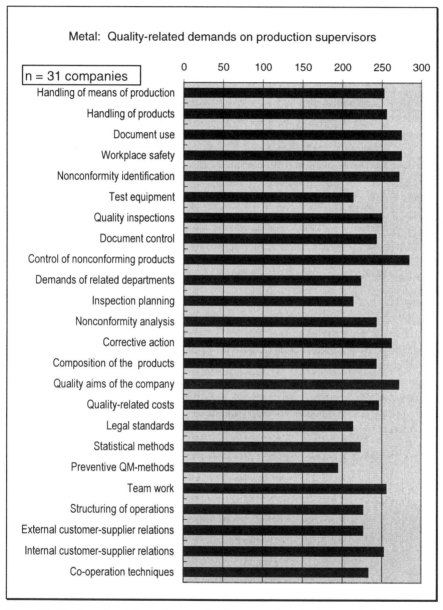

Figure 16: Quality-related demands on production supervisors in the metal industry

Supervisors in production are mainly expected to carry out "control of nonconforming products". Nonconforming products should not be worked further or even come into the market and to the client. This is considered the main quality task in monitoring the production. The following requirements in the rating - "document use" and "workplace safety" - correspond to traditional tasks of production supervisors consisting in job instructions and work organisation. But relatively high ratings for "nonconformity identification and documentation", "quality aims of the company" and "corrective action" indicate a new quality-oriented increase of tasks of supervisors in the production.

Strikingly low values attained quality assurance methods such as "data collection & statistical methods", "test equipment", "inspection planning" and "preventive quality management methods". This finding can be interpreted in a double sense. On the one hand, SMEs of the metal industry find it hard to adapt the existing methods to their operations and personnel resources. The relatively low rating of the requirements "structuring of operations of the company", "external customer-supplier relations", "quality demands of related departments" allows also the interpretation that in the surveyed companies the job profile for production supervisors is still mainly functional-specific and specialised tasks of quality assurance are left to specialist staff responsible for quality.

Quality-related demands on production skilled staff

The priority of "proper handling of means of production" and "workplace safety" as demands on skilled staff in the production corresponds to traditional job profiles. It is striking that "control of nonconforming products", "quality inspections", "document use (work, procedures instructions)", "nonconformity identification and documentation" and "test equipment" are nearly equally highly rated. This shows the tendency that at least operative tasks of quality control and quality assurance are transferred back into the production activity. This suggest that in the surveyed metalworking companies steps are undertaken to introduce shopfloor self-inspection, thereby extending the job profiles.

For this employee group the following profile was identified:

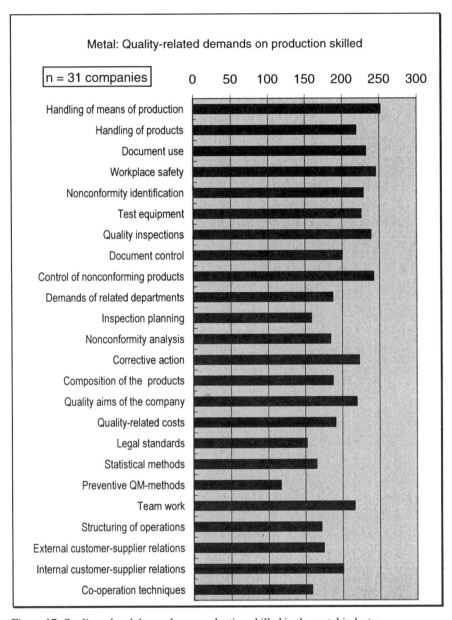

Figure 17: Quality-related demands on production skilled in the metal industry

Quality-related demands on production semi/unskilled staff

The following profile was identified for this staff group:

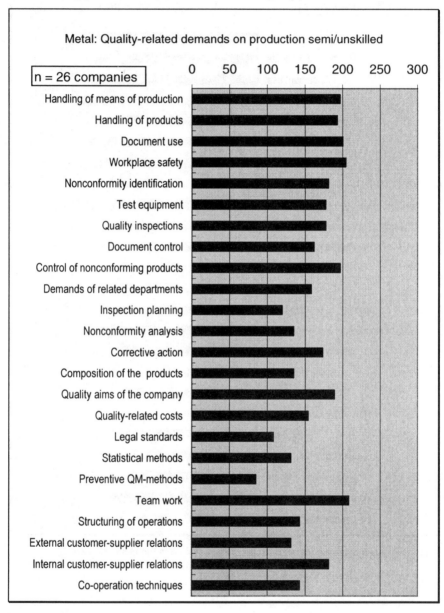

Figure 18: Quality-related demands on production semi/unskilled in the metal industry

The priority of the requirements "team work", "workplace safety", "document use (work, procedures instructions)" and "proper handling of means of production" corresponds to the traditional job profile of operative employees who are bound to directives. The fact that "team work" is on the first place in this context suggests that this term is in many companies less understood as reorganisation of work forms than the functioning co-operation in the existing work organisation. This interpretation was confirmed in the qualitative expert interviews.

It is striking that the requirement "control of nonconforming products" is attached the same importance as "proper handling of means of production". This confirms the fact identified with the production supervisors that the first quality task in production is regarded to be avoiding that nonconforming products are worked further or even come into the market and to the client.

Comparison: Production

Extrapolating a hierarchy of the five best rated quality-related job requirements from the occupational group-specific ratings, the following picture is obtained

Table 6: Best rated quality-related job requirements in the production (Metal industry)

Production supervisors	Production skilled staff	Production semi-/unskilled staff
1. Control of nonconforming products 2. Document use (work, procedures instructions) 3. Workplace safety 4. Nonconformity identification and documentation 5. Quality aims of the company	1. Proper handling of means of production 2. Workplace safety 3. Control of nonconforming products 4. Quality inspections 5. Document use (work, procedures instructions)	1. Team work 2. Workplace safety 3. Document use (work, procedures instructions) 4. Proper handling of means of production 5. Control of nonconforming products

Some department-specific as well as hierarchy-specific statements can be deduced from this picture:

In the production department the surveyed metalworking SMEs attach a crucial importance for the implementation of their quality system to the requirement "control of nonconforming products". The equally great importance, across the hierarchies, of "workplace safety" and "document use" appears, on the one hand, to be adequate in the specific function but it also allows the interpretation that the production is still strongly regarded to be merely an operative department in the quality system of the company. Cross-departmental quality tasks do not seem to be of priority responsibility of the production staff.

From the hierarchy-specific point of view a certain maintenance of the pattern "instruction & monitoring versus execution" can be observed.

Extrapolating a hierarchy of the five lowest rated quality-related job requirements from the occupational group-specific ratings, the following picture is obtained

Table 7: Lowest rated quality-related job requirements in the production (Metal industry)

Production supervisors	Production skilled staff	Production semi-/unskilled staff
• Data collection & statistical methods • Test equipment • Inspection planning • Legal standards • Preventive QM methods	• Data collection & statistical methods • Inspection planning • Co-operation techniques • Legal standards • Preventive QM methods	• Data collection & statistical methods • External customer-supplier relations • Inspection planning • Legal standards • Preventive QM methods

The generally low rating of "legal standards" is not quite department-specific. It corresponds to the finding about the assessment of the reasons for and aims of the introduction of quality management in the surveyed companies.

Strikingly low ratings attain across the hierarchies quality assurance measures such as "data collection & statistical methods", "test equipment", "inspection planning" and "preventive quality management methods". It seems to be difficult for metalworking SMEs to adapt these methods to their production operations and personnel resources. But this finding also allows the interpretation that specialised tasks of quality assurance continue to be left to special staff responsible for quality.

Quality-related demands on staff

Summarising the quality-related job requirements for the different staff groups across the departments, the following profile emerges:

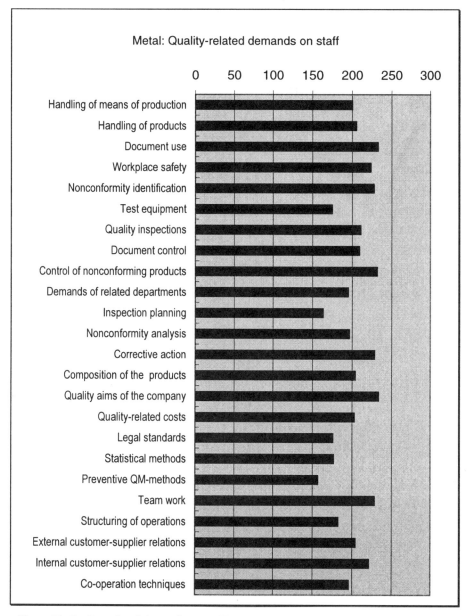

Figure 19: Quality-related demands on staff in the metal industry

The interviewed companies attach particular significance to the requirement for staff across the departments to be guided by the "quality aims of the company".

Insisting on "document use", the quality related demands on staff correspond to the average state of developments of quality management in the surveyed small and medium-sized enterprises which are still essentially oriented by the ISO system on the basis of reliable work and procedure instructions. The emphasis of the quality tasks "control of nonconforming products", "corrective action" and "nonconformity identification and documentation" focuses the quality responsibility of staff on the aim to prevent nonconforming products from reaching the customer. The high rating of "teamwork" indicates a sector-specific job requirement especially in mechanical engineering companies.

Table 8: Rated quality-related job requirements cross the staff (Metal industry)

Best rated quality-related job requirements	Lowest rated quality-related job requirements
1. Quality aims of the company	• Preventive quality management methods
2. Document use (work, procedures instructions)	• Inspection planning
3. Control of nonconforming products	• Test equipment
4. Team work	• Legal standards
5. Corrective action	• Data collection & statistical methods
6. Nonconformity identification and documentation	• Structuring of operations of the company
7. Workplace safety	• Quality demands of related departments

The assessment of an implementation of quality management essentially still remaining within the framework of the ISO system corresponds to the low rating of special quality methods and techniques, especially preventive methods. Low rating of "structuring of operations of the company" and "quality demands of related departments" indicates that "teamwork" is mainly required within the department boundaries and less cross-departmentally.

Comparison: cross-departmental

Table 9: Best rated quality-related job requirements across the departments (Metal industry)

Development supervisors	Development skilled staff
1. Quality aims of the company	1. Team work
2. Composition of the company products	2. Document use (work, procedures instructions)
3. Corrective action	3. Nonconformity identification and documentation
4. Team work	4. Corrective action
5. Nonconformity identification and documentation, Nonconformity analysis and assessment, Internal customer-supplier relations	5. Quality inspections
6. Preventive QM methods	
Purchasing supervisors	**Purchasing skilled staff**
1. Quality aims of the company	1. Document use (work, procedures instructions)
2. External customer-supplier relations	2. Control of nonconforming products
3. Document use (work, procedures instructions)	3. External customer-supplier relations
4. Internal customer-supplier relations	4. Internal customer-supplier relations
5. Nonconformity identification and documentation	5. Corrective action
Production supervisors	**Production skilled staff**
1. Control of nonconforming products	1. Proper handling of means of production
2. Document use (work, procedures instructions)	2. Workplace safety
3. Workplace safety	3. Control of nonconforming products
4. Nonconformity identification and documentation	4. Quality inspections
5. Quality aims of the company	5. Document use (work, procedures instructions)
Production semi-/unskilled staff	
1. Team work	
2. Workplace safety	
3. Document use (work, procedures instructions)	
4. Proper handling of means of production	
5. Control of nonconforming products	

Table 10: Lowest rated quality-related job requirements across the departments (Metal industry)

Development supervisors	Development skilled staff
• Quality inspections	• Test equipment
• Data collection & statistical methods	• Inspection planning
• Inspection planning	• Legal standards
• Proper handling of means of production	• Structuring of operations of the company
• Test equipment	• Data collection & statistical methods
Purchasing supervisors	**Purchasing skilled staff**
• Handling of products	• Data collection & statistical methods
• Inspection planning	• Structuring of operations of the company
• Proper handling of means of production	• Test equipment
• Preventive QM methods	• Inspection planning
• Test equipment	• Preventive QM methods
Production supervisors	**Production skilled staff**
• Data collection & statistical methods	• Data collection & statistical methods
• Test equipment	• Inspection planning
• Inspection planning	• Co-operation techniques
• Legal standards	• Legal standards
• Preventive QM methods	• Preventive QM methods
Production semi-/unskilled staff	
• Data collection & statistical methods	
• External customer-supplier relations	
• Inspection planning	
• Legal standards	
• Preventive QM methods	

"Nonconformity identification" and "control of nonconforming products", on the one hand, and "document use", on the other, appear to be priority demands on staff across the departments. In metalworking SMEs the focus of quality is still the final product, not so much the processes. In the surveyed companies this corresponds to a quality management which is directed by experts, especially development engineers, and which orientates itself essentially by the ISO standards. A broader division of these tasks across departmental and hierarchical barriers can be recognised. This corresponds to the tendency not to leave the task "quality" to a special quality department alone.

The low rating of statistical and preventive methods corresponds to the assessment of the implementation of quality management as essentially still remaining within the framework of the ISO standards. But it also suggests that metalworking SMEs regard especially statistical methods a less suitable quality instrument in their little standardised operations often producing small series or unique products, which are often oriented by individual customer requirements.

Customer orientation demands on the staff

Does the customer orientation proclaimed especially by SMEs result in extended quality demands on the job of the employees? The marketing executives in the surveyed companies were asked the following semi-standardised question:

Question: "The satisfaction of the customer is the crucial measure of quality!" - Does this statement imply new demands on your employees? If so, what are the implications for training? Is training required to meet gaps in knowledge? **Rate answers according to following key:** 0 = unimportant, 1 = plays a role 2 = important, 3 = very important

The quantitative evaluation identified the following picture:

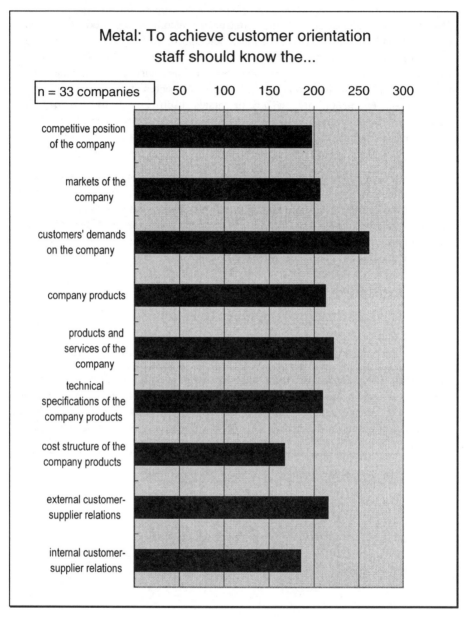

Figure 20: Customer orientation demands on the staff in the metal industry

Company experts for the customer contact consider improved knowledge of staff necessary mainly with regard to "customers' demands on the company", "products and services of the company" and "external customer-supplier relations".

These statements, which concern the entire staff, are in a certain contrast to the data of the companies on the "quality-related demands on the staff", in which the customer relationship was stated as a priority requirement only for the purchasing department. But in the qualitative expert interviews, the companies which have independent departments for assembly and service gave analogue assessments.

Quality-related actual training issues

The survey intended to identify an actual state of enterprise training and examine whether or how these training efforts correlate with the indicated quality-related demands of the companies on their staff in general and also on certain staff groups.

But those standardised questions met with greatest difficulties in the companies which, broken down to departments and staff groups, asked about training programmes and courses relevant to quality management. It was particularly hard to obtain quantitative data concerning topics and duration of training tailored to the specific needs of the participants. Furthermore, the qualitative expert interviews showed that a considerable proportion especially of in-house training reacts to an actual need, thus varying strongly according to participants and topics, particularly since there are uncertainties about which training really is relevant to quality management.

Due to the situation of these data, only the statements of personnel managers regarding a generalised question are evaluated.

> Question: Where are the most important areas of training for the quality management system of your company at the moment? **Rate answers according to following key:** 0 = unimportant, 1 = plays a role, 2 = important, 3 = very important

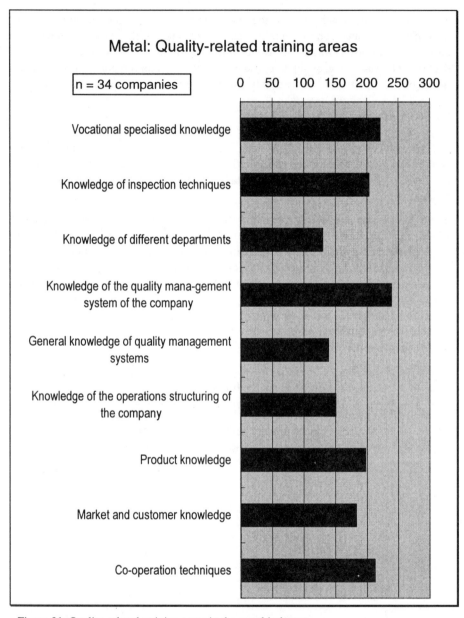

Figure 21: Quality-related training areas in the metal industry

A clear priority is given to training in "knowledge of the quality management of the company". Little importance is comparatively attached to training in "general knowledge of the quality systems". This is based on the view, which was confirmed in the qualitative expert interviews, that companies tend to focus employee training on a company-specific implementation of quality management. For that reason it seems to be a contradiction that the subjects "knowledge of the operations structuring of the company" and "knowledge of different departments" are not treated as the focus of training. Possibly, small and medium-sized enterprises rely on an existing knowledge basis of their employees or they consider these subjects to be sufficiently covered by the quality system training. The relatively great importance attributed to the subject "knowledge of inspection techniques" also allows the interpretation that the surveyed companies on average still concentrate on a training for the first implementation of new quality assurance tasks of the employees when introducing a quality system.

Furthermore, "vocational specialised training" and training in "product knowledge" also rank high. This reflects the sector-specific need to respond effectively to stiffened competition by innovations in products and technologies as well as by extending service provisions.

A high rating attains also training in "co-operation techniques". The qualitative expert interviews identified here a training focus especially for executives and middle-management staff.

Qualitative findings: Barriers, critical points, examples of good practice

The following description pursues the question about which human resources policy-related tasks metalworking small and medium-sized enterprises in Europe are facing through the introduction and implementation of quality management and which conclusions they draw. It is based on open-ended expert interviews with managerial staff which were first evaluated in case studies at company level.

Anticipating one result: Quality management leads in the surveyed companies generally to a new consideration of the employee competencies, of the practical competence to act as well as the necessary qualifications of the employees; but there is still a struggle going on in the companies for the right answers about the personnel policy and personnel development policy.

This description of identified barriers, critical points and examples of good practice is to make these "experiments" and discussions in individual companies accessible for the general discussion. The evaluation is based, on the one hand, on the thematically structured summary of the direct information of company experts about identified implementation problems and problem-solving experience, which are partially documented in statements and, on the other hand, on meta-analyses of generalisable personnel-related problems with the implementation of quality management and already recognisable tendencies of personnel-policy concepts in the respondent companies.

Personnel and qualification structures

For identifying the new skill needs arising in the companies by the implementation of quality management, the existing personnel and qualification structures have been taken as a point of reference. The analysis of the results makes it inadequate to extrapolate average personnel and qualification structures in metalworking small and medium-sized enterprises in Europe. To a relatively small extent definition problems are responsible for this as a result of different vocational training and education cultures in the European partner countries. Decisive is the differentiation of the personnel and qualification structures in the sample of the surveyed companies which is representative for these problems both in the metal sector and the SMEs in Europe. The identified great differences result from

- the country-specific and regional development of basic vocational training

- the country-specific and regional long-term competitive development in the sector

- the specialisation strategy and position of the companies in the division of work

- the performance and manufacturing penetration of the companies

- product-related higher and lower demands on the skills of the employee

- the age of the company

- the period of employment in the company and staff turnover

- the staffing costs estimate by the companies

As most effective factors having an impact on the company-specific personnel and qualification structures appear to be, in the light of this survey, the specialisation strategies of metalworking small and medium-sized enterprises in the chain of work division between companies and the selected policy of performance penetration, with product and market features representing essential framework conditions. These specialisation strategies decide which departments, their staffing and qualification level exist in the companies and how distinct they are in terms of quality and quantity. In the investigated sample fully integrated companies contrast with components supplying companies whose staff is concentrated in production while system developers specialise in commercial, research/development, project-planning and service functions while covering large parts of the production through suppliers.

The description of general personnel and qualification structures as a point of reference for identified quality management-driven new skill needs thus appear to be inadequate. Instead, the survey identified some structural framework conditions for the staff-related implementation of quality management and its skills implications which can be attributed both to the specifics of the sector and of SMEs.

As small and medium-sized enterprises most of the surveyed companies show **organisational and personnel structures** which contain favourable elements for the implementation of quality management. These organisational and personnel structures originated both in a rather traditional development of family-owned small and medium-sized businesses and in specialisation strategies of metalworking small and medium-sized enterprises in the international competition in Europe (e.g. outsourcing, supplier etc.)

- The **executive level** is, as a rule, staffed with few people and rather little graduated. Often the executive personnel assumes tasks of the middle management, which leads to flat hierarchies, short, direct communication ways and management experience with the concrete processes and technologies in the company.

- On the side of the **employees** it is rare to have a strict division of functions with highly specialised tasks. Particularly in the systems engineering there are forms of teamwork between departments and between specialists within the departments, multi-functional job profiles and beginnings of inter-occupational skill profiles, which are not to be attributed to restructuring of the work organisation for the implementation of quality management, but which are, rather, to be seen as typical for the structure of the company, the product and the production. Especially in this direction there are in some companies efforts towards a flexible fulfilment of specific customer demands and a predominant production of unique items.

The **qualification structure** of the surveyed companies also shows some favourable conditions with regard to the requirements of a modern quality management. These conditions are essentially product- and sector-related.

- In many cases the qualification of the **executive personnel** is oriented towards technologies. This suggests an objective handling of nonconformity and quality problems. With a widening of the quality concept in the companies from the technology of the product to customer satisfaction follows from the strong orientation towards technology the concentration on application conditions of the products of the own company on the premises of the customers and on user problems. Customers belong mostly to the same sector. Pioneers in customer orientation are those companies which are used to extensive and detailed specifications and high product reliability standards from their traditional clients, for instance in the military area or automobile industry and/or whose products need to comply with safety standards regulated by law.

- The qualification structure of the **employees** in the surveyed metalworking companies is characterised by a sector-typical tradition of high skills partially associated with craftsmanship and received vocational education. The metalworking industry and particularly mechanical engineering in Europe remains a sector which is based on the co-operation of different special technologies - metal engineering, surface technology, pneumatics, hydraulics, processor engineering etc. - and which has to organise a co-operation - changing from order to order - between the respectively highly qualified specialists. A constant difference between the required latent staff skills and the ones applied in the current orders is characteristic. The rapid innovation in the processed materials, the products, control and production technologies requires from staff a constantly growing specialist and cross-occupational knowledge which, at least within the framework of the internally applied knowledge, increasingly blurs the border between engineering and occupational qualifications also for operatives. Fairly often are employees with knowledge gained by experience quite indispensable human resources for the companies.

Statements

"The company bets on a permanent staff of skilled workers. It is a company that provides training by conviction. In all responsible positions there are people we trained ourselves. We are proud of it." (116/F R Germany/40 employees/certification > 2 years/ISO 9001)

"Direct labour is the most important. Structured training is required for this group. Engineers and technical staff are fully aware via formal education and self learning which is well covered." (713/United Kingdom/110 employees/certification > 2 years/ISO 9001)

"On going training is always required but in a company of less than 50 employees one has to concentrate on essential training e.g. production skills, quality procedures. Most employees have been with the company for many years and staff turnover is very low. As a result there is quite a high level of skill in the organisation." (414/Ireland/49 employees/certification < 2 years/ISO 9002)

Personnel development and company strategy

The ISO-9000 series of standards requires of the companies that they systematically identify and document training needs and carry out employee training. This requirement is fulfilled by the surveyed companies for the certificate.

However, findings of the survey and statements of the interviewed managers show a discrepancy between the documented and the real personnel development in the company practice.

In the interviews those standardised questions encountered the greatest difficulties with the questioned experts, which inquired, broken down to departments and groups of employees, about quality management-related new skill demands on the staff and corresponding company-specific training programmes and courses. It was particularly difficult to get quantitative data about the amount of training, its topics and participants. To avoid terminological difficulties, these thematic areas have been described, to a wide extent, using standardised terms of the ISO standards or generally accepted terms of the quality management theory. Such difficulties were felt in only one case due to the fact that the management did not want to "publish" any details about the internal personnel structure and development.

In answers to open-ended questions some managers stated frankly that the documentation of staff-related measures for the ISO certification is one thing, but that in reality sometimes extensive measures of personnel development are planned and carried out according to other criteria. From the explanations of the company experts it is possible to characterise more closely some barriers for the implementation of the ISO demands on systematic staff training in the company-specific personnel development:

- In particular in some companies that are still seeking certification according to ISO 9000 it turns out that a more systematic identification of the human resources of the company and a more strategic planning of their skills development is only pushed by the ISO process.

- In the questioned companies it was, as a rule, strictly differentiated between quality-related and other job-related skill demands on the staff and corresponding training actions, on the one hand, but according to very different criteria from company to company, on the other. Attributing these demands was often considered to be a problem. This is probably because in these companies these qualification elements are not sufficiently identified in their interfaces.

- A critical assessment is also advisable for the view manifested in some of the surveyed companies that the ISO elements "training/staff" are to be dealt with as a special demand on the personnel development for passing the audits instead of making use of these audits as an opportunity to proceed to a company-specific framework planning of the human resources management. In contrast, "only to write down what we are doing anyway" seems to be the better approach.

- Some of the surveyed companies rely on the existing skills structure of the staff for managing the new demands on their staff for the certification of the company according to ISO 9000 and for the continuing implementation of their quality management. In contrast to the confidence in the traditional skills structure are, however, statements of other company experts that modern quality management can be implemented with less frictions with younger employees than with those of many years' standing.

The analysis of these findings shows strengths and weaknesses both of the ISO system and the personnel development of the questioned small and medium-sized enterprises of the metal industry:

1. It shows as a strong point of the ISO standards, especially in small enterprises, that they insist on skill needs analysis and on staff training, its systematisation and planning. At the same time, for many of the surveyed companies the ISO system is not suitable as an adequate planning instrument, but it is necessary for the formal fulfilment of the standards.

2. As a constant strong point of the surveyed companies it shows that they seek to maintain their capability to innovate and to react to the market also in the staff area with a multitude of work-based and problem-related training. With all due caution, it has also to be presumed that in the reality of personnel development of many of the surveyed companies there exists a lack of systematic identification of existing human resources or skill needs and of a strategic orientation of the personnel development.

In clear contrast to the findings of a little systematised management of human resources and a rather formal fulfilment of the ISO standard for staff training instead of a strategic personnel development within the framework of a company-specific quality policy is the constant view of the questioned experts that a high level of professional qualification of the employees is desired at the sectoral level and an essential component part of the strategy of their companies. This goes along with the indication of a multitude of continuing as well as selective training actions. Specialist knowledge and generic knowledge with a clear focus on information and data technologies. They stress that this is also the basis of quality-oriented work. Explicit quality training is carried out in addition to that.

Typical shortages of personnel concepts of the surveyed companies can thus be concretised on the basis of these statements:

1. Training activities for specialist knowledge are not sufficiently analysed with regard to their quality-critical and quality-promoting points and designed accordingly so that they could be integrated into a quality system-related training. This often leads to a competition for time and money between vocational further training and ISO training.

2. If training for the ISO system is undertaken primarily as a special demand on personnel development, companies have only insufficiently succeeded in

transferring the system into a company-specific quality policy that in formulating periodic quality aims makes up, at the same time, a framework for a strategic personnel development that also allows companies to react with training to the enormous external pressures.

These survey findings about the quality-related personnel development specify general findings about the state of development of the personnel management in small and medium-sized enterprises. The company-specific competition requirements to react rapidly and flexibly to market opportunities and customer wishes as well as quick technological innovation, create a great demand for the acquisition of new skills in the short term, which is, in fact, partially covered in the framework of limited financial and time resources. A systematic identification of the existing human resources and a strategy of personnel development driven by internal company aims which integrate these external demands in the long term is not common. This tendency is increased in some questioned companies by

- a great general change of the markets or competitive conditions of the small and medium-sized enterprises (e.g. reorientation in the European single market, new competitors from the new industrial countries etc.)

- rapid company-specific growth processes and/or employee turnover

Companies are most likely to operate with skill profiles, which are based on their long-term aims, when employing new persons. Above all, the personnel management of the permanent staff often goes down to haphazard short-term securing of special skills. Smaller companies rely on the fact that "you know who knows what to do". Medium-sized enterprises need to pursue a more methodical staff identification and policy but they allow it to be driven by external necessities. This applies often also to the fulfilment of the ISO standards whose element 20 demands systematised personnel-related and training actions. Many of the questioned companies, which admit discrepancies between the ISO documentation and the reality of their personnel development, justify these discrepancies with the competitive pressures to comply with the ISO standards also in the staff area.

The strongest awareness of strategic demands on personnel development by quality management is shown among the questioned managers by those who

- seek to fulfil new quality-related requirements with low-skilled staff (e.g. in areas of mechanical serial production)

- seek to integrate highly developed quality techniques in highly developed skills (e.g. self-control of operatives, FMEA etc.)

- implement a comprehensive reorganisation of work processes for a comprehensive quality system.

Statements

"HRM : The company feels it has not done enough in this area. The amount of time and effort required to introduce teamworking both initially and on an on-going basis means this is not an option for the company at present. While the operations manager wishes to go down this road at a later stage, the continuous growth and resulting pressure on production which the company is experiencing means that training, in this area, will not take place for some time.

For a number of reasons the company does not find it easy to provide training:

1. The company is rapidly expanding and training is concentrated on providing new employees with basic skills. Turnover doubled in 1993 and trebled in 1994 and has continued to grow significantly since. This has put enormous pressure on human resources.

2. There is no one solely responsible for training / personnel. As a result a training needs analysis has not been undertaken and ongoing training is not documented." (412/Ireland/130 employees/certification > 2 years/ISO 9002)

"Although I consider proper the company training policy, there is no such think as a never failing training plan, especially when we view it under a strategic perspective. Thus, having into account the need to adapt to future markets and being evolutive the surrounding reality, training also must be so. As new opportunities appear in the horizon, e.g. those concerning the new developing market of cryogenics, the need for new qualifications to meet these new products will arise. On the other hand, we will continue insisting on the behavioural-type training, inferred in the valuation we make of our human resources, considered as one of our best assets. However, to end and under a short/medium term perspective, I must say that if the company will increase its involvement with different markets, stocks management as well as transport management must be bettered." (512/Portugal/85 employees/certification > 2 years/ISO 9001)

Qualification-relevant new demands by quality management

ISO certification

The introduction of in the surveyed companies generally of the employee competencies. On the first hand in a more formal way: The ISO-9000 series of standards requires of the companies that they systematically identify and document job profiles and training needs and carry out employee training. On the second hand the work to introduce the ISO-System leads to a new consideration of the practical competence to act as well as the qualifications of the employees. But there is still a struggle going on in the companies for a proper identification of human resources and for the right answers about the personnel development policy.

The acquisition of the certificate according to ISO 9000 ff faces, in the first place, the senior- and middle-management levels with extensive tasks. All interviewed companies identify skill needs due to the introduction of the ISO system with the executive personnel. In the narrowest sense this concerns only the responsible person for quality.

The companies in the sample, which identify further-reaching needs of quality-related skills with the employees, can be typified, according to their stated reasons, as follows:

- Companies intending to translate the expenditure for the certification into strategic investment bet on activating existing and extended employee skills for the improvement of the formalised processes.

- Companies restructuring an elaborated old quality-assurance system (inspection department) identify retraining needs with the employees for the reintegration of quality responsibility.

- Companies with otherwise justified inter-departmental organisation need to implement quality management in these co-operation structures and, therefore, secure the qualification basis of divided responsibilities on a broader basis.

- Companies introducing quality management as a supporting measure of a repositioning in the market or of innovation of products or production technologies seek the integration of the necessary extensive personnel-development measures.

- But some executives identify simply in the expenditure of the documentation the skills and working experience of the employees as an indispensable support for establishing quality management. In many of theses companies these efforts lead to a rediscovering of the skills and work experiences of the employees and to a revaluation of their importance for the company. External consultants can help, even if at a fairly high price, to adapt the standards system of the ISO series and to make them manageable for the company and its specific processes. But many of the interviewed managers state, sometimes more critically, sometimes more self-critically, that the performance of external consultants for the establishment of a tailor-made quality system for the own company was limited. With the task to examine the concrete processes of the company for strong and weak points, to systematise and document them, the employees are discovered as experts on the spot who know the processes and weak points from their daily practice, and who have already, at least partially, also developed individual strategies for coping with the problems when they arise.

Resorting to knowledge and experience of the employees to establish a quality system is adequate to solve problems and achieve the aims. Many quality methods and techniques are, on their part, scientific generalisations of experience-based knowledge or scientific methods for systematisation and analysis of experiences of operating processes and technical performance processes.

This rediscovering of the human resources, which is induced by the certification process, is differently realised in the inquired companies.

- The importance of employee knowledge and experience is higher estimated with complex operations and production processes (e.g. in systems engineering and assembly) and in such functional areas of the company which require, as a rule, high specialist knowledge of the employees (e.g. in design, operations planning etc.)

- Staff participation is less estimated with highly mechanised production processes (e.g. in subcontractor companies). In these cases occurred some staff-related problems with the new quality-related methods (e.g. statistical process checking) and supporting methods (e.g. tasks of computer-aided manufacturing, preventive maintenance). These problems can be interpreted in such a way that these measures have not been developed from the beginning with the employees as an improvement of their method of working.

- The inclusion of employee skills and experience is more limited in larger companies, which are more structured according to functions, than in smaller ones or in companies with multi-functional and extended job profiles of the employees.

ISO process

In quite a few of the inquired companies it is possible to identify a rupture between the rediscovering of the existing employee skills and the practical involvement of the employees during the introduction of quality systems according to ISO 9000 ff and the management of the human resources after successful certification.

On the one hand, this proves to be adequate in those cases where the necessary next phase of routinisation of the new system is introduced. Because the companies are concerned with the next step of the implementation of their certified quality system, which consists in the fact that clarified and defined operations, methods and quality techniques need to be learned, mastered and observed in the everyday practice.

On the other hand, it is problematic when the awareness in the company gets lost again that the skills and the concrete job experiences, by this time also with the quality system, are an indispensable internal source for the preventive development of concrete steps towards conservation, continuation and improvement of the company-specific quality system, preventive as opposed to external assessments and demands due to customer complaints or the reaudit.

Good experiences are shown, however, by a minority of the respondent companies which intend to make use of the expenditure for the maintenance of the ISO certificate directly as a strategic investment also in the field of human capital. The ISO audit routine provides, according to their statements, especially small and medium-sized enterprises with limited time resources, a useful framework for company-wide training cycles which combine the preparation for an audit with efforts towards the improvement of the formalised processes activating and extending therefore employee skills. Company-wide training makes it obvious that it is not the individual employee that has to overcome skill shortages but that it is the whole organisation that reviews and learns its quality system in order to improve itself.

Changes of the internal processes and the work organisation

A clear majority of the respondent companies do not associate the introduction of quality management with the necessity of extensive changes of the processes and the work organisation. This can be attributed to two reasons:

- As changes of the processes and the work organisation the interviewed experts understand clear and obvious technological or organisational restructuring of the company.

- Technological, economic and structural reasons for such restructuring measures are of prime importance or at least of equal importance as requirements of the quality system.

Since, from this perspective, quality management is not a decisive reason for extensive changes of the processes and work organisation, the interviewed managers do not identify preponderantly from this perspective new job requirements and skill needs with the staff.

Insisting on the priority of technological, economic and structural reasons for the existing operation structures and their restructuring include, in many cases, sector- and company-specific quality aims as orientation, especially

- product quality

- service quality

- co-operation quality.

Being focused on such specific quality aims, the interviewed managers identify new job requirements and implicit skill needs as being of prime importance:

- function-related: in the functions preceding and following the productive functions and

- hierarchy-related: in the clerical and process-conducting staff groups.

On the other hand, the analysis of individual-company experiences shows that also at the operative level already the implementation of the ISO system changes the character of the work organisation and the way the companies refer to the skills of the employees. Since these changes do not have the obvious character of a restructuring, they are not always consciously perceived and organised as such by the interviewed managers. Where this occurs, the observations and reflections of the interviewees allow the following conclusions:

At the operative level the implementation of a systematic quality management in the operations of the company and in the work of the employees has two contrary effects on the demands on the skills of the employees.

- On the one hand, there occurs an objectivisation of specialist and process skills which before had been more in the responsibility of individuals. Already the documentation of detailed methodical and job instructions for the respective workplaces leads without greater work reorganisation this effect. Furthermore, quality technologies and thereof derived controls of processes such as the statistic process control and preventive maintenance are based on the specialist and experience knowledge of the staff, but as scientific methods they replace decisions and measures taken before by individual employees on the basis of skills they acquired by experience. On this objective basis rests also the tendency of quality management to flatten hierarchies. However, from this tendency arise fears in some companies - at least temporarily - of employees regarding loss of qualification, status and job.

- On the other hand, experiences prove in the surveyed companies a contrary tendency of the effects of quality management on the necessary skill profiles of the employees. Already with the documentation of the jobs are small-step instructions of superiors replaced by larger jobs and responsibilities of the employees, often without greater reorganisation of the work. The development of understanding for the documented job descriptions and of routine by using them at work, including the new documentation duties, often represent an essential first step towards the implementation of the quality system. Especially in cases where this was connected with new information and control technologies, new demands on employee skills arose which in some companies were identified as training needs. Relevant to training is also the following experience in some of the respondent companies: Only if the employees recognise in the new documentation and control methods not only an additional "bureaucratic" duty, but rather an improved means for the development of a more extensive responsibility for their own field of work, is the foundation laid for more autonomous quality-oriented control of this entire field of work by the employees.

Statements

"Concerning the question that quality training may result in vocational skills downgrading, let us say that machines became the key element, while previously an excellent tool involved an excellent professional, nowadays, with new industry equipment, we almost have no further use for excellent professionals." (513/Portugal/130 employees/aspiring certification/ISO 9001)

"Yes. There is a well identified lack of qualification, not in technical but in basic issues like writing a report or clearly summarising a problem using only a few words. In production, a shop-floor worker usually corrects an error instead of reporting it precisely defined in some procedures." (514/Portugal/431 employees/certification > 2 years/ISO 9002)

"Actually the workers checked their work themselves before, too, the checking methods and checking steps were not completely new to them. The inhibition level is where they assume responsibility themselves. To sign the record oneself, that is the inhibition level." (115/F R Germany/520 employees/certification > 2 years/ISO 9001)

Changes of the external relations

In an above-average number of times the respondents stated new quality management-related demands on the skills of the staff with regard to the *external* customer-supplier relations of the company. In a generic sense the inquired companies want, above all, improve their relationship with the customers and thus seek that employees

- develop an extended understanding for the application requirements and conditions of the products of the company with the customers

- internalise the justification for task-specific quality and work demands on the respective employees by customer wishes and in the company aim "customer satisfaction".

In the analysis in the individual company this picture differentiates, yet not mainly according to the degree of fulfilment of these aims. Due to very different demands of customers on the companies, the generic aims "customer orientation" and "customer satisfaction" set very different staff-related tasks in putting these demands into practice, require company-specific skills of the entire staff which differentiate, on their part, from company to company more or less according to functional employee groups. As crucial factors impacting these modifications were identified: the structure of the products of the company, the position and specialisation of the companies in the division of tasks, the size of the companies.

Thus

- are producers of serial bulk goods and suppliers of technologically simple components facing the task to raise the awareness among the employees for quality requirements whose quality-deciding importance is only perceivable on the premises of the customers or in the functional context of the end product;

- are providers of customer-specific system solutions - especially in mechanical engineering and systems engineering - facing the task to develop consulting, problem-solving and customer-service skills of their employees. This concerns, at first, especially functional groups and employees with tasks that have to do directly with customers: marketing/distribution/development & design, assembly & customer service;

- there are, in addition, analogue demands on the employee skills for the collaboration with suppliers and for co-operations within the company, according to the performance penetration.

The size of the company plays an important role for the company-specific degree of the function-specific distribution of such skills among employee groups. In small companies, in particular, such a function-specific distribution becomes practically irrelevant.

Some of the respondent companies undertake the interesting trial to use the external working relations of their employees to customers and suppliers deliberately as training opportunities and for gaining information for the training of internal supplier and customer knowledge. Measures have been taken by small as well as medium-sized enterprises which bring their employees from different departments in direct contact with suppliers and customers and thereby deliberately seek the development of a profounder understanding of the employees for the market partners of the own company and a spreading of such a supplier and customer knowledge in the staff. In some cases companies made decided arrangements with supplier and customer companies for employee coaching. The direct insight into production processes and operations of suppliers is for employees to learn what otherwise is only accessible in the internal documentations of incoming inspections and supplier assessments. The same applies more strongly to intensified customer contacts of employees: Employees can study concretely the utilisation conditions of the product of the company and the practical significance of the customer demands on quality, but also identify problems with the utilisation on the premises of the customer and develop service-specific skills. This helps to overcome departmental barriers of information and departmental thinking of quality responsibility in the own company.

These external contacts of employees, however, often do not seem to be systematically prepared, and the experiences subsequently assessed and multiplied. Smaller enterprises often rely on intensive informal communication. But already in small companies, and much more in more differentiated larger ones, is this concrete way of extending the market and customer-specific skills of the own staff in this sense still to be developed and improved.

Statements

"In our nail production prevailed the saying: "You can't make an omelette without braking eggs." Complaint statistics, quality-cost accountings don't mean much to people. Therefore, we once didn't, as an example, repay the customer an entire nonconforming batch with a credit note; instead we brought it back to the company. The employees had to sort out their own products. This way the employees get an objective and financial picture of what they have done. This was an educational measure and its effect was striking. We haven't had complaints, which would be worth mentioning, for years."(112/F R Germany/90 employees/certification < 2 years/ISO 9002)

"Operatives now view the 'box of electronics' leaving the factory , not as a low value item but as the million dollar product that leaves the customers premises." (412/Ireland/130 employees/certification > 2 years/ISO 9002)

"The focus of training is the company, and training takes place as a "pragmatic job rotation". Employees in the production are also assigned to materials purchasing in order to gain knowledge of suppliers and their production conditions. They work, on the other hand, in assembly and customer service on the clients' premises and are there expected to identify utilisation conditions of and practical demands on the products of the own company. Therefore, the management makes arrangements with suppliers and customers, now and then also informal agreements, in order to make sure that the own employees are coached by their specialists." (113/F R Germany/20 employees/aspiring certification/ISO 9001)

"Also employees go to the premises of the customer in order to make themselves more familiar with customers and their needs. One aim is to learn to communicate better with the customers. There is need for this kind of visits. It is very important to know all customers and their needs." (212/Finland/26 employees/aspiring certification/ISO 9002)

Training issues, areas and methods

Training issues and training areas

It was mentioned that there is still a struggle going on in the companies for a proper documentation of job profiles and for a clear identification of existing human resources as well as for the right answers about the personnel development policy. It was particularly difficult to get quantitative data about the amount of training, its topics and participants. In the interviewed companies a distinction was, on the one hand, made between quality-related and other occupation-specific and generic training measures, and, on the other hand, according to very different criteria varying from company to company, and very often the interviewed experts pointed out that it was a problem to give clear allocations.

This indicates a sector-specific challenge. The rapid innovation in the processed materials, the products and production technologies as well as increasing customer-specific projects and new forms of company co-operation requires from staff a constantly growing specialist and cross-occupational knowledge also to fulfil multi-role jobs. It is obvious that specialised quality training does not cover these needs. Therefore, a conflict between specialist training and quality training easily occurs in metalworking small and medium-sized enterprises. But this also indicates lacks of personnel strategy or the challenge to integrate quality issues as an orientation into the - otherwise often haphazard - approach to training.

Specialist training

Most of the respondent companies recognise a permanent need to improve and renew the specialist knowledge of their employees by training, and they state corresponding activities. But only a minority of the interviewed experts regard personnel-related requirements for the implementation of quality management to be the decisive source and guideline for specialist training in their companies. With regard to training contents, this means that only a small section of specialist training has been attributed to this aim. The following issues have been clearly attributed to the implementation of quality management:

- Training in understanding and handling of new quality documents, job instructions and documentation tasks
- Training in new checking technologies and methods
- Training in new quality-assuring control techniques.

In most cases the interviewees do not state implementation requirements of the quality system as source of training needs and as guideline for specialist training. As a rule, more specific requirements are decisive for the provision of training:

- Customers, or new customers, require new performances and product specifications

- The company creates innovative products, or it extends its tender by additional customer services

- New materials or materials with changed specifications are worked, or the company works with new suppliers

- New technologies are used in production, material flow and administration (for which the innovation of information and data technologies in all these areas produce permanent training needs)

- Changes in the organisation of the structure and operations of the company require training of employees for changed workplace documents.

These reasons for employee training often occur in combination and they are address by combined training, but even so is this specific training essentially related to individual cases and occurs in most cases as reactive actions. Elements of quality knowledge occur chiefly in the narrow sense of new specifications so that in this respect, too, a reactive quality concept still prevails which fulfils external demands.

Only in a minority of the respondent companies a more strategic orientation by quality aims and a proactive handling of the specialist employee training could be identified, and they could be attributed to three very different motives:

- basic reorientation of the company towards new markets and products

- strategic orientation of the company towards highly demanding products and processes

- general necessity of the company to improve the basic skills of the employees.

Especially in the last case the identification of training needs was directly linked to implementation requirements of the quality management.

First steps towards the embedding of specialist training of the company in a quality-oriented personnel development strategy were detected where

- specialist knowledge as an indispensable basis of quality awareness and quality-oriented working of the employees are identified

- identified occupation-specific skill shortages of employees lead to workplace-related training in quality management

- the company provide up-dating of existing specialist knowledge as an element of training routines in quality management.

Statements

"Performance requirements of the customers call for R&D work, new ways in design. This leads to new production materials and methods. The result

is permanent specialist training needs." (115/F R Germany/520 employees/certification > 2 years/ISO 9001)

"Giving "very important" to "vocational specialised knowledge" and "important" to "product knowledge", I intend to stress the difficulties people feel in dominating the most advanced technologies in the world in this sector. Everything happened so rapidly and equipment was so quickly developed that we were more concerned about training in that area." (513/Portugal/130 employees/aspiring certification/ISO 9001)

"We always focus on upgrading our employees' technical skills. On the job training is most important. We believe that as long as skills are upgraded, this will improve quality assurance." (311/Greece/146 employees/certification > 2 years/ISO 9001)

"Training is needed according to jobs accomplished. For example, if we have a new product for a new customer, which might need certain specifications (different taper, coil, heater etc) we give specific instructions to the foreman. The foreman describes to the production team concerned, verbally, what has to be done. This is not done through ISO. If a new machine is purchased, training is needed for the workers so that the best quality will be produced by this machine." (314/Greece/170 employees/aspiring certification/ISO 9001)

"Most important area is knowing their 'craft' - regarded as highly skilled work. Things that are relevant to that area are targets for QM training." (711/United Kingdom/44 employees/certification > 2 years/ISO 9001)

"As markets change it is inevitable that new demands will be put on the employees within the business for which training must be provided. Training is an integral part of all business and as such it is relevant to all employees within the business. Whatever change is taking place training is necessary if the best result is to be achieved." (712/United Kingdom/120 employees/aspiring certification/ISO 9002)

"At the moment the company feels all staff have sufficient training in quality related issues. However on-going training is required, especially

when product specifications are altered or new production methods are introduced." (414/Ireland/49 employees/certification < 2 years/ISO 9002)

"The performance of the workers is appraised according to the quality of their work. If a worker gets less than 5 points in the quality field on the occasion of performance appraisal, this worker has to submit to training actions in order to overcome knowledge deficiencies." (512/Portugal/85 employees/certification > 2 years/ISO 9001)

"Training is preponderantly project-oriented and provided internally. Experiences and training materials of foreign companies of the same group are made use of. The focus is the introduction of new technologies and their impact on the departments such as purchasing/new specifications for raw materials, production/operating machines and preventive maintenance, sales/modification of the range of goods and services offered etc. Autonomous learning processes are organised according to a project plan. External consultants are only called in when difficulties arise, while we encourage self-initiative in such cases too." (112/F R Germany/90 employees/certification < 2 years/ISO 9002)

Cross-occupational training

In most of the respondent companies there exists an awareness that for the internal implementation of quality management the co-operation between departments is of crucial importance. It is widely spoken about "internal customer-supplier relations". Some managers also stated communication and co-operation between the departments as critical points or weak points of their quality system to be overcome.

Compared with this management approach of the company experts, a systematic identification of interfaces, of corresponding needs for generic and specialist skills of the employees and therefore tailored training programmes, still needs to be improved. Often the interviewed managers inferred the need for social *key skills* such as "communication and team ability" directly from the aim of getting an improved inter-functional co-operation. Little widespread was the idea that inter-functional quality requirements such as "understanding quality requirements of closely-related departments", "manufacturing-oriented design" etc. also require an *objective cross-occupational* basis of knowledge in form of *elements of specialist knowledge* from the other departments. Quite often it was assumed that a solid basic vocational education and the everyday co-operation experience in the company secure this basis by themselves, without having to undertake deliberate efforts in personnel development.

This critical finding does not mean that cross-occupational training does not exist in the inquired companies. Characteristic is rather the fact that elements of such a training are induced by very heterogeneous motives so that requirements of the ISO system act at the same time haphazardly with requirements of new internal information technologies, product-related co-operation among employees of different occupational specialisation, company interests in flexibly employable staff, restructurings of the company structure according to aspects of division, matrix or project management. An improvement of the internal training needs analysis aimed at a quality-oriented integration of these training efforts thus seems to be desirable.

The following disparate approaches to the development of quality-related cross-occupational training could be identified in the inquired companies:

- The ISO standards represent an impetus to identifying cross-occupational training needs, especially with the demands for documentation of operations and document control.

- This impetus has a stronger effect in companies which at the same time introduce new information technologies. On the other hand, the in-plant interdepartmental training of employees is often limited to an immediate acquisition of computing skills.

- Companies increasingly identify training needs for securing cross-occupational skills, e.g. to develop user-specific offer packages, above all among employees with external contacts to suppliers and customers. From these departments the necessity to harmonise complex customer requirements with the internal abilities induces the identification of needs of corresponding cross-occupational skills among employees in internal departments.

- Product-related or sector-specific forms of inter-occupational co-operation are identified as a bases of a quality-assuring collaboration to be secured and improved by training. This also applies to the co-operation in small companies, which was unplanned and informal before.

- Originally rather economically founded inter-functional organisation structures and multi-functional job profiles are, on the one hand, identified as a good basis of quality management and, on the other, as a learning field to be organised.

Statements

"The demand for interdisciplinary skills is growing fast in such a culture as ours which is developing its own performance activities. Also the significance of problem-solving techniques and co-operational skills is increasing." (211/Finland/38 (1250) employees/certification > 2 years/ISO 9001)

"Circulation of the jobs and tasks is one way of training. A monitoring system is being developed for gathering information on the effects of circulation." (211/Finland/38 (1250) employees/certification > 2 years/ISO 9001)

"1. Marketing is one area. Marketing oriented thinking. It is needed also in production. That understands the business oriented way of working and what it means in production.

2. Computer skills

3. Quality system training for new employees.

4. Employees with interdisciplinary skills are needed. In the future an employee should have abilities to interact with customers and should have skills to express themselves so that they are understood also on the customer side. Ability to translate the request of a customer into technical questions and answers that could be analysed and solved." (213/Finland/55 employees/certification > 2 years/ISO 9002)

"All employees must have a perfect knowledge of the products' technical specifications, because they all are very important in the process of detecting and correcting mistakes." (513/Portugal/130 employees/aspiring certification/ISO 9001)

"Our company is now implementing a global management information system, chosen after a strategic diagnosis which identified insufficient and unprecise information as one of the major problems in the company's decision making process. So, in order to extract all the potential of new IT and related procedures it is essential to assure an extensive training programme for all employees." (514/Portugal/431 employees/certification > 2 years/ISO 9002)

"The main issues that should be addressed in the future are employee flexibility and utilisation through multi-skilling initiatives." (712/United Kingdom/120 employees/aspiring certification/ISO 9002)

"New requirements due to design or production engineering are coped with in form of internal job instructions. Production staff are to be utilised in a

flexible way, e.g. should manual lathe operators also be able to operate the CNC technology in order to be able to step in when necessary. Skilled employees are assumed to have basic technical knowledge and social abilities such as responsibility." (116/F R Germany/40 employees/certification > 2 years/ISO 9001)

Training of quality system knowledge

Generally, the respondent companies reject non company-specific employee training in the general system of the ISO standards or in theoretical systems of quality management with the argument that such abstract system knowledge is not useful for the practical realisation of the concrete quality aims of the company. The generic theoretical basic training is reserved for the responsible quality managers or representatives. With regard to the internal quality training of the employees, the interviewees take quite homogeneously the view that it has to impart the company-specific quality system. The picture becomes irregular with regard to the methods companies adopt in this system training.

As a practical key issue of the internal planning of an effective system training of the staff have crystallised in the expert interviews the decision on the right mixture of overview knowledge of the quality system of the company and of workplace-related special knowledge of quality elements:

> How far does the system training in the quality system and in the quality policy of the company support the training of the employees in the detailed quality tasks of their specific work field or, conversely, how far does specialised workplace-related quality training underpin, the understanding of the employees for the company-wide quality system and promote the engagement of the employees in its care and in the improvement aims of the quality policy?

The following deciding factors have been preponderantly identified for the different decisions on these issues in the companies:

- Differences of the company size, the complexity of the internal division of labour and the resulting differentiation of the documented quality elements and instructions are crucial factors.

- Furthermore, a different stressing between generic system knowledge and function-specific knowledge of elements of the system, according to the stage of development of the quality system used in the company was recognisable. Generic system knowledge is in the foreground in setting up and in reorganisation phases of the company-specific quality management. After it training in the detail comes to the fore when the quality instructions are to be carried out in the working routine and in self-responsibility of the employees: "Where are the manuals expected to be used?", "Where is this or that to be found in the manuals?", "Where are there the relevant methodical and work instructions for the own work area?" etc.

The necessary scope of such training needs is not to be underestimated. But now and then some statements of interviewed managers on an unexpected lengthiness of these training phases, lacking motivation and barriers with the employees also point to deficiencies in the training concept. Training in knowledge of elements neglects necessary generic system knowledge, the awareness of the cross-functional relevance of the "own" quality element. For example, techniques of checking and quality control on ones own responsibility - the "what, when, how" - require the awareness of the "why and for whom", labelling and documentation duties find their intrinsic motivation in the orientation at the "what for and for whom".

A sector-specific problem of the connection between cross-functional orientation knowledge of the quality policy and the quality system of the company and the function-specific knowledge of workplace-related quality tasks results from the production of metalworking companies for industrial customers. The quality requirements of industrial customers are essentially based on commercial and engineering expert knowledge, which is not available to many employees especially at an operating level. Training in quality system that intends to embed workplace-specific quality tasks in an orientating company-wide quality awareness of the employees faces, therefore, the difficulty of not being able to resort to such expert knowledge among many employees nor to quality concepts of end consumers. In a narrower sense, this problem was identified by some interviewees in the difference between product-related and manufacturing-related quality requirements. This difficulty arises chiefly in the quality training of operating employees in production. Specifications for dimensional accuracy in production of parts cannot easily be represented in their quality-deciding function context of the end product on the premises of the customer. But, at the same time, the experiences of some of the interviewed company experts prove the necessity of training that promotes such a generic quality awareness of the employees.

Examples of good practice were achieved in companies which

- impart workplace-specific quality elements in their concrete system context ("interfaces")

- put practice training and repetition training of function-specific quality elements in the perspective of a critical review of the practical suitability and improvement of the documented elements.

- combine workplace-related quality training with exemplary familiarisation with quality elements of closely related and other functional areas. In "other" areas employees obtain, in the first place, access to the "sense" of the formalised quality instructions and then, by deduction, they understand more easily the instructions they are directly concerned with.

The forms in which the respondent companies institutionalise their quality system training can hardly be systematised. It is relatively usual that

- the introduction to the quality system and the quality aims of the company is part of the employment training
- the audit cycle constitutes the framework of a company-wide brush-up of the system knowledge.

Apart from that, continuing job-accompanying training was preponderantly stated.

Statements

*"I don't think much of external survival seminars for the certificate."
(111/F R Germany/167 employees/certification < 2 years/ISO 9001)*

"Each new employee is trained in the company quality system procedures, the focus being dimensional and fitting accuracy. Internal audits are carried out regularly. Producing quality is part of the organisational climate." (116/F R Germany/40 employees/certification > 2 years/ISO 9001)

"The integration of the employees of the different departments in different project pools presupposes clear procedural and working instructions, but it also makes training in these fields difficult. Training in the quality system of the company is, therefore, to be ensured in a plant-wide training of the employees by the quality department. Therefore we focus on job-specific or workplace-related issues. It has been regretted that a regular in-house magazine, in which quality issues were also dealt with, has ceased publication. I can't expect employees to know the whole manual in all sections. But they must know the instructions they need to follow. The employees know where they can look up something they need. They are also encouraged to do it. That is the quality policy of the management." (115/F R Germany/520 employees/certification > 2 years/ISO 9001)

"At this moment we have a running training program, that covers all employees, beginning with the Managing Director and ending with the production workers, covering the following issues: General management, Quality in the company, Team leader training course, Quality and human behaviour. I think that extensive training is essential for quality development." (511/Portugal/181 employees/certification > 2 years/ISO 9001)

"Primarily, the training has been focused on quality issues relevant to the employees' job position. Also a less intensified general quality training has been implemented. Most of the personnel in this sector are older with little or no educational background and they accomplish the work based mainly on experience." (312/Greece/47 employees/certification < 2 years/ISO 9002)

"When people are interviewed they are asked for their views on quality. When approved, they get induction training and they must sign a form to agree to follow quality procedures. On-going audits keep "quality issues in peoples' minds". Training is integrated to working practices. Focus groups meet regularly." (711/United Kingdom/44 employees/certification > 2 years/ISO 9001)

"Quality system first comes into personnel function when candidates are interviewed for jobs. Also comes into the selection process. QA is responsibility of all - it's built into everybody's job." (711/United Kingdom/44 employees/certification > 2 years/ISO 9001)

"The company has a system in three steps;

1. Repeating of former quality training programmes

2. General training in ISO 9002 and going through the manual

3. Detailed training programme individually adapted for functions/groups at the company"(613/Sweden/186 employees/aspiring certification/ISO 9002)

"Each new employee receives training in quality management "detached from the day-to-day operations" ... But we also run regular training in the quality system of the company for small groups of employees (about 5) from different departments. In general, the aim and object of quality management is explained as well as the organisation of the ISO elements. On the basis of practical examples the participants develop an idea also of the quality elements which do not concern them directly, e.g. an assembler of "contract reviewing". Then they go through documents directly concerning the own workplace. For the reaudit they receive work-based area-related additional training, where practical quality problems are also dealt with. Approaching the employees this way we want to pave the way

*for them to take the initiative to report and solve quality problems." (111/F.
R Germany/167 employees/certification < 2 years/ISO 9001)*

Training of process competence

The relatively young imperative of the quality management theory to develop not product- but process-oriented quality awareness of the employees encounters, at least in the exaggerated version as an alternative, scepticism with the experts in small and medium-sized enterprises. On the one hand, as a typical feature of the sector, product knowledge and orientation of the employees as a guideline for the internalisation of job-specific quality tasks is a very demanding programme. The understanding of products for industrial customers, for their application conditions and for quality requirements of these customers mostly presupposes engineering and commercial knowledge. When imparting this knowledge to employees which are not adequately trained, it is only partially possible to build on their working experience - e.g. working competence - but not on their experience as end consumers. On the other hand, the aim "process orientation" differentiates in the company practice, especially according to the products of the respective company: process stability and mastery with machine-based serial production and project mastery with special production.

Deliberate approaches to training of quality-related process competence have been developed, above all, by those companies which are determined to develop their quality system towards TQM.

Under the slogan "Discovering the employee", the following practical definition of process competence has been given:

> The job experience of the employees are to be made profitable for the identification of quality-related critical points in the process, the specialist knowledge is to be activated and developed from a mere basis for operative tasks in the company towards competencies in preventive analysis of such critical points; practical job experience and developed specialist knowledge are to lead the wealth of knowledge and experience into the development of improvement measures.

This aims at a bringing together the imparting of system knowledge - explaining the management system of quality (top-down) including training in documented procedural instructions and quality engineering - with the development of specific and generic skills and a practical competence extension of the staff (bottom-up).

First signs of such an integration were identified also in companies which so far do not pursue it deliberately as a strategy towards a comprehensive process-related quality system. For in many of the inquired companies training in occupation-specific skills is explicitly considered important also because it is regarded to be a substantial basis for the implementation of quality management and for achieving quality aims in the concrete work of the employees. It is also common to attribute quality and process problems to shortages in the skills of the employees or gaps in the utilisation of the skills. In some cases, companies also control training activities of employees on the basis of an identification of process malfunctions.

Even so, in these cases personnel development oriented towards process quality has so far only been realised in first steps. For if the occupation-specific skills and job experience of the employees are to become the "lively" competence for the identification of critical points of the company processes and the source of preventive improvement measures, then this orientation should be a decisive aim, an integral part of the contents and essential success criterion of specialist and generic personnel development. Examples of such a proactive planning were only identified in the first-mentioned companies with explicit TQM targets.

Overall, it is evident in the sample, that in company practice the planning of process competence as training target is connected with starting a continuous improvement process as quality policy of the enterprise.

Two special impulses for the development of process-oriented quality and training concepts for the personnel have been identified in the sample of the inquired companies.

- Companies whose products pass through complex production processes or vary strongly according to individual customer wishes, quickly encounter barriers of a rigidly structured quality system, e.g. within the framework of the ISO standards. Maintaining the indispensable flexibility sets limits to standardisation and formalisation of operations for the assurance of quality limits. Progress in the process quality and process competence of the employees are thus obvious steps to improve quality management.

- An increased effort towards process quality has also been identified in companies which are, for different reasons, undergoing a basic repositioning and restructuring. This applies e.g. to companies facing the necessity to position themselves in the internal market in the course of the expansion of the EU in the north of Europe or for companies which, driven by competition, feel themselves compelled to great changes in their range of goods and services offered as well as extensive technological readjustment.

Statements

"I think extensive training might be needed. As training techniques we strongly suggest on-the-job training for non-executives and the seminars for all. The issues are the following:

1. Quality Assurance System Implementation Gaps

2. *Technical Training - Programming CNC power, Programming central process, Programming surface protection." (311/Greece/146 employees/certification > 2 years/ISO 9001)*

"We always work new types of projects, sometimes in international co-operation. Therefore, the information must get to the employee, in order that he/she knows what he/she actually has to work. We want to be a large team. The company demands a lot of the employees: self-responsibility, self-checking. Therefore the qualification of the employee in relation to the product is required. A first group of employees is being trained in FMEA. Here the company sees itself as a pioneer in the sector." (115/F R Germany/520 employees/certification > 2 years/ISO 9001)

"More training is needed mainly on the following topics:

1. new types of products

2. extensive knowledge of the production process and the new techniques developed world-wide

3. communication of production information to other departments." (313/Greece/260 employees/aspiring certification/ISO 9002)

"As the company seeks product quality through process capability, the quality of the work of each employee becomes crucial. Here the information loop of the top-down task "quality management" closes which, according to ISO 9000, begins with error detection, search for the cause and debugging." (111/F R Germany/167 employees/certification < 2 years/ISO 9001)

"This is the main issue; making the personnel understand that the customer is using our products." (611/Sweden/110 employees/aspiring certification/ISO 9001)

"The quality training as a separate job doesn't exist. It is integrated into our training as a part of training. Quality training is integrated into initiation training that a person receives when he/she starts to work in the company. Separate quality management training is arranged only to persons, who are responsible for the quality management system, as a quality manager or auditor." (211/Finland/38 (1250) employees/certification > 2 years/ISO 9001)

"We emphasise as extremely as necessary to raise the level of "perception" of quality as a company philosophy at all hierarchical levels, and, most especially, at the production sector, by seeking that shop floor workers do not confine themselves to carrying out established procedures but actively participating in the process, by means of improvement suggestions, for instance; therefore, we think it necessary to afford general training on quality, and, on the other hand, a special behavioural-type training. Anyhow, our greatest needs fall upon the technical level, and this concerns not only very particular aspects, as, for instance, the aluminium welding techniques, where qualification is more difficult to attain, but also other general aspects. The raising of individual and collective qualification demands great efforts, however it will allow to reduce failures and to increase quality. Finally, we point out a great effort on the part of the semi-skilled staff, consisting of employees who are not yet prepared to assure internal training programmes." (511/Portugal/181 employees/certification > 2 years/ISO 9001)

"People are considered in our company as one of its most important assets, and are deeply engaged with our business in general. For the next five years, our most urgent goal is the search of new products and markets, able to progressively fill in the reduction of demand concerning our present products. We also know that our training planning must take into consideration creativity and innovation ability, in parallel with new technical qualifications for the production of new products." (512/Portugal/85 employees/certification > 2 years/ISO 9001)

"Training should be at three levels:

Level 1:

Orientation training to cover policies, products, markets of the company and technical training on the production methods and quality practices relevant to a particular job.

Level 2 :

Three months after employment commences, further training should be given to encourage operatives to work independently and to take responsibility for their work. At this stage employees should be actively engaged so that the quality process becomes self sustaining.

Level 3 :

Continuous training e.g. every six months, to ensure staff do not forget skills and to enable them to learn new ones as needs arise. Usually training is driven out of a need for corrective action." (411/Ireland/150 employees/certification > 2 years/ISO 9001/2)

"Malcolm Baldridge workshops have been organised for experts: information of real cases is gathered from the own company and others too." (211/Finland/38 (1250) employees/certification > 2 years/ISO 9001)

Training of social competencies

The majority of the interviewed managers gives social key skills such as "communication ability", "team capability", "responsibility", "problem-solving competence" in the open talk a decisive position in the personnel-related implementation of quality management and considers training necessary to achieve a high degree of fulfilment. It was, at the same time, striking that mainly companies with long experience in quality management stated the most difficult implementation tasks in this field.

Caution seems, therefore, to be advisable in the interpretation of these statements when using these examples for quality-oriented personnel development concepts and training. This focusing of personnel development on social key skills or "behaviour" of the employees quite often seems to arise from the desire for a passe-partout intended to replace the detailed and extensive training of the employees to be supporting subjects in the company-specific quality system. A careful review seems to be advisable especially in those cases when "the everyday life in the company" "learning by doing", "by work", "ongoing training", etc. are preponderantly stated as company-specific methods of training social key skills. On the one hand, social skills only develop in the practical social context but, on the other hand, the desired result of quality-oriented collaboration of the employees is not to be attained without efforts to develop the necessary skills, more or less automatically from the continuing work routine in the production process.

A key issue in the expert talks was the following:

What can be achieved by training, or by which kind of training can success be achieved when the change towards a quality culture of the companies and towards a quality-conscious behaviour of the employees is the main focus of interest and not a series of clearly identifiable abilities.

From the answers of the interviewees, the necessary interplay of the following factors can be retained:

1. "Social skills" of employees are necessary as a precondition to set up a company-specific quality system with the support of the employees, to carry out the necessary learning and multiplying processes among the employees and to apply the new quality knowledge in the everyday working practice. Otherwise the quality system remains an effort of special managers and on paper, and employee training remain "secret expert knowledge" in the double sense: the employees retain it in their head and it does not help promote quality.

2. Without imparting concrete new quality-relevant elements of occupation-specific and generic skills as well as action-relevant skills in the company processes, appeals for "employee motivation" and "self-responsibility", "quality awareness" and "team spirit", "problem awareness" and "conflict capability" remain without substance even if they are issues of training.

3. Social key qualifications require to be embedded in company structures and forms of work organisation, in which they can really be "lived". In the inquired smaller companies the managers often rely on a natural basis of confidence. But examples also show in these companies the necessity to deliberately institutionalise these structures in order to stand growth and restructuring processes. Larger companies are equipped with differentiated, formalised and more anonymous social structures. In these companies the demand for special forms of organisation for the development and practise of quality-promoting social employee skills such as quality and innovation circles are felt but not always put into practice.

The most important finding from the questioning of company experts seems to be the experience of some interview partners that before learning quality-promoting social skills it is necessary to "dislearn" old established social behaviour patterns of instruction and execution, labour and supervision, work and control, which otherwise act as a blockade. Hierarchy-supported instructive behaviour devalues objective authority and hampers the integration of employee competence for the identification and solution of quality problems; resulting from the old separation of supervision and labour, the paralysing confusion of objective self-responsibility for the identification, documentation and elimination of nonconformity with personal liability is still alive.

Statements

"Couldn't really pick out any one group as more in need of training - it applies to all levels of employee "from me to the delivery man". We carry out (informal) in-house training constantly - we run regular focus groups which include all staff from apprentices to senior managers. It's seen as a means of raising a general awareness." (711/United Kingdom/44 employees/certification > 2 years/ISO 9001)

"Building on quality training for employees and superiors, another training for superiors is carried out, especially for the superiors working as team leaders of small groups. The superiors must motivate the quality awareness of the employees. The wealth of experience lies with the employees, and we must dig it out." (115/F R Germany/520 employees/certification > 2 years/ISO 9001)

"It appears to me that there is need for training concerning the facility for independent working and willingness to take responsibility as a holistic approach. The lack of these facilities appears as carelessness." (212/Finland/26 employees/aspiring certification/ISO 9002)

"Team working skills. Languages and knowledge of other cultures." (211/Finland/38 (1250) employees/certification > 2 years/ISO 9001)

"If we go towards teamworking the attitude the work of one's own must develop in the direction of multi-disciplinarity. In team working it is a question of abilities and attitudes more than skills." (214/Finland/145 employees/certification > 2 years/ISO 9001)

"Henceforth, we would like our employees to assume themselves as self-starters concerning knowledge acquisition, being able on their own to detect problems and give rise to possible forms of solution. Greater responsibilities in an atmosphere of enlarged autonomy and, most of all, a sharp criticism ability are features to set a value on. Now, this kind of considerations shows us the need to invest strongly in training in the behavioural area, which presently still has an incipient weight, in percentage, in the costs of our yearly training planning." (513/Portugal/130 employees/aspiring certification/ISO 9001)

"The employees of our company, particularly those working in production, have a high average level of age, and lack of behavioural qualification skills, but in technical issues there are not any important knowledge gaps." (514/Portugal/431 employees/certification > 2 years/ISO 9002)

"Communication and purpose are often more effective than formal training where cultural training is concerned." (712/United Kingdom/120 employees/aspiring certification/ISO 9002)

Training methods and training conditions

The in-plant organisation of training with work-based or work-related methods is clearly the prevalent way in which the respondent companies seek to cover the quality-related skill needs in the narrower sense (ISO or quality system knowledge) and in the broader sense (quality-relevant specific and generic knowledge and social skills).

External quality-related training provisions are essentially reserved for managerial staff (especially quality managers, quality representatives etc) and for the acquisition of supplementary skills required from employees for the certification (nondestructive testing, welder certificate etc).

This summary evaluation can be made although incomplete quantitative data and partly incompatible statements were given. The qualitative statements of the experts support this finding. Moreover, they reveal the essential reasons for the decisions taken by the companies:

Quality-related training

• must be justifiable in the face of the limited time and capital resources of the companies

• is expected to be applicable and useful to the specific needs of the company

The majority of the inquired companies seek to fulfil these criteria through in-plant and work-based training.

The interviewed company experts showed only little awareness of the strained relation between the rather restrictive budgeting of training efforts as a guideline and the rather demanding aim of making training really useful to the company. Only first signs of *methodical* considerations and arrangements to tackle this strained relation by making the internal training more effective have been identified; they were explicit only in a minority of the questioned companies.

Where such first signs were identified, the tendencies can be summarised as follows:

• Supplementary skills of executives and superiors (middle management) are to secure and improve the multiplication of quality-relevant know-how and promote the learning interest and the integration of skills of employees.

- The size of training groups, their make-up from different functional and hierarchical groups and the work-based positioning of training are to secure the learning capability, problem orientation and utilisation.

- Companies support external training employees undertake on their own initiative in order to limit the internal training expenditure and to promote the integration of extended employee skills in the company processes.

- The selection of external training bodies and provisions is to guarantee tailor-made training units.

- A special case of such an approach consists in using company co-operations and networks for company-related employee training.

In-company training methods and training conditions

With regard to internal training methods in the respondent companies, strictly speaking only the prevalent criteria can be generalised:

- they must be job-related and
- profitable.

Apart from quality training relevant to the ISO audit, employment training and elements of vocational skills compulsory for the certification, the internal training methods of the surveyed companies can hardly be significantly typified.

The results of the interviews show that the companies operate with little formalised, pragmatic methods. The dividing lines between work and work organisation, on the one hand and training and communication, on the other hand, in the company practice become fluid in a range of job instructions, coaching - partially through partner companies -, working discussions and training units.

Special forms of organisation such as quality circles, focus groups, improvement groups etc were not often mentioned. Some examples suggest the conclusion that small and medium-sized enterprises usually only set up such forms for the introduction of quality systems, taking them back to work-relevant structures afterwards.

On the other hand, first signs could be noticed that - initiated by requirements of the quality management - internal information and control structures are being increasingly reflected as places of quality-related learning, structures which served before exclusively for the corporate management and performance organisation. Companies review from this perspective their communication and work forms to find out whether they promote or rather hamper learning. In the average of the surveyed companies this tendency can so far only to be recognised in rudiments. The concepts of the respondent experts about necessary changes of the behaviour especially of superiors are clearer than about necessary changes of the organisation.

The result of the survey of internal training methods for the personnel-related implementation of quality management can thus be best summarised in a key question in the majority of the surveyed companies, although generalisable and transferable concepts for solutions cannot yet be identified:

What are the adequate organisational impulses for the employees to internalise the quality system and quality policy of the company?

Statements

"Problems along with some prejudices existing were faced in the beginning of our effort. Through training and communication we have reached a level where the employees press the management for the ISO certification at first and then for its implementation." (313/Greece/260 employees/aspiring certification/ISO 9002)

"We can only send people to training when teamwork is established, then they pass their knowledge to the colleagues." (112/F R Germany/90 employees/certification < 2 years/ISO 9002)

"While teamwork, especially cross functional, is important, it is only possible to have a limited number of teams operational at any one time. In the respondent firm the ideal number is 6 - 8 teams as each team requires approximately two hours per week for discussion groups etc. This is the maximum disruption the production department can sustain without falling behind schedule. As a result the change process takes a little longer to implement." (411/Ireland/150 employees/certification > 2 years/ISO 9001/2)

"Training is important. But training is subsidiary, the attitude must be there. The attitude towards training and education."(612/Sweden/125 employees/certification < 2 years/ISO 9002)

"The main issue is that the organisation itself should work with education." (611/Sweden/110 employees/aspiring certification/ISO 9001)

External training

Only about a third of the respondent companies stated that the national basic vocational training covers sufficiently the skill needs of the employees for the implementation of quality management. In this context it is advisable to assess critically statements expressing the expectation that the basic vocational training should provide quality-related skills for employees but do not work out concrete requirements out of the own company experience.

The majority of the companies consider training also for the continuing implementation of quality management as indispensable and, therefore, resort also to external training provisions.

The resort to external training concentrates on know-how in managing quality management and remains predominantly reserved to executives responsible for quality. The input of this external knowledge in the companies occurs by

- new employment of externally trained quality managers

- external training of executives as quality managers and auditors

- resort to external consultants for the setting up and actualisation of the quality system.

In the segment of management training the respondent companies are predominantly satisfied with the obtainability, contents and cost-to-performance ratio of external training provisions. The ISO certification wave has created the provision, often the certifiers participate in the provision of quality management training. For the satisfaction an advantage of the metalworking sector - in spite of some criticism of the "sector-unrelatedness" of the ISO system - plays a role: The automobile industry is a pioneer in the (further) development of quality systems and quality techniques so that these subjects are often trained on the basis of sector-related examples.

In spite of the basic satisfaction with the external provision of know-how in managing quality management, the majority of the interviewed experts express the criticism that external quality training is not sufficiently "company-related" as regards contents and organisation, and they call for "tailor-made" provisions. They criticise an overweight of generic system knowledge in the external training provisions while missing problem-related implementation knowledge. These critical assessments relate above all to the provisions of large widespread training organisations.

Some companies have, therefore, decided to utilise consultants already at the input of management know-how, giving priority to private business consultants in order that the quality system is tailor-made for the company and not the company for the quality system.

In contrast with the fundamental satisfaction with the training provision for managerial staff, the majority of the surveyed companies do not consider the quality training of the employees with current provisions of external training institutions to be in the best hands.

A similar picture is shown when external training provisions for quality-relevant qualifications in the broader sense are utilised. For managers social qualifications for the development of a co-operative management style are in the foreground, while external training for employees is concentrated on specialised knowledge.

A promising way not only for the company-specific adaptation of quality systems for metalworking small and medium-sized enterprises but also for establishing more company-related training schemes for employees is seen in companies of various countries participating in the survey in setting up company networks. Companies come to this approach on different ways

- through good experiences with the preparation of the certification according to ISO 9000 in networks which are partially promoted by the region, nation or the EU

- by using external customer-supplier relations for employee training on their own initiative

- through inter-company forums for the exchange of experiences in quality issues

- through the company interest in orienting itself on new markets by benchmarking.

Statements

"The more unqualified the staff is the more difficult it is to get quality management in. But in this company one stays two weeks or thirty years. We are now rejuvenating the staff, and the Jung people bring already quality with them from the vocational school." (116/F R Germany/40 employees/certification > 2 years/ISO 9001)

"All Quality Systems have been included in the NVQ which is the dominant training vehicle for shopfloor personnel within this business." (712/United Kingdom/120 employees/aspiring certification/ISO 9002)

"For new products the employees are trained externally. The same applies to the setting up of the quality system and the preparation for the

certification. Probably there will arise training needs in connection with quality management. We are still at the beginning." (114/F R Germany/22 employees/aspiring certification/ISO 9001)

"The company regards itself in a leading role in utilising external training. The integration of external experiences, in particular also from other companies of the sector, is part of the philosophy of the management. One reason lies also in the necessity of being capable for international projects." (115/F R Germany/520 employees/certification > 2 years/ISO 9001)

"For quality management the quality manager should be trained externally as quality manager and auditor. The employee training should then be basically done internally by these managers as multipliers in order that the company-specific quality system is trained. I would never place training in quality system externally, there you learn all theory but get no notion of our practice." (111/F R Germany/167 employees/certification < 2 years/ISO 9001)

"Training is needed. Direct labour can be all 'on-the-job'. Supervisors need external training. 'Auditors' need external training." (713/United Kingdom/110 employees/certification > 2 years/ISO 9001)

"In external seminars with a broad range of participants the information which is exciting for us goes lost in a jumble of the overall description of the subject matter." (113/F R Germany/20 employees/aspiring certification/ISO 9001)

"Even in big training institutions training is carried out by only one person. The training programmes also have characteristics of one-man performance. In institutions you can usually find only one person who is an expert and knows the subject. In that way in big training institutions the base of knowledge is thin." (211/Finland/38 (1250) employees/certification > 2 years/ISO 9001)

"There is an excess of external training provision. Most important training was provided by the consultant who helped them to design our QM system at the start of accreditation. It was custom-built for our needs. Much of the

training provision is not geared to the particular concerns of SMEs. We require very focused (short periods) of training. Two areas which could be addressed.

1) General awareness of quality issues at the beginning of accreditation process.

2)   Internal   quality   auditing." (711/United   Kingdom/44 employees/certification > 2 years/ISO 9001)

"The provisions of external training should contain more precise indications in the presentation and there should be more possibilities to select partial areas. It is difficult to sort out the right one." (116/F R Germany/40 employees/certification > 2 years/ISO 9001)

"There is a network of SM companies, where management can meet one another and discuss about quality management and developmental questions of the companies. 17 companies take part in this network and it is considered as developmental work." (212/Finland/26 employees/aspiring certification/ISO 9002)

Quality and personnel concepts of metalworking SMEs Summary

Competition, specialisation strategies & quality management

Sensitivity to cyclical influences, global competitive pressures, in particular with standard products, also from the new market economies in Eastern and Central European countries, as well as cost pressure in West Europe, are the framework conditions for metalworking small and medium-sized enterprises which constitute the core of this key industry of Europe. The companies respond with product innovation and with specialisation and co-operation strategies (e.g. fully integrated providers of complex products, system developers and service providers, suppliers, penetration of the own production, vertical and horizontal company co-operation). Customised product diversification and service components gain whereas mass production with efficiencies of scale lose weight. This is drastically reflected in the functional and work organisation as well as in the staff and qualification structures of the companies, and it leads to a very differentiated company landscape which is partly specifically marked in the European partner countries. More than the company size according to the number of employees, these tendencies of the sector modify the implementation conditions and tasks of quality management in the companies.

ISO 9000 is becoming a competitive standard - despite criticism

Currently, quality management in metalworking SMEs remains to a large extent in the fulfilment of the ISO system. Two reasons for it can be mentioned: On the one hand, the decisive motive of the companies is the ISO certificate that satisfies customer requirements and is generally recognised in the international competition. On the other hand, the ISO requirements fully occupy the rather scarce management capacities and resources of SMEs, the employees are for a longer term fully occupied with learning and routinisation of the formalised quality elements. Expenditure and benefit of quality management are calculated rather as cost of market access than as investment in internal improvement.

Prospectively, many company experts do not regard the ISO system as an optimal set of quality instruments. They criticise the

- orientation at the large-scale industry

- rigidity

- lack of relation to the sector

In their view, the formalisation secures multi-grade operations in big industries, but it is less suitable to improve the short, often informal paths in SMEs. The department-oriented degrees of demonstration ISO 9001, 9002, 9003 do not correspond with the specialisation profiles and co-operative relations of SMEs. Quality strengths of SMEs in the metal industry such as customer-oriented flexibility and rapid product innovation can even be constrained.

In dealing with the ISO system, which is not done without conflicts, the companies orient their sector-specific adaptation of quality management and their company-specific quality policy at demanding product, customer and specialisation strategies. Under the aim of maintaining competitive strengths of SMEs such as the ability to react quickly to the market and customer-oriented flexibility, many interviewed experts regard preventive and process- or project-related quality management as a means of choice, existing quality techniques (e.g. QFD, SPC, FMEA) and supporting methods are very little used in the surveyed companies. The company experts criticise the expenditure they cause and their inadequacy for the performance profiles and operations of SMEs in the metalworking sector (e.g. statistical methods in single-item production, small batch sizes and highly flexible operations). **Customer orientation & product innovation are priority - suitable quality methods are sought for**

None of the companies indicated the introduction of the ISO system as the decisive impetus to restructure the company, process and work organisation. For such kinds of - currently running and far-reaching - restructuring processes, product and production technologies, economic and company structures are more important reasons than the requirements of the quality system. But such kinds of reorganisation measures very often include quality aims, though sector- and company-specific ones, such as **The reorganisation effects of the ISO system are limited**

- product quality
- service quality
- co-operation quality

Quality-related reorganisation is at the moment focusing on management & customer-related functions

Normally, quality management changes the structures and the working methods of the company management. Particularly at mechanical engineering companies, the implementation of the managerial task "quality management" very often met with already existing cross-departmental structures and/or methods of the management. At the middle and operative level, quality-induced cross-departmental work and teamwork within the departments can be found predominantly in the pre- and post-production, rather more directing functions. Customer orientation and/or the improvement of the capability of the company to meet specific customer demands flexibly was clearly the main drive of the company to introduce teamwork. Therefore, this restructuring affects first of all the customer-related functions.

Production level: critical area of the quality policy

Currently, quality management at the operative level mainly brings about the formalisation of the existing work organisation and less their reorganisation. Changes at production level focus on transferring quality inspection to an earlier stage and on the reorganisation of the material flow and maintenance. The introduction of operator self-inspection as an extension of the job profiles is in its beginnings and is mainly considered as being a difficult and lengthy process. The production seems to be the critical point in the implementation of cross-departmental quality responsibility. One often mentioned reason is the difference between product-related and production-related quality requirements. Especially the implementation of customer-related quality concepts at the manufacturing level seems to have hardly been operationable so far. The sector-specific technological complexity of demands of industrial customers leads at the manufacturing level, based on the division of labour, to technical specifications as quality requirements which are difficult to be related back to the benefit of the total product for the customer. Interestingly enough, however, many of the surveyed companies - of suppliers of final products as well of sub-suppliers - indicated as a critical point of the implementation of quality management at the operative manufacturing level the awareness of staff of the crucial value of their contribution to customer satisfaction.

Exceptionally often new quality requirements of the external customer-supplier relationships were pointed out in the companies. For component suppliers the customer relationship at management level is an important task. For suppliers of final products this is also true a the operative level, particularly if customer services are to be rendered, that is, in assembly, staring up, maintenance and repair and other extended customer services. Here, companies develop new forms of organisation of a cross-departmental involvement of these staff in the company as well as extended job profiles of these staff. This affects first of all the work tasks and the functional groups of the staff who deal directly with external suppliers or customers: marketing/distribution/development & design, sales/purchase, assembly & customer services. Originating from these functions, issues of the processability of pre-products, the manufacturability of products and, in general, the harmonisation of complex customer requirements with the internal-company capabilities induce necessities of a quality-related reorganisation of the whole company.

External customer-supplier relationships as trail-blazer and motor

A quality policy going along two more or less markedly different lines is currently characteristic of metalworking small and medium-sized enterprises. Apart from maintaining the ISO system, the companies orient their concrete quality aims by the innovation of product and production and by requirements of an extended co-operation with suppliers and customers. This going along double lines is very costly and not always free of friction. As an obvious way of a practicable improvement towards TQM the integration of the two sides suggests itself. Examples of good practice can be found in companies which operationalise their ISO system for the company needs from audit to audit and, the other way round, carry out concrete quality tasks more and more strategically, that is, developing the ISO system of the company further towards a flexible organisation of planing, carrying out and controlling.

Sectoral tendencies & future

For the future it can be expected: The specialisation strategies of European small and medium-sized enterprises as suppliers of customised system solutions require as quality management the cross-functional and cross-company ability to master changing complex projects.

Sector-specific personnel structure & quality management

As small and medium-sized enterprises, most of the surveyed companies show personnel structures which have quite favourable elements for the personnel-related implementation of quality management. Normally there is lean management. Often senior executive staff carry out tasks of the middle management as well so that there are flat hierarchies, short and direct communication channels and profound experiences with concrete operations and processes in the company. On the part of staff the restriction to strict and small-stepped functional division is rather seldom. Teamwork among specialists within departments, multi-functional job profiles and beginnings of cross-departmental teamwork can be found.

The qualification structure also shows some favourable prerequisites with regard to the requirements of a modern quality management. In many cases the qualification of the executive staff is mainly oriented towards engineering which suggests an objective dealing with nonconformities and a sector-specific customer orientation like the focus on the condition for the use of the company products at the customer. The qualification structure of staff is characterised by a high degree of specialist staff with cross-occupational knowledge and/or work experience. Quite often personal handicraft-like knowledge based on experience form an important human resource of the companies.

Effects of the ISO system on the personnel development are relativised

The companies see relatively little challenge to their personnel development policy by the introduction of the ISO system. The documentation of existing work tasks is considered to result seldom in skill shortages of staff but rather to make the execution of tasks with the existing qualifications easier. Similar to the two lines of their quality policy, the companies identify the bigger challenges to their personnel development in

- innovations of the product and production technologies

- repositioning of the company in the market and customer relationships.

This is the basis for a number of further training measures in small and medium-sized enterprises of the metalworking industry and their manifold predominantly problem- and work-related nature.

Job-specific training is still clearly the focus of personnel development of metalworking small and medium-sized enterprises. Currently, this training takes place mainly independently of quality training, it imparts specialised adaptive qualifications and rather responds in a short term to the following requirements: **Current training of specific qualifications**

- new product specifications by the customers

- new materials

- product and process innovations (particularly new information and control technologies)

The sector-specific high degree of technical communication and co-operation is often still considered as a sufficient, frequently informal ensuring of competencies by experience of staff for the quality-related responsible co-operation within the internal customer-supplier relationships. Cross-occupational training takes place rather selectively and is driven by heterogeneous company motives: requirements of the use of new information technologies, co-operation of specialists required by the product engineering, the company's interest in flexibly employable staff, demands of the ISO system etc.. A systematic definition of interfaces within the company for the identification of needs of more strategic cross-occupational training programmes is still in its beginnings and has its starting point, by using examples of good practice, in requirements in market and customer contacts. **Current cross-occupational training**

Most of the companies reject a general training of staff in the systematics of the ISO standards or theoretical systems of quality management arguing that such an abstract system knowledge is of little use for the practical realisation of the company's concrete quality aims and leave this training in basics up to the quality manager. The in-company quality training of staff is intended to impart the company-specific quality system. At the moment, this holds the danger that **Current training in quality system knowledge** quality training is reduced to a mere instruction in the documented job instructions which are partly extensive and based on the division of labour and/or that it is supplemented by a rather formal training imparting just an overview of the quality system.

Current approaches to the promotion of process competence

The current approaches to the development of process competence of staff is as diverse as is the company landscape of the metalworking industry. Already the efforts for process orientation of the quality management diverge in the aim essentially according to the products of the respective company: process stability with machine-based series, mastering a project with items made to order. The tasks of the personnel development diverge accordingly.

Being typical of the sector, product knowledge and product orientation of the staff is the guideline and this is a demanding programme. The understanding of products for industrial customers, for their operating conditions and for the quality demands of these customers requires elements of engineering and commercial knowledge. In imparting this knowledge to staff who are not qualified, it is only partly possible to build upon their work experience - e.g. work safety - and not on their experience as final customers.

On the other hand, especially those companies whose products undergo complex manufacturing processes and/or strongly vary according to individual customer wishes rapidly meet with the restrictions of a rigidly structured system of work instructions. Therefore, for maintaining and improving the flexibility, above all advances in the process quality and in the process competence of staff suggest themselves.

Social key qualifications

Very often the emphasis of the quality-decisive significance of social key qualifications of staff such as "capability to work in teams", "quality responsibility" etc. still has rather the nature of an appeal. A real quality-induced change of the vocational tasks, which metalworking small and medium-sized enterprises already support with special training for superiors and/or "train the trainer programmes", is currently emerging at the level of the middle management. Needs for new social key qualifications are identified especially with supervisors for the following new tasks in the quality system:

- motivation of staff for proactive quality commitment

- harmonisation of the quality requirements of the own department, other departments and the quality aims of the company

- multiplication of external quality knowledge and experiences from customer and supplier relationships

- identification of training needs with staff

- organisation of job-accompanying training

The personnel development in metalworking small and medium-sized enterprises takes mainly place in the company and is related to the job. The training must justify itself in the face of limited time and financial resources of the companies and is to be directly applicable to the specific needs of and beneficial to the company. In the companies, there is little awareness of the conflicting relation between the rather restrictive budgeting of training measures and the rather demanding expectation that they are directly beneficial to the company.

Barriers of the in-company training

External quality-related training provisions are essentially left to managerial staff (particularly to quality managers, quality representatives etc.) and with employees it is restricted to acquiring additional qualifications (non-destructive tests, welding certificate etc.) which are compulsory for certification. In addition, most of the companies find that external quality consultants and quality training providers are lacking in "customer orientation": Sector- and company-oriented implementation know-how useful to train broad groups of staff according to organisational form, content and method is seldom provided. In several countries, companies see a promising way towards an input of sector- and company-related external (quality) knowledge in the establishing of company networks, emerging either from customer-supplier relationships or from ISO certification networks.

Benefit and deficiencies of external training provisions

In summary, both the ISO system as well as the personnel development of the surveyed metalworking SMEs show strengths and weaknesses:

Weak point: personnel strategy

- It occurs as a strength of the ISO standards, particularly in small enterprises, that they demand personnel training, their systematisation and planning. At the same time, the ISO system is not suitable as an adequate planning instrument for many surveyed companies, but it forces to formal fulfilment.

- It appears to be a general strength of the surveyed companies that they seek to maintain their capacity of innovation and responsiveness to the market also in the personnel area with a multitude of work- and problem-related training measures. With all due caution, one has to assume that in the reality of personnel development of many companies there is a lack of systematic identification of human resources and of a strategic orientation of personnel development. In the personnel development of metalworking SMEs the introduction of quality management according to ISO 9000 is often considered as an extra work load apart from competitive efforts in the market and the coping with technological innovation. Instead of creating synergy, ISO training and vocational further training compete with each other.

Sectoral tendencies & future

With an, on average, intense - technically oriented - cross-departmental and cross-hierarchical co-operation, current qualification strategies for the implementation of quality management are limited to executive staff and specialists in customer-related functions. The current personnel development of operative staff is mainly reactive and focuses on vocational specialist adaptive qualifications.

The following is to be expected in the future:

The metalworking industry, especially mechanical engineering, in Europe remains a sector based on the co-operation of different specialist technologies - metal construction, surface technology, electrical technology, pneumatics, hydraulics, processor technology etc. and which needs to organise the co-operation of the respective highly qualified specialists. The accelerated innovation of the processed materials, the products, control and production technologies requires of staff a continuously growing specialist and generic knowledge which, at least within the framework of the applied knowledge in the company, blurs also with operative staff the dividing line between engineering and vocational specialist qualification.

The competitive requirement of increasing service provisions for mostly industrial customers with individual requirements demands adequate competencies of ever more members of staff which at the same time assumes technical, commercial and directing know-how. The re-positioning in the industrial division of labour, forms of outsourcing and company co-operations require to implement external customer supplier relationships directly as an orientation of internal processes of the output of goods and services by the staff.

The rather increasing need for a broad range of engineering-related special qualifications and for quality knowledge requires the integration into a concept of **project competence**. Project-related learning suggests in-company work-related forms of learning - e.g. in project teams.

Part 2: Food-Processing

Food-processing SMEs: Target group and sample

Food-processing industry in Europe
Reasons for the selection of the sector

1. The European food industry attained a leading position in the world market, which its companies intend to retain and extend with high-quality products. SMEs of this sector are in a competitive situation which is determined by a stagnating demand and concentration tendencies, and to which they can only stand up by specialising in products of high quality.

2. For the food industry, sectoral framework conditions apply for the implementation of modern quality systems. Traditionally, consumers, the public and legislators used to demand a secured quality of products and production conditions. Nowadays, the full responsibility for the whole food chain is expected from the companies. Within the companies, on their turn, the increasing implementation of quality management according to global standards of the ISO 9000 series goes along with the modernisation of processes and the purchasing and distributing chains. The development of sector-specific manuals (ISO 9004-3) seeks to meet the particularity of process-technological products in the otherwise cross-sectoral ISO 9000 series.

3. The food industry is a leading employer in Europe. While the job profile in small companies, which continue to form the bulk of companies, is still characterised by manual work, a new job profile of industrial food producers is developing in modernised SMEs whose quality capability should be secured by training.

*

Food, beverages and tobacco industry (NACE 41)

> *"In the year 1990 more than 90 % of the companies in the Member States had less than 20 employees, 6 % of the companies had between 20 and 99 employees, and 2 % of the companies had 100 or more employees. It follows from these data that the sector consists of numerous smaller firms mainly operating on the basis of manual work. These small enterprises attain only 12 % of the total turnover of the sector, while the middle-sized enterprises, which account for 6 % of all EU companies of the sector, attain 20 % of the total turnover .... In general, a strong concentration process in the industrial food production is to be observed as a tendency in Europe. Entire sub-sectors, such as the sugar confectionery industry, are in*

the hands of quite a few multi-national groups. SMEs maintain their hold on the market in other sub-sectors .... Three essential tendencies can be discerned in takeovers. First, the majority of the deals is done through marketing companies trying to extend their presence in the sector. Second, the takeover of marketing companies corresponds to the strategy of pursuing a vertical integration as it is pursued by certain producer groups, while the acquisition of production companies by marketing groups occurs rarely. Third, it turns out that in nearly all takeovers done by buyers from EU countries mostly companies from the own country of at least from EU or EFTA countries are bought. Such company acquisitions aim primarily at strengthening the presence of the companies in the European or also the national markets".

Panorama of the EU industry 95-96, European Commission (Editor), Luxembourg 1995

"The European food, beverages and tobacco sector is, from the point of view of demand, characterised by a high degree of saturation. Measured by the value, the EU was in 1993 the world-wide most important producer of food followed by the USA and Japan .... With regard to the external trade, Europe stands out for it extraordinarily high level of activity. This is true of the trade within the community as well as the exchange with third countries. ... In the food, beverages and tobacco industry two crucial tendencies are persistently influencing the development of the sector. An increasingly health-conscious consumption pattern causes that those products are given preference which have a low content of harmful substances, are highly nutritive and have low calorie and fat contents. On the other hand, an increased demand exists for convenience foods characterised by high quality and good taste. ... For the future, it has to be assumed that demand for consumer goods will not increase substantially in spite of the current cyclical economic recovery. ... A high product quality, which is recognised by certificates Europe-wide, will increasingly determine the competitiveness of EU companies of the sector."

Panorama of the EU Industry 95-96, European Commission (editor), Luxembourg 1995

"Key success factors for operating successfully in the food industry are as follows:

- *Commodity products must be produced under least cost manufacturing conditions*

- *A strong ability to understand, predict and act upon changing consumer and customer requirements*

- *Product research an innovation*

- *Strong brand or company reputations*

- *Products must be produced to the highest of quality and safety standards*

- *Products should be available in the correct state and at convenient locations*

- *Products must be perceived by customers as value for money"*

Centre for Quality & Services Management, University College Dublin, Sectoral Report, 1997

Overview of the sample
"Food-processing SMEs in 7 European partner countries"

The sample of the survey is not a representative average of SMEs of the European food industry.

For one thing, the smallest and small companies, which form the bulk of companies in this sector, are not represented in it. For the other, all the surveyed companies deal with quality management, are ISO 9000 certified or seeking to be certified.

But the sample of the survey does represent some typical tendencies in SMEs of this sector. For one thing, the preponderance of middle-sized companies reflects the concentration tendencies in this sector just as much as the fact that various surveyed companies are integrated in supra-ordinate company structures or, at the time of the survey, on the way to such structures. For the other, the sample represents, on an average, companies with progressive strategies for the competitiveness at a European level.

Table 11: Countries/enterprises according to products, total number of employees, ISO certificate (Food industry)

Code no. & country	Products	Company size	State & of type certification	
121 F R Germany	spices; spice mixtures	160	certification > 2 years	ISO 9001
122 F R Germany	tinned fish	12	certification < 2 years	ISO 9002

Code no. & country	Products	Company size	State & of type certification	
123 F R Germany	egg products	100	certification < 2 years	ISO 9002
124 F R Germany	roasted ground coffee	70	certification < 2 years	ISO 9002
125 F R Germany	frozen products	688	certification < 2 years	ISO 9001
221 Finland	salads, meat products	40	certification < 2 years	ISO 9001
222 Finland	ice-cream	250	certification > 2 years	ISO 9001
223 Finland	Milk products	289	certification > 2 years	ISO 9002
224 Finland	biscuits	250	aspiring certification	ISO 9001
321 Greece	ice - creams, fresh juices	437	certification < 2 years	ISO 9002
322 Greece	toast	258	certification > 2 years	ISO 9002
323 Greece	puff pastry, strudel leaves, frozen vegetable, pizza	231	aspiring certification	ISO 9001
324 Greece	pasta, tomato products	336	certification > 2 years	ISO 9002
325 Greece	cooked pork meat	226	certification < 2 years	ISO 9001/2
421 Ireland	All animal feeds	39-44	certification > 2 years	ISO 9001/2
422 Ireland	Butter	49	certification > 2 years	ISO 9002
423 Ireland	Full range of fresh dairy products	246	certification > 2 years	ISO 9002
424 Ireland	Full range of milk products	343	certification < 2 years	ISO 9002

Code no. & country	Products	Company size	State & of type certification	
425 Ireland	Canning of food and vegetables; beverages; packing dry pulses	295	aspiring certification	ISO 9002
521 Portugal	Milk products	281	certification > 2 years	ISO 9002
522 Portugal	Milk	406	aspiring certification/ certification > 2 years	ISO 9002
523 Portugal	Coffee	297	certification < 2 years	ISO 9002
621 Sweden	Wheat- and rye flour, rice, peas, beans	95	certification < 2 years	ISO 9002
622 Sweden	Ice-cream & frozen desserts	91	certification < 2 years	ISO 9001
623 Sweden	Potato chips and other snack products. Sales and distribution of Mexican food	330	certification > 2 years	ISO 9001
624 Sweden	Development and production of fruit preparations and chocolate products	130	certification > 2 years	ISO 9001
625 Sweden	Soft drinks, beer, mineral water	100	certification > 2 years	ISO 9001
721 United Kingdom	Tea	500	certification > 2 years	ISO 9001
722 United Kingdom	children's sugar confectionery	610	certification > 2 years	ISO 9002
723 United Kingdom	Infant and dietetic foods	280	certification > 2 years	ISO 9002
724 United Kingdom	edible cake decorations, sugar and chocolate confectionery, popcorn	160	certification > 2 years	ISO 9002

Code no. & country	Products	Company size	State & of type certification	
725 United Kingdom	Peanut butter; Gales honey; Tablet jelly	300	certification > 2 years	ISO 9002
726 United Kingdom	confectionery aimed at children	350	certification > 2 years	ISO 9002

From the 33 surveyed companies 4 fell in the group of 10-49 employees, 11 in the group of 50-249, and 18 in the group of 250-500 employees.

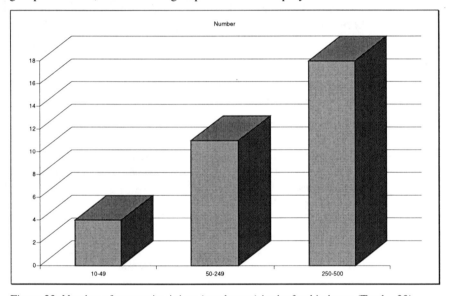

Figure 22: Number of companies / sizes (employees) in the food industry (Total = 33)

From the 33 surveyed companies 4 still sought ISO certification, 2 of which for ISO 9001 and also 2 for ISO 9002.

11 companies were certified for less than 2 years, 4 of which according to ISO 9001 and 5 according to ISO 9002.

18 companies were certified for more than 2 years, 7 of which according to ISO 9001 and 11 according to ISO 9002.

A certificate according to ISO 9003 was not represented in the sample.

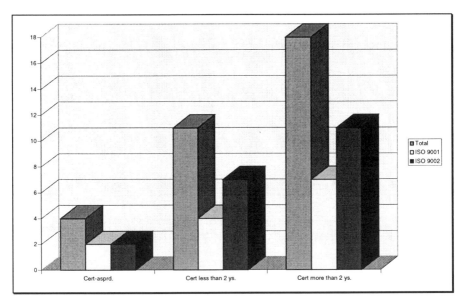

Figure 23: Number of companies / type and state of certification (aspiring/less than 2 years/more than 2 years) in the food industry (Total = 33)

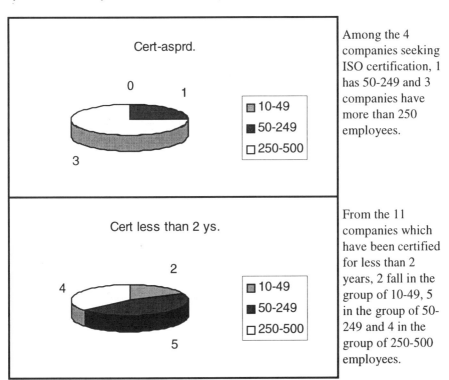

Among the 4 companies seeking ISO certification, 1 has 50-249 and 3 companies have more than 250 employees.

From the 11 companies which have been certified for less than 2 years, 2 fall in the group of 10-49, 5 in the group of 50-249 and 4 in the group of 250-500 employees.

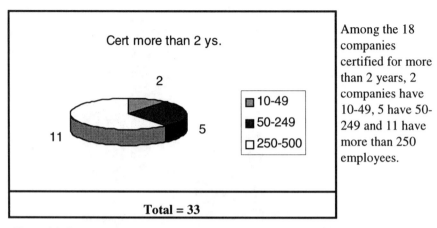

Among the 18 companies certified for more than 2 years, 2 companies have 10-49, 5 have 50-249 and 11 have more than 250 employees.

Figure 24: Sizes (employees) / state of certification in the food industry

The sample

The following brief descriptions are extracts of country-specific overview studies on SMEs of the food industry and of the individual-company case studies of the project partners

Federal Republic of Germany

The German food, beverages and tobacco industry is, according to real net output, the largest in Europe and an important sector in the German economy. In 1992 it attained a turnover high and accounted for about 12% of the total turnover of the producing sector (mining and processing sectors). In 1994 the sector accounted for about 10% of companies, about 11.5% of the turnover and about 8% of the employees of the producing sector. In spite of a continuing concentration process in the 90s, the food, beverages and tobacco industry is characterised by SMEs. In 1994, the companies with 10-499 accounted for over 96% of the companies of the sector, companies wit 20-49 employees accounted for 39% and companies with 50-99 employees accounted for about 23%. For 1995 the sectoral association calculated that about 5080 companies in the German food, beverages and tobacco industry had 103 employees and a turnover of 43 million DM, on an average..

Apart from the rapid increase in turnover and number of employees in the years 1990-92, essentially due to the German reunification, the economic development in the German food, beverages and tobacco industry corresponds with the sector in the EU as a whole. With a hardly increasing turnover, a reduction in company and employee numbers due to concentration and rationalisation is taking place. In particular the pricing policy in commerce as opposed to a limited purchasing power and propensity to consume of the consumers forces the food producers to rationalise. In 1995 the German food, beverages and tobacco industry attained about 13% of its turnover in the international business.

In mid-1996 a total of about 15500 companies were certified according to ISO 9000. An exact attribution of the certificates according to sectors and size of companies could not be identified. Taking a listing made by the market leader of the certifiers of 1996 as a basis, about 5% of the certificates go to the food, beverages and tobacco industry with an increasing tendency. According to an estimate of the sectoral association at the beginning of 1997, about 800 companies of the sector were certified. This corresponds to about 16%-17% of all the companies in the sector.

121 F R Germany	spices; spice mixtures	160	certification > 2 years	ISO 9001

121 was until recently an independent corporation with fully developed company structures. Corporate governance and structure were at the time of the survey undergoing a change. After the integration into a group, the company is an autonomous unit of production and brand marketing company. 121 produces in the second stage spices and spice mixtures out of natural raw material imported from all over the world for the end consumer. The company runs mass production with mechanic production techniques.

The company has been certified for over 2 years according to ISO 9001. Due to its integration into a group, research and development is centralised in the supra-ordinate corporate structure. Therefore, the company will change the demonstration of its quality system to ISO 9002. The HACCP concept is in the phase of introduction, and it will be integrated into the quality system.

122 F R Germany	tinned fish	12	certification < 2 years	ISO 9002

122 is a purely production company. It belongs to a group of three small companies with a total of 80 employees under a single owner. All the administrative functions, purchasing, production planning, distribution, personnel as well as development and laboratory are centrally organised for all three companies in the headquarters. The company produces tinned fish in two variants, both in oil. The company is in the core business a supplier for a few bulk buyers, especially from the catering industry. It runs mass production with mechanical production techniques which still include a large share in manual work.

122 is the only company in the group with a certified quality system. It has been certified for less than two years according to ISO 9002. After the integration of the European Directive for the food industry into the national law, the group will

introduce a system according to the HACCP concept. In this company it can be integrated into the ISO system.

123 F R Germany	egg products	100	certification < 2 years	ISO 9002

123 is an independent production company as subsidiary of a holding company with headquarters in Denmark. It processes raw eggs to egg products which are intermediate products for further processing steps. Customers are at home and abroad mainly bulk buyers from the food, cosmetics and pharmaceuticals industries and, to a smaller extent, by the baking trade. The raw material is purchased internationally, yet mainly on the European single market. The company runs mass production in continuous processes which are partially automated.

123 has been certified according to ISO 9002 for less than two years. This degree of demonstration was selected because the company does not run own product development, except for product variations, mainly mixing ratios or degrees of concentration according to customer wishes. The quality assurance representative recently transferred the system to another German company of the holding. An HACCP concept has been introduced and integrated into the quality system.

124 F R Germany	roasted ground coffee	70	certification < 2 years	ISO 9002

124 is an autonomous production company within the framework of a holding. At the time of the survey, a merger took place at the level of the holding which led to a restructuring of company 124. The company produces ground roasted coffee in vacuum and bag packing in a wide range from espresso to mild coffee in customised portions for the home and foreign markets. The main customer is the holding which distributes the product over its own marketing network and the grocery retailing industry; but which also supplies external areas such as the gastronomy. The company runs widely automated mass production. The production has been modernised to state-of-the-art technology in recent years. The retooling to vertical process engineering ensures short ways and minimises the influence of oxygen, it serves above all to avoid oxidation of flavour.

124 has been certified according to ISO 9002 for less than two years. The introduction of the ISO system coincided with the change from a divisional structure to a horizontal division of responsibilities within the holding so that ISO 9002 has been chosen as system for the production. The introduction lasted one year. Presently, HACCP is being implemented in the entire enterprise, and thus a previous project of a cross-departmental quality management has been postponed for the time being.

125 F R Germany	frozen products	688	certification < 2 years	ISO 9001

125 is a production company within a group set up in the last two years. The company produces frozen products in a range of fish, fruits, finished products and vegetable convenience. Customised products are developed and produced for system gastronomy and menu producers. The products are distributed internationally, in particular in the European single market as brand products, but also as dealer brands. The company runs mass production in automated flow line production.

The company has been certified according to ISO 9001 for less than two years. The HACCP concept has been integrated into the system. The introduction of this quality system supported the restructuring of the previously more autonomous and locally oriented companies to the new group. The ISO project was used as a tool for the organisational development. The company operates according to yearly organisational and quality aims in the perspective of a continuous improvement process. At present, quality assurance and product development are being centralised in the area of product service. A production planning and control system is in use. Environmental management is being discussed.

Finland

Finland's gross domestic product in 1995 was some 546 billion FIM. Income per capita was 85,543 FIM. Of the total value added basic agriculture accounted for 2.6 % while the share of food industries was 2.6%. In terms of agriculture and food production, Finland is largely self-sufficient. Raw materials used in production are largely of domestic origin (over 80 %). Of all industries here, food production ranks third whatever criteria are applied, after metal manufacturing and forestry industries and it accounts for 13 % of its total industrial production The gross value was 45.6 billion FIM in 1994 while the value added of the food industry was 11.7 billion FIM. The population directly or indirectly dependent on farming and food industries totals 0.282 million, while the total labour force in 1995 was 2.067 million. Finland is characterised by a high percentage of female workers. In food industries some 50 % of employees are women. The number of food processing companies in Finland is over 800. The great majority of them, however, are small family owned bakeries. Food exports in 1995 totalled some 4.042 billion FIM. Finland's main export markets were the EU (38,5 %), Russia (29.5 %), the Estonia (6.9 %) and EFTA (4.1 %).

For the food industry 1996 was a fairly good year. Production rose by 2 per cent, mainly because of exports, which soared by 25 per cent since 1995 to over 5 billion FIM. Food consumption in Finland increased by 2 per cent. Producer prices in the food industry were brought down as a result of the EU accession. Last year the decrease halted and turned into a slight increase of 1 per cent compared to 1995. Other costs of the industry, and labour costs in particular, increased as a faster rate. However, the overall profitability of food companies was fair and somewhat better than in the year before. Consumer prices of food remained steady while the entire consumer price index rose by a mere 0,8 per cent, the lowest rate of the EU member states.

The production technologies in Finnish food enterprises are at advanced level. Due to the internationally small size of the companies, the Finnish food enterprises have recognised the ever growing need for faster technological development and specialisation. The R&D inputs are growing and the food companies are concentrating their resources on their real technological strengths. The most promising areas in the future for the Finnish food industry are functional foods, process optimisation through information technology and use of biotechnology. The development of functional foods has long been a key research and development goal for many Finnish food enterprises. Research in the food industry therefore has close links with nutritional and clinical research. Several important health-promoting products have been developed by the Finnish food industry.

221 Finland	salads, meat products	40	certification < 2 years	ISO 9001

221 operates independently as a subsidiary within the framework of the corporation. The corporation organisation structure is divided in three different unites. 221 is one factory under one of the units. It is specialised in salads. It also operates in the field of subzero treated meat and meat products. The core business consists of different kind of salads. The main production method is mass production and the processes are continuos.

The enterprise has certified recently according to ISO 9001. This enterprise was first under the corporation umbrella that got the certificate. HACCP is also in place.

222 Finland	ice-cream	250	certification > 2 years	ISO 9001

222 operates independently as a subsidiary within the framework of the corporation. The enterprise is managed on the principles of corporation and management principles of its own. It is specialised in ice-cream. The enterprise produce and deliver the products to the warehouse of the corporation. Corporation marketing and sale takes care of the final sale and distribution to customers, retail

shops et. The main production method is mass production, partially automated and the processes are discontinuous.

The enterprise has been certified four years ago according to ISO 9001. There is HACCP in use as well as some problem analysis and creativity techniques. Development department use QFD (Quality function deployment). Statistical process control is also in use applied by company. Data collection & statistical methods are in use but limited.

223 Finland	Milk products	289	certification > 2 years	ISO 9002

223 is an independent company. It is owned by 1100 different milk producers. Representative body of milk producers is the body that define the main strategically definition. The company produces a range of dairy products: milk, cream, soured white milk, yoghurt and butter . It also operates in the field of UTH-products and less lactose products. The enterprise is also a producer of special kind of home made cheese. Dried milk powder as well is the production line of its own. The main production method is discontinuous processes and fully automated production.

The enterprise has certified according to ISO 9002. HACCP is also in place. Now there is a tendency to look environmental management system more closely although the building process has not started yet.

224 Finland	biscuits	250	aspiring certification	ISO 9001

224 operates independently as a subsidiary within the framework of the corporation. The enterprise is managed on the principles of corporate level and the principles of its own. To be a part of large corporation have happened very recently. Because of that there is confusion in the air, what are the principles and how does it effect here in Finland to be a part of a corporate in European level. The company produces biscuits. The main production method is mass production. Processes are continuos and fully automated.

The enterprise has not been certified yet. But it is building management system according to ISO 9001. HACCP is in use.

Greece

The food processing industry is of primary importance among Greek manufacturing sectors contributing to 11,9% to the total Industrial Output. According to the last industrial census (1988) the food processing industry included 19.776 establishments with 104.306 employees representing 13,7% and 14,8% of total industry. About 93% of the establishments had less than 10 employees representing 46,8% of the employment, while only 1,2 % had more than 50 employees (1 % for total industry). The average size was 5,27 employees per establishment slightly over the total industry average size (4,88). In the large scale industry (i.e. establishments with more than 10 employees) the average size was for the food sector 41,5 employees per establishment (43,1 for total manufacturing).The main feature of the food sector is the seasonal character of the employment which is estimated to be 85% to 115% in average. The SMEs with 50-500 employees represented 1,15% of the establishments but 28% of the employees of the food processing sector (Industrial census 1988).

In the period 1980-1992 (Industrial survey) the number of establishments of the large- scale food industry decreased by 2,7% but the number of employees increased by 3,2% and the Industrial Output Index increased by 33%. In the same period the number of establishments of the total large scale manufacturing sector decreased by 2,4% and the number of employees by 15,6% while the total Industry Output Index remained essentially unchanged. In 1992 the large scale food industry included 1146 establishments and 48936 employees representing 13,7% and 15,1% of the total large scale manufacturing sector. The contribution of the food industry to the total large scale industry gross output value increased from 15,6% in 1980 to 20% in 1992 and to the total large scale industry value added from 11,9% to 17%.

However, the high degree of seasonality and the geographical dispersion of raw materials did not allow a high degree of productive capacity utilisation to be achieved.

In the middle of 1996 the total number of firms certified according to ISO 9000 in Greece was about 250, about 54% of them are SMEs with 50-500 employees and only 10% have less than 20 employees. About 80% of the certified firms belong to the manufacturing sector and 18 of them (8,5%) are food processing firms. The percentage of the food processing firms among certified industrial firms is lower than the sector's share in the Greek large scale industry as well as in manufacturing SMEs, although the numbers are not directly comparable.

321 Greece	ice - creams, fresh juices	437	certification < 2 years	ISO 9002

321 is the operating unit of a large firm. The company has a tradition of 63 years in the production of milk products (ice-creams) in Greece. It possesses a big percentage of the Greek market and also achieves significant exports. Since it became in the last decade the operating unit of a large firm, its activity has expanded to the production of fruit juices as well. The production takes place by using serial, mechanical and fully automated production methods.

Because of the seasonal nature of the products the company works fully during the summer period whereas in the winter it passes to a stage of maintenance with reduced production . The standard number of employees is 137 throughout the year, 54 (40%) of them are semi- or unskilled personnel .During the summer the number of employees increases to 437 by the addition of 300 seasonal workers. From the 300 seasonal workers 280 are unskilled and work mainly in the production and stock departments.

The company is certified with ISO 9002 for less than two year. The system also covers the marketing and exportation department. The company is actually making the preparations needed for the implementation of the ISO 9001 standard. The implementation of the system HACCP has also been adopted because it is considered to be necessary for prevention reasons.

322 Greece	toast	258	certification > 2 years	ISO 9002

322 is an operating unit of a large firm. It consists of two separate production departments: the one producing several types of bread and the other producing toasted bread. The production of toasted bread represents a well known product possessing a very high share of the domestic market. The production methods include continuous and discontinuous processes, the production line being only partially automated.

The company has not its own marketing and sales department since it functions as a supplier of a large firm and the distribution of the products takes place by the customer's distribution/sales department.

The company has been certified for more than 2 years with ISO 9002 covering only the production of toasted bread. The main reason for the implementation of the Quality System was the assurance of the quality of the product. The toast that the company produces is a well-known product for more than 20 years, so its quality concerning its taste can't be changed. All customers trust its taste which has been stable throughout the course of time.

323 Greece	puff pastry, strudel leaves, frozen vegetable, pizza	231	aspiring certification	ISO 9001

323 is an operating unit of a large firm. The company produces different types of food products including mainly puff pastry, strudel leaves and pizza as well as frozen vegetables. A great variety of production methods are used including serial, mass production and continuous processes. Manual production as well as mechanical production methods are used while some processes are partially and others fully automated.

The company has started the preparation procedure for the certification according to the original ISO 9001 standards but the procedures change so fast due to the high rate of development of the company (20 % yearly), that it is difficult for the bureaucratic system to keep up with. The company aims directly at the implementation of ISO 9001 because the design of new products is very important for the company. A HACCP system has been implemented for one year and a half and it is considered important since it gives the customers a communication code.

324 Greece	pasta, tomato products	336	certification > 2 years	ISO 9002

Company 324 is the operating unit of a large firm with two factories located in different places in Greece. The one is producing various types of pasta, the other tomato products. The company's products are mainly sold in the domestic market but there also are important exports concerning countries of the EU and, in the last years, of East Europe and Asia. The production process takes place continuously using serial, mass and mechanical production methods. Some processes are partially while some others fully automated.

Company 324 has been certified since 1994 with ISO 9002 and still remains the only pasta industry certified with ISO in Greece. An internal quality system already existed before the certification while HACCP has also been recently implemented and its function is still explored.

325 Greece	cooked pork meat	226	certification < 2 years	ISO 9001/2

325 is the operating unit of a large firm. The company is producing several meat products, mainly cooked pork meat. It possesses a big share of the domestic market and also makes some exports to Balkan or Middle East countries. The production takes place based on a variety of methods including serial and mass production , continuous and discontinuous processes, manual as well as mechanical production. The production processes are partially automated.

The company has been certified with ISO 9002 15 months ago and with ISO 9001 two months ago. The company lays special emphasis on the quality of its products, therefore it didn't content itself with the implementation of the ISO 9002 standards, which was sufficient for advertising purposes, but went further into the implementation of ISO 9001 standards, while a HACCP system has also been adopted. After the certification the main target of the enterprise is the constant improvement of the system.

Ireland

The food and drink industry is of major importance within the Irish economy in terms of output, employment and trade. The industry accounts for 37% of the total manufacturing industry output, the highest percentage of value output in the manufacturing industry. In terms of employment the industry is second in importance after metals and engineering, accounting for 22% of manufacturing employment. Food exports accounts for 40% of foreign exchange earnings. In 1992 there were a total of 937 establishments operating within the food (establishment is defined as any economic unit engaged in activity within the sector). The degree of concentration can be seen from the fact that these establishments are owned by 691 companies (where company is defined as the largest unit). The industry is characterised by small to medium sized companies with 74% employing less than 50 employees and with 29% employing less than 10 employees. 5% employ over 200 people. The largest source of employment in the food sector is in plants of less than 50. The next most important employers are in the plant size category 100-199 and 200-400.

The output of the food sector increased by over 50% in the period 1985 to 1992. This masked a steady decline of 23% in the bakery sector, a decline followed by a recovery in the dairy sector, erratic growth for the chocolate, sugar and confectionery and meat sector. Most dynamic of all was the Other Foods sector. While the industry has grown rapidly over the last 20 years, employment has declined from 38,245 in 1986 to 37,900 in 1992. The greatest percentage employment loss was in large plants employing over 500, followed by plant size 100-199. This is due to the closure and rationalisation of many traditional companies within the industry in the face of market pressures and international competition as well as the impact on investment in new technology and increased international competition. Part of the rationalisation process also involved the contracting out of activities which, previously, were carried out within companies i.e. collection and delivery, maintenance, security and catering.

According to Forbairt (1996) approximately 150 food companies are known to be registered to ISO 9000 alone, accounting for 10% of all ISO registered companies. Under a third of all plants are currently accredited to ISO, compared to less than a fifth of plants who have the Q Mark. Accreditation is significantly higher amongst large plants - over half of all large plants compared to only one-third of small plants. Under a third of all plants claimed to operate a full HACCP system and only slightly more (38%), have implemented all elements with the exception of a reviewing mechanism.

421 Ireland	All animal feeds	39-44	certification > 2 years	ISO 9001/2

421 is a private limited company owned by a co-operative. The company manufactures high-nutrition animal feed for dairy cows, beef cattle, calves, sheep, lambs and pigs.

The customer base is geographically dispersed across the country. Branches were set up to serve the customers in each of the key areas. From these branches the customers place their orders. These are forwarded directly to the mill for processing using a sophisticated computer ordering system. The company also provides technical and marketing support to their customers.

Quality system certification to I.S. EN ISO 9002 was awarded in 1994. The laboratory also achieved the ISO 9001. The company is also evolving its systems towards a Hazard Analysis and Critical Control Point (HACCP) procedure to further ensure the food safety of their products.

422 Ireland	Butter	49	certification > 2 years	ISO 9002

422 is a private limited company owned by a co-operative. It is one of four business units in the Dairy products business. The company manufacturers butter. The product is sold over a wide geographical spread, and to a broad customer base in the retail Quality raw materials and a careful handling of the potatoes is important. The enterprise has developed a unique a system for the transport, storage and processing of potatoes. The potato storage centre is located a few miles from the factory close to most of their contract growers. The centre has been expanded and modernised and has today a storage capacity of 23 000 tons of potatoes. When the potatoes are needed for production, they are transported in a special closed truck where a constant temperature is maintained from the warehouse to the factory. and food ingredient sectors in Ireland, the UK (many of whom are large confectioners), Continental Europe, and the US. This constitutes approximately 80% in exports. A variety of production processes are used: continuous processing, partially automated production and fully automated production.

The company is one of the first food processing companies to be awarded the Q Mark in the 80s. Since then they were awarded ISO 9002 in 1989. Prior to this the company operated a Total Quality Management system. The company also operates Total Production Maintenance (TPM) in the plant. They are currently in the process of installing a Hazard Analysis and Critical Control Point (HACCP) procedure to enhance the existing quality system.

423 Ireland	Full range of fresh dairy products	246	certification > 2 years	ISO 9002

423 is a private limited company owned by a co-operative. The company produces a full range of fresh dairy products: yogurts, cottage cheeses, soft cheeses, and fresh fruit desserts. They have export markets in the UK, Sweden, France, Spain and Portugal. A variety of production processes are used: continuous processing, partially automated production and fully automated production.

The company were awarded ISO 9002 in 1990. The company proudly acknowledges they were the first yogurt producing company in Europe to be awarded ISO. They also operate a Hazard Analysis and Critical Control Point (HACCP) procedure.

424 Ireland	Full range of milk products	343	certification < 2 years	ISO 9002

424 is a subsidiary company of a larger firm. It is responsible for the assembly, processing and dispatch of liquid milk. The full range of milk products is: full cream milk, low fat milk, fortified low fat milk, fortified slimline milk, buttermilk and cream. All of these products are produced in a range of pack sizes and types. The company employs a variety of production methods: continuous processing, partially automated production and fully automated.

The Plant within the last two years was awarded the I.S. EN ISO 9002. The company has also been awarded the Q Mark and are presently installing a Hazard Analysis and Critical Control Point (HACCP) procedure.

425 Ireland	Canning of food and vegetables; beverages; packing dry pulses	295	aspiring certification	ISO 9002

425 is a subsidiary of a larger company. The company is responsible for the canning of food and vegetables: peas, beans, prunes, mixed vegetables. It also has a beverage section which produces a variety of juices. A new packaging for its juice products recently launch has boosted sales. In addition, the company also packs dry pulses. The company also factors 250 other products and it is an agent for certain brands of food. It supplies products to supermarkets all over the country. The company employs four different production methods: continuous process, discontinuous process, partially automated production and fully automated production.

The company has been using a Hazard Analysis and Critical Control Point (HACCP) procedure since 1993. It is in the process of seeking ISO accreditation and has been preparing for it vigorously over the past year and a half.

Portugal

The foodstuffs and beverages industries play an important part in Portuguese economy. These industries represent about 20% of the GDP (Gross Domestic Products) and about 15% of the GAV (Gross Added Value) of the whole manufacturing industry and 10% of national exports. During the last years the major rates of increasing were in " Fruit and Vegetables Conserves " industry. The foodstuffs and beverages industries give direct employment to about 122000 people (12% of the manufacturing industries' total), and most of their products are of a good technological level when compared with similar foreign products. In 1994 the companies with 10-499 employees accounted for 24% of the companies and 69% of the employees in the sector, companies with 1-9 employees accounted for 76% of the companies and 18% of the employees.

The development of the Portuguese agroindustry was conditioned by the strong penetration from new competitors, some of considerable international dimension and renown, and by increasing and aggressive competition within the European and world markets of products from third world countries, where production is being direct more and more. Though the foodstuffs and beverages industries fall within the set of traditional industries, in recent years considerable efforts have been made to modernise them. These have occurred practically everywhere in the country and a large number of small and medium firms have been set up, with good organisation and dimensioning in order to occupy segments of the home market that are as yet unexploited and with a view to export possibilities now opened up by the agreement with the EEC for free circulation of products, besides enlarged opportunities under agreements with the Portuguese-speaking African countries. These sectors produce some of the products for which Portugal is well known abroad on account of their high quality, such as tomato conserves, olive oil, wines (Oporto wine and "vinho verde"). The main destination for the products of Portuguese "Foodstuffs and Beverages" industries is the internal market, except for the "Port Wine" and the "Industrialised Tomato".

Competitiveness of national products in foreign markets was seriously affected by the continuing policy of exchange stability, which caused the escudo to stay close to such currencies as the DM. Meanwhile the currencies of other countries, over competitors or important end markets, developed unfavourably, placing our exports in ever-increasing difficulties. Finally, the positive effect of a continued fall in the inflation rate should be stressed. The average of the investment is around 10% of total manufacturing industry and these sectors also show a considerable penetration of foreign capital.

In Portugal more than 500 certified companies are in accordance with ISO 9000, only 16 (3%) belong to "Foodstuffs and Beverages". The percentage of certified firms in the food-processing industry is slightly under the sector's overall percentage in the Portuguese manufacturing industries.

521 Portugal	Milk products	281	certification > 2 years	ISO 9002

521 is a subsidiary within the framework of a holding company. In 1994, it starts its organisational restructuring, subdividing its business areas. In the top of the group was the original co-operative, that, by means of SGPS, a society for the management of social participation, controlled the other structures, as for instance a commercial and an industrial structure, presently self-managed. The company here analysed is the industrial structure, whose main goal is milk and milk products (yogurt, milk deserts, butter) processing. The main production method is continuous mass production which is fully automated.

It was the first Portuguese company of the dairy industry to be certified according to the Portuguese standard NP EN 29002 (presently NP EN ISO 9002), in May 1993. The problem of quality was considered as the decisive factor for the changes the company had to go through in order to be prepared to increase its competitiveness, which was likely to happen after the abrogation in 1993 of product trade barriers.

522 Portugal	Milk	406	aspiring certification/ certification > 2 years	ISO 9002

522 is a corporation in form of a union of 46 co-operatives providing milk reception and treatment. The main production method is manual production. What started 1949 as a union of co-operatives of milk producers transformed into a great industrial company, disposing of its own milking post, becoming again, from 1997 on, just a union of co-operatives of milk producers. The company suffered in 1997 a strong reduction of its assets and turnover, on account of its participation in a new company. With 406 employees in the end of July the number of full-time employees was substantially reduced to 297 in the end of the year.

In 1994, the Quality Manual of the company declared that the main goal of the Union of Co-operatives was the leadership of the dairy industry in the national market. Due to the deep modifications undergone, the company is proceeding to the revision of the system, since the certification obtained according to ISO 9002, dated from May 1996, is connected with the industrial structure (premises, equipment and workers) that became a constituent of the new company. However, the present structure maintained the laboratory, certified according to NP EN 45001.

523 Portugal	Coffee	297	certification < 2 years	ISO 9002

523 is an independent company. The company produces coffee in a continuous process of partially automated production. Everything started in 1961 when an entrepreneur and three collaborators founded an individually owned coffee-processing company. It leads the internal market, exporting into Spain, France, Belgium, the Netherlands, Luxembourg, Germany, United Kingdom, Canada and United States of America.

It got its first certification according to NP EN 29002 in 10 of August of 1994 and according to ISO 9002 in 16 of May of 1996.

Sweden

The Swedish food industry is characterised by being very heterogeneous with about 15 different sub-branches, big differences in size, owner structure etc. The industry is spread all over the country but is concentrated to the areas where people live. The industry is one of the largest in the country and employs 9% of the total number of employees in the manufacturing industry.

The export value in 1990 was 6.300 and the import value during the same year was 17.500 million Swedish crowns. Import focus mainly in products that cant be produced in the country e.g. coffee and fruit.

Between 1970 and 1990 the number of companies has decreased with more than 50% from 1.609 to 734 while the number of employees has decreased with only about 10% from 71.976 to 65.201. This development shows the concentration strategy for the industry where the number of employees per company has increased from 45 to 89 during this period. The concentration tendency was first established in the mill-, sugar and food-oil industries and during the last years the same tendency has been implemented in malt- and soft-drink industries as well as in the bakery industries. The concentration strategy has also taken place in the structure of the owners where we today see fewer and bigger than before. The government owned shares has during this period decreased and the private companies today employs 60% of the total number of employees in the industry.

According to political decisions and customer restrictions the industry is still very concentrated to the Swedish market. The possibilities to growth is assumed to be very limited.

The consumption volume of food products in Sweden shows rather small changes and the increase follows approximately the increase in population. On the other hand from 1970 to 1990 the numbers of articles in the consumer market has increased from 2.500 to 3.800 according to the introduction of new brands, products and variants.

The national and international legal limitations have traditionally put a lot of restrictions for the industry and it is used to work with standardised control systems. On the other hand this tradition has slowed down the speed for implementing quality systems like ISO 9000 and up till 1997 only a very limited numbers of the companies have got a ISO-certificate. In 1997 a total of 27 Swedish companies in the food sector have been certified according to ISO 9000 (1.2% of the total numbers of ISO-certified companies).

621 Sweden	Wheat- and rye flour, rice, peas, beans	95	certification < 2 years	ISO 9002

621 is an independent corporation and a subsidiary within the framework of a holding company. The company has two different mills at two different geographical locations in Sweden. The most important products today are wheat- and rye flour, rice, peas and beans. The primary products are delivered to the mill by boat or truck from the farmers in the region. Short transports and primary products raised in the region is a motto within this corporation. The total amount of different flours in the assortment is 50. This means that both ecological and conventional flours are produced. The main production method, is a continuous process which is fully automated.

The enterprise has recently been certified according to ISO 9002.

622 Sweden	Ice-cream & frozen desserts	91	certification < 2 years	ISO 9001

622 is an independent corporation and a subsidiary within the framework of a family holding company. The enterprise develops, manufactures and sells ice-cream and frozen desserts. The total amount of different products in the assortment is 120. Parts of the assortment is produced on license for a foreign company since 1986. The main production method is a serial production which is partially automated. The company is a family owned enterprise with roots in the mill business and with a history within the same family that goes back thirteen

generations. The enterprise received a honourable mention by Veckans Affärer (Weekly Business in Sweden) in 1993 as being the "Best family business".

The enterprise has been certified according to ISO 9001 for less than 2 years, they received their certification in November 1995. The enterprise had a early start with the implementation of the quality system which appointed them for being the first ice-cream producer in Sweden being ISO certified. During autumn 1997 they will be ready with the HACCP system as well. This is not optional since it is regulated by the Swedish health and food legislation. Beyond this a system of QACCP - Quality Analysis Critical Control Point - is introduced at the enterprise. This is to analyse both the effects of the failures and the risks for reduced quality.

623 Sweden	Potato chips and other snack products. Sales and distribution of Mexican food	330	certification > 2 years	ISO 9001

623 is a corporation and a subsidiary company of an international larger firm since 1993. The company started up Sweden's first potato chip production line. Besides potato chips, popcorn was produced and other snack products were imported. During the 60's the foundations were laid for a period of development and expansion which have made the enterprise the market leader in Scandinavia today. The main production method is a continuos process according to the different production lines. Quality raw materials and a careful handling of the potatoes is important. The enterprise has developed a unique a system for the transport, storage and processing of potatoes. The potato storage centre is located a few miles from the factory close to most of their contract growers. The centre has been expanded and modernised and has today a storage capacity of 23 000 tons of potatoes. When the potatoes are needed for production, they are transported in a special closed truck where a constant temperature is maintained from the warehouse to the factory.

The enterprise has been certified according to ISO 9001 for more than 2 years. Quality management and environmental management are implemented in the strategic planning of the enterprise. They are approved according to the quality system HACCP since last year. Their aim is to be approved according to ISO 14000 or EMAS within two years. Currently they are in the middle of comparing the two environmental management systems. The enterprise has an internal quality concept with internal rules which is quite extensive. The quality concept is established by the international parent company. The concept is integrated in ISO 9001. Some of the internal quality structure are based on the following: GMP - Good Manufacturing Process, SSE - Security, Safety, Environment, QSAE - Quality System Audit Expectation.

624 Sweden	Development and production of fruit preparations and chocolate products	130	certification > 2 years	ISO 9001

624 is a corporation and an operating unit of a large firm. The enterprise produces chocolate for the bakery and ice-cream industry with a wide range of specially developed dip coatings. They also produce fruit preparations for use in ice-cream and yoghurts. They supply the bakery industry with special fruit-based products for all kinds of cakes and pastries. The main production method is a partially automated production. However one of the production lines is fully automated. Approximately half of the current annual production is exported. They have made a number of strategic choices to enlarge the amount of export. One example is the extension of their network of agents in Europe.

The enterprise has been certified according to ISO 9001 for more than 2 years, they received their certification in May 1994. The enterprise is also working with the quality system HACCP. Their aim is to be approved according to HACCP during 1998. The aim of the enterprise is to get the environmental assurance according to ISO 14000 and possibly also EMAS. The enterprise has a totally integrated computerised administrative system. The quality handbook is integrated in the system and all the changes are done directly in the system.

625 Sweden	Soft drinks, beer, mineral water	100	certification > 2 years	ISO 9001

625 is an independent company and a corporation. The business is still run with a total ownership of one family. It is their firm conviction to keep it the same way in the future. The family has a long and strong brewing tradition of six generations of brewers. This gives them a unique position in the Swedish brewing industry today. The brewery has developed beers that are highly rated by experts and juries in international competitions. They have since 1990 been given five international awards. The main production method is a continuous process according to the different production lines.

They are seeking ISO certification according to ISO 9001 and will probably be accredited at the beginning of 1998. The enterprise has made a strategic decision to postpone their application for ISO 14000 or EMAS due to circumstances concerning the geographical location of the brewery. The buildings on the premises are protected by Swedish cultural laws and no reconstruction's are allowed. To be able to fulfil the demands of the environmental management systems a major reconstruction of several buildings are required. The enterprise is now planning to build a new brewery at a different location within five years. These new buildings will be built according to the environmental demands.

United Kingdom

The food and drink manufacturing industries in the UK account for some 3 per cent of GDP and 1.7% of employment. In 1996, there were 10,580 companies in food products, beverages and tobacco, comprising 6% of total manufacturing units. Of these companies, 4,315 were SMEs with employees in the range 10-499. Food products SMEs comprised 8% of all SMEs of this size in manufacturing, a slightly greater percentage than their contribution of 6% to the overall manufacturing sector. 41% of the companies in the food products, beverages and tobacco sector are SMEs (10-499 employees), a much greater number than the national average of 30% of SMEs as a percentage of manufacturing companies.

The volume of output of food and drink manufacturing has increased steadily over the last twelve years. Taking 1990 as 100, output rose 93.9 to 104.3 in the decade from 1985 to 1995. Employment in the sector fell over this period, from 105.6 to 90.7, reflecting an increase in labour productivity from 89.6 to 115.0 over the same period. There has been a small decline in the number of companies in the food processing industries in relation to other manufacture, the percentage having fallen from 7.2% in 1987 to 5.9% in 1996, and this is reflected in the numbers of SMEs in the sector, the percentage having fallen from 8.8% of manufacturing units in 1987 to 7.9% in 1996. SMEs as a percentage of companies in the food processing sectors have, however, risen slightly, from 39.2% to 40.8%.

In the UK, the number of small firms and their share of output and employment has been steadily rising for at least 20 years. Although the food industry is dominated by a small number of giant firms, the SME sector remains healthy. There were 4,315 SMEs in the food industry in 1996, in comparison with 4,361 in 1987 and 4,285 in 1992. Although this apparent stability will inevitably mask a number of starts and closures, food SMEs can nevertheless be said to have coped successfully with the recession.

Overall, exports of food, feed and drink increased by 102% between 1985 and 1995 and by 1995 exports were equal to 60% of imports, compared to only 49% in 1985-1987.

Concern about BSE in the human food chain led to a crisis of confidence in the UK food and farming industries in March 1996 and a considerable allocation of government spending was needed to allay public fears and contain the problem. The UK beef market suffered from an initial fall in demand of 25% in the home market and the complete loss of export trade, which had accounted for 30% of production. The home market has now recovered somewhat, reaching 85% of its former levels by the end of 1996. It is difficult to assess at the present time what overall impact on the food industry this crisis will have had.

Overall in the UK there are 60188 companies which have some ISO certification and of these 2798 (4,6 %) are involved in food processing and manufacturing.

721 United Kingdom	Tea	500	certification > 2 years	ISO 9001

721 is a subsidiary of a very large company which specialises in the production of hot beverages: tea, fruit and herb tea, food beverages (e.g. hot chocolate and malt-based drinks) and coffee. 721 specialises in tea production. The brands of tea produced by 721 are the most popular and best-selling brands in the UK. Production methods at 721 are partially automated. The beverages the company manufactures are mass produced by continuous methods. The parent company has been established in the area for many years and has the reputation of being a company which 'looks after' its employees well.

The company has been certified according to ISO 9001 for more than three years. Their main reason for deciding to seek quality certification was in order to keep their 'competitive edge'.

722 United Kingdom	children's sugar confectionery	610	certification > 2 years	ISO 9002

722 is an independent company. The company was established as two separate companies who worked together. About 20 years ago they came together with the two current joint managing directors who are joint owners of the present company. The general impression is not of an up-to-date modern factory but of an old-fashioned, traditional factory which 'has seen better days'. The range of products the company makes are children's sweets which sell quite cheaply ('pocket-money sweets' for younger children) and which have a rather old-fashioned image. These include: high boiled sweets, low boiled sweets, compressed powder, marshmallows, gums and jellies, chocolate brazils, popcorn, rainbow drops. Production methods are mechanical and partially automated. A number of the products require hand-finishing. Both continuous and non-continuous production processes are in use.

The company has been certified according to ISO 9002 for more than 3 years. The decision to seek quality certification was taken about five years ago as part of a move to improve operations and generally bring the factory up-to-date.

723 United Kingdom	Infant and dietetic foods	280	certification > 2 years	ISO 9002

723 is a subsidiary of a larger company. The company manufacture infant and dietetic foods - mainly the former - and so they pay great attention to health and safety and hygiene. There are two 'core' production areas within the factory: one which manufactures spray-dried 'intermediates' (bulk products) and a secondary area which blends those products (i.e. combines the bulk intermediates with vitamins, minerals, carbohydrates and flavours etc) and then packs them. The main manufacturing methods are serial production and non-continuous process. Some sections of the factory are fully automated; others are partially automated. The factory has been given 3 and a half million pounds investment money from the parent company to buy new packing equipment.

723 has been ISO 9002 certified for more than 3 years and also has HACCP in place.

724 United Kingdom	edible cake decorations, sugar and chocolate confectionery, popcorn	160	certification > 2 years	ISO 9002

724 is owned by a consortium of 5 who are the present directors. It is an independent company. The main items produced are edible cake decorations, sugar and chocolate confectionery and popcorn. Production methods are manual, partially automated and discontinuous.

The company has been ISO certified (ISO 9002) for more than 3 years. They also have HACCP and EFSIS (third part audit).

725 United Kingdom	Peanut butter; Gales honey; Tablet jelly	300	certification > 2 years	ISO 9002

725 is part of a very large multinational food manufacturing company. Within the UK, the company is divided into 4 separate divisions: Confectionery, Foodservice, Grocery, Food. 725 is part of the food division and is one of a group of three discrete factories. The management of all three factories centres around 725 with local managers at the other 2 factories having specific operational responsibilities. The other 2 factories are said to function as 'satellites' of 725 each requiring support from it with regard to certain specialist functions. Products manufactured are diverse as jellies, sweet and savoury spreads. They are sold under major brand names associated with a particular section of the business. Many variants of each

product are also sold under the specific labels of the major supermarket chains in a variety of pack or case sizes. Production methods are a combination of mechanical, partially and fully automated.

The factory has been ISO 9002 certified for more than 2 years. HACCP is also in place. The priority now is HACCP as this is required by the Food Safety Act and *'it's more important to the company than ISO 9000'.*

726 United Kingdom	confectionery aimed at children	350	certification > 2 years	ISO 9002

726 is an operating unit of a large company based in Finland. It makes confectionery aimed at children. The main production methods are continuous and a combination of partially and fully automated.

The company has been ISO 9002 certified for more than 2 years and is also soon to implement HACCP.

Quality concepts of food-processing SMEs

The interviewees were allowed to rate multiple criterions. The scale of 0 - 300 results from the rating scale of 0 - 3 and from the fact that the survey results based on different quantities of respondents have been extrapolated to a number of companies of 100 in order to obtain data that are comparable between the sectors.

Quantitative findings

Reasons for implementing quality management

In order to identify the motives and aims small and medium-sized enterprises of the food industry connect with the introduction of quality management, all interviewed experts were asked the following semi-standardised question:

Question: Implementing a Quality Management system has cost implications - particularly for SMEs. What were the main reasons for your company deciding to invest in Quality Management? **Rate answers according to following key:** 0 = unimportant, 1 = plays a role, 2 = important, 3 = very important.

- Customer commitment (supplier duty)
- Competitive pressures (new competitive standard)
- Legal pressures (liability precaution)
- Impact of advertising
- Costs of quality (reducing complaints; nonconformity costs/costs of its correction)
- Improvement of internal processes (clear working aims; co-operation of the departments)
- Shorter processing times
- Improving management procedures/systems
- Customer satisfaction
- Company philosophy
- Working atmosphere/employees motivation
- Changeover to teamwork

Reasons in the view of company experts

90 executives from 33 companies have been interviewed as company experts in the implementation of quality management.

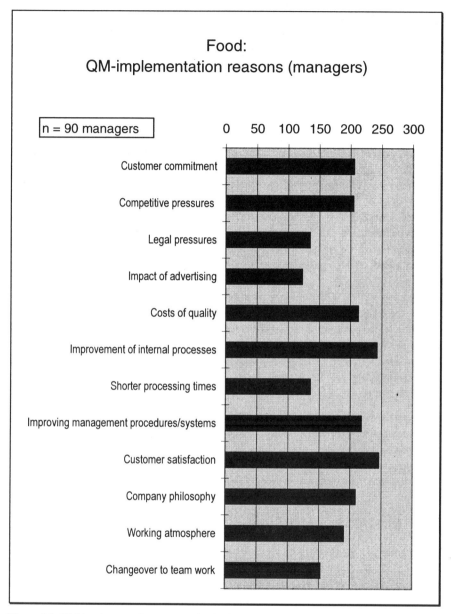

Figure 25: QM-implementation reasons in the food industry (managers)

In the cumulative evaluation "customer satisfaction" reaches the highest rating. Thus quality management is predominantly understood by the interviewed managers as an instrument of the company to fulfil customer wishes, be those customers the consumers or further processing and distribution companies. The aim of a proactive customer orientation is underlined by the fact that rather reactive motives such as "customer commitment" and "competitive pressures", that is adjustment pressures resulting from already manifest demands, are rated rather low.

"Improvement of internal processes" and "improving management procedures/systems" as well are named as priority reasons for the introduction of quality management. This also documents an active understanding of quality management as an instrument of the company and is oriented towards the effective internal implementation instead of external demonstration of norm conformity. The combination of the two motives shows where the company experts predominantly see the improvement potential resulting from quality management. The focus is on the method and the cross-functional collaboration of the management. Quite to the contrary the experts of the food industry attach rather low expectations to the implementation of quality management with regard to "shorter processing times" (rank 10) and - proved by low ratings for "changeover to teamwork" (9) and "working atmosphere/employees motivation" (8) - particularly with regard to changes of the operative performance processes and for the operative staff. The qualitative expert interviews showed two reasons for this. First, the interviewed companies of the food industry were characterised structurally by a relatively strict division of the administrative planning level and the operative level. Second, the interviewed managers considered the technological modernisation of procedures as the decisive factor of the work organisation and as the crucial instrument of the company to rationalise the performance processes.

The relatively high rating of "costs of quality" (4) shows that quality management is valued as an instrument to balance the result of the companies in the main aims "customer satisfaction" and "improvement of internal processes" also in its economic effects. Though it was frequently mentioned in the expert interviews that an exact determination of costs was rather difficult. Many companies were working on the improvement of data collection and evaluation.

It is striking that only the lowest rating is attributed to the "impact of advertising" of a demonstrated quality system. This rating probably reflects the fact that quality management is meanwhile becoming common as a competitive standard also for small and medium-sized enterprises in Europe, that an ISO certificate distinguishes a company less and less from others in the market. More striking still and at first sight rather surprising is that the interviewed experts attribute a very low rating to "legal standards" when introducing quality management. The qualitative expert interviews brought out the following explanations. The "legal standards" have long been a matter of course and have been understood as a minimum demand on quality. Quality management however is to organise the self-responsible response of the companies to much higher quality demands of consumers and the general public. Moreover, quality systems according to international ISO standards are viewed predominantly as internal economic and not as public legal quality guarantee in the global market.

Reasons from different functional views

The survey intended to identify whether the motivation of the experts for quality management varies according to their managerial function or whether there are significantly different views. Among the interviewed 90 executives 28 were responsible for marketing, 33 for production, 29 for personnel. The deviation of the number of interviewed functional managers from the number of the surveyed companies (33) results from several factors. In some companies managers of not all functions had time for an expert interview, also some managers held different functions, in some companies operating within company co-operations the marketing function was centralised, some companies have deliberately delegated the personnel function to the line manager. The function-specific evaluation of the answers shows the following picture. The graph essentially shows a consonance in the assessment among the functional managers in the surveyed companies.

However, some deviations are remarkable.

Responsible staff in marketing value external pressure - such as "competitive pressures" and "legal standards" as a motive for the introduction of quality management even lower than production and personnel managers. Significantly lower is also their expectation of "shorter processing times" as an effect of quality management. Above all, it can be regarded as a function-specific interest that marketing managers clearly emphasise "customer satisfaction" as orientation for quality management.

Personnel managers significantly deviate with their low rating of "improvement of internal processes" from the assessment of their colleagues from other functions. It is to be interpreted as function-specific interest that they put more emphasis on the improvement of "working atmosphere/employees motivation" than marketing and production managers.

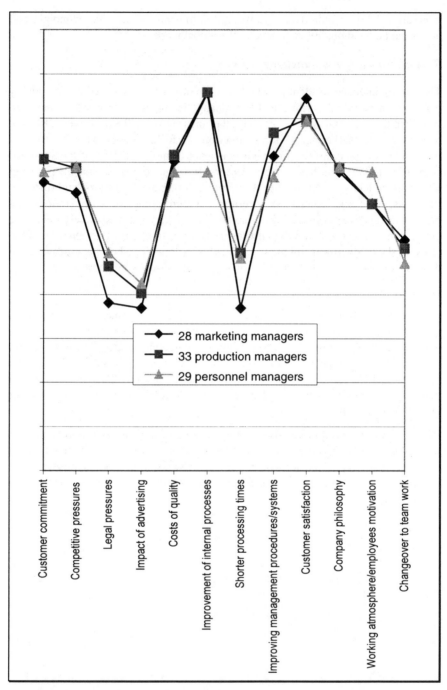

Figure 26: QM-implementation reasons from different functional views (managers)

Reasons at the level of companies

On the basis of the identified values for each company, the following picture emerges at the company level regarding the motives for the introduction of quality management:

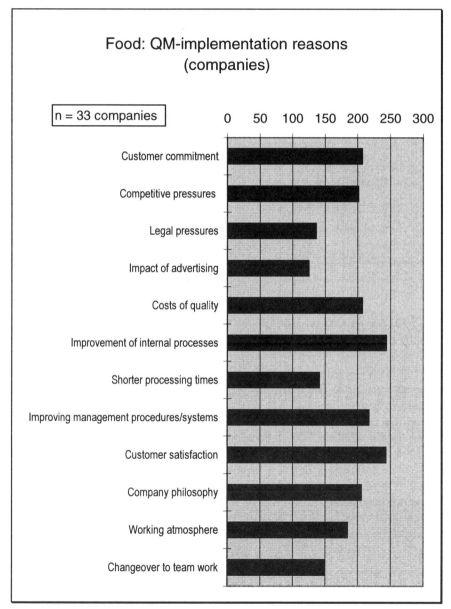

Figure 27: QM-implementation reasons in the food industry (companies)

Extrapolating a hierarchy of motives the list is as follows:

1.	Improvement of internal processes (clear working aims; co-operation of the departments)
2.	Customer satisfaction
3.	Improving management procedures/systems
4.	Customer commitment (supplier duty)
5.	Costs of quality (reducing complaints; nonconformity costs/costs of its correction)
6.	Company philosophy
7.	Competitive pressures (new competitive standard)
8.	Working atmosphere/employee motivation
9.	Changeover to teamwork
10.	Shorter processing times
11.	Legal pressures (liability precaution)
12.	Impact of advertising

Qualitative findings: Barriers, critical points, examples of good practice

The following description of qualitative findings about quality concepts of the surveyed enterprises with regard to barriers, critical points and examples of good practice orientates itself to the aim of making available practical company experiences and practical management know-how concerning the implementation of quality management. This is to allow practical key actors to learn from the difficulties of others as well as to prevent them from having to re-invent transferable solutions. Therefore, company practice is directly quoted as "case examples" deriving from the underlying case studies and from "statements" of the interviewed managers.

Quality: Traditional and new demands on the food industry in the EU

Traditional and new demands

To demonstrate on the basis of standards to external instances that internally the quality of products and production is assured systematically and in a verifiable way: this demand on enterprises of the food industry has not only just come up since quality systems according to ISO 9000 have become generally accepted as a competitive standard. The tendency towards ISO certification also in SMEs of this sector appears to be more of an entrepreneurial attempt to respond comprehensively to the traditionally high and increasing quality demands which the different instances of the enterprise environment make.

SMEs of the food industry in Europe are facing a number of external demands with quality implication:

- Standards, laws and monitoring instances of the nations and the EU deal with health protection and hygiene, legal restrictions concerning food, marking and packing regulations, consumer protection and product liability. The responsible secretaries of the EU currently intend to apply the latter also to the agricultural production.

- Dietetics and food technology work out scientific and technical standards which become generally accepted in the economic competition and become the guidelines of "Good Manufacturing Practice" in the sector.

- Commercial enterprises in the international competition increase and globalise quality demands (e.g. product stability) as do multinational companies of the food industry, particularly in their brand policy. These quality demands also affect suppliers of primary products.

- Sensible eating has become a part of lifestyle particularly with European consumers developing a sophisticated health awareness.

- There is an increasing environmental awareness in the European general public particularly focusing on the entire food chain.

- Food scandals and catastrophes such as BSE show companies the economic significance of quality issues.

The various quality-related demands of the different external instances on the companies overlap but they are not always identical. They might even clash as can be illustrated with a few examples:

- What is considered to be food of high nutritive value according to science and technology is not necessarily in accordance with traditional or new customer wishes.

- Marketing requirements concerning e.g. packaging may contradict environmental requirements.

- Legal standards at a national, European and international level are clashing last but not least in trade conflicts (see GATT and CAP).

The establishing of quality systems

All the same the tendency has been generally accepted, that is a new extended definition of the notion of quality. Traditionally food quality focused on product features particularly on:

- consumption value
- nutritive value
- hygiene
- toxicology
- suitability.

Not only did this comply with the monitoring practice of the authorities but also with the quality assurance practice of the companies through final inspections. Now there is an increasing necessity for companies to integrate on the one hand

- the entire internal as well as the external process chain of food processing

and on the other hand

- the expectations of the consumers and the general public

into their quality concept.

Here particularly SMEs in Europe are facing a confusing variety of provisions offering systems for the solutions of these tasks: ISO 9000, HACCP, environmental management according to ISO 14000 or EMAS. In company practice the quality system according to ISO 9000 appears to become generally accepted as to details. This surely is not least due to its acknowledgement in the increasingly global market. Basic advantages of the ISO system for companies are

- the reversal of the burden of proof to external auditors from authorities and the trade and industry who have to substantiate nonconformities of the systems of certified companies
- the suitability of the ISO system as a framework for a company-specific integration of further quality-related systems such as HACCP and environmental management.

The latter already indicates that the ISO system should only be the basis for the companies to fill it with life by a company-specific quality policy.

New approaches of the legislators

The authorities are also facing the task to harmonise framework demands on quality so that they are suitable for a global market. To this end some crucial steps have been taken at a European level.

In the Horizontal Directive 93/43 of the European Commission general hygiene demands on food and procedures to enforce legal regulations were defined. The Directive has a wide field of application. It does not only apply to all sectors. It lays down hygiene and safety regulations for all phases of the industrial production process - from preparation via production to transport and sales. The approach to harmonise and integrate existing quality concepts is obvious. The Directive contains

- principles of "Good Hygiene Practice"

- voluntary "guidelines for Good Hygiene Practice" of the sector

- the HACCP concept

- product-related criteria

- new competencies of the authorities for the monitoring of the companies' self-inspection

The companies of the sector have the obligation to carry out procedures for maintaining standards concerning food hygiene and to monitor the risks of each and every work process. The concentration on political framework requirements corresponds with the increasing importance of the companies' self-inspection. Companies are explicitly recommended to establish a quality system which is oriented towards the ISO 9000 standards.

Organic products and environmental management

Not so much driven by the legislator but rather by consumers and the public awareness do SMEs of the food industry increasingly rely on the production of organic products and on environmental management. A considerable number of the companies in this survey is already working with environmental management or at least working on its implementation. Without doubt this causes costs for the changeover and generates new tasks of quality assurance. Since for example organic products and their primary products do not contain additives and preservative, microbiological and chemical tests might be increasingly necessary and the storage time has to be kept to a minimum. The latter is also in accordance with cost-effective rationalisation objectives. The same is true for cutting down on supplies such as water or energy with an efficient environmental management.

ISO 9000 and food-processing SMEs

Barriers

The ISO standards face all sectors and types of companies with the same requirements. When implementing a quality system according to ISO 9000 the following general barriers came up in the surveyed SMEs of the food industry:

Expenditure of time:

For many surveyed companies the expenditure of time for the systematisation and documentation of operational processes according to ISO elements creates a considerable barrier. This is true for both the preparation of the initial certification as well as for the maintenance and up-dating of the documentation with regard to re-audits.

Cost expenditure:

The costs for obtaining the certificate and for maintaining the quality system meet with structurally thin capital resources in SMEs. This is particularly true when external consultants are made use of extensively.

Lacking support by the company management:

Particularly in traditional family-owned companies the company management is very often not familiar with new management systems. In small enterprises the company management is fully occupied. Although responsibility for the certification is delegated, the "quality manager" does not get sufficient support in his or her task. In some cases where the leadership function lies with a higher company unit the lack of communication was a barrier.

"Bureaucracy" and outdated organisation structures:

The criticism of too much bureaucracy indicates in most cases an insufficient company-specific implementation and use of the ISO system. In some cases a documentation is devised for formal compliance, which is neither useful nor helpful as a practical instruction. In some cases outdated and inefficient organisation structures are reproduced in the quality system instead of making use of the expenditure resulting from a systematic analysis anyway to get rid of weaknesses in the organisation.

These barriers are rather unspecific for the surveyed food industry yet quite typical for SMEs. They often show that *the same weaknesses* of the company structures are responsible for the fact that difficulties occur in the simultaneous dealing with current company tasks, competitive requirements and internal changes as well as with quality management and that only seemingly there is an "overburden". In these cases elements of the quality system are not used as *contributions* to the solution of company tasks, which by nature they could very well be: e.g. clear allocation of tasks, reliable information and control channels, quality-related product, technology and process strategies. The demonstration of a quality system is much rather understood as an externally induced additional task which is to be dealt with *formally.*

The following barriers are more specific problems of the food industry:

"Secret knowledge", divisional thinking and fear of rationalisation:

Indeed, the certification wave in the food industry is following a process of modernisation and rationalisation which has already been going on for some time. A number of employees and also some employee organisations therefore want to keep up production lines and procedures in which they consider themselves as being irreplaceable for their companies. However, what is in many cases true for modernisation and rationalisation, that traditional skills and also staff become redundant, does not really apply to the implementation of quality management. Wherever this barrier occurs it is, therefore, very often a sign of a lack of information and participation of staff.

Processes which are difficult to standardise:

On the one hand, this applies to points in the process which involve natural processes or which handle primary products strongly varying due to nature. The same is true of traditional manufacturing methods with a high proportion of manual work which is essentially directed by knowledge and experience of craftsmanship.

Case examples and statements

"There is always a time pressure. Now we are living quite hard times. Many kind of changes have happened in very short period of time. In production 80 products have changed its place because of the re-organisation in European level." (224/Finland/biscuits/250 employees/aspiring certification/ISO 9001)

The managerial task of quality management falls completely into the responsibility of the quality representative and is limited to quality inspections and the maintenance and up-dating of the established system. There are ambitions to further develop the system with regard to the transfer of the system and the certification to the other two companies. But they have not yet had the consent of the upper management. *(122/Germany/tinned fish/12 employees/certification < 2 years/ISO 9002)*

"I have my background in the metal-working industry which means that when I began to work here in 1992 I already had been working with Quality issues. This was why I initiated the discussion with the managing director. However he did not respond to my signals. In 1993 we recruited a new manager for the finance department and the two of us finally managed to convince the managing director who in 1994 took the decision to seek for ISO certification. It had taken me two years to convince the company

management." (621/Sweden/wheat and rye flour, rice, peas, beans/95 employees/certification < 2 years/ISO 9002)

"We have a problem with a low interest in the subject in the managerial group. They do not really know what this is all about, the interest is low and they do not support this to 100%." (623/Sweden/potato chips and other snack products/330 employees/certification > 2 years/ISO 9001)

"Quality system means more paper work and it takes resources. But our world has changed totally. We are working in different enterprise than before certification. The awareness of follow-up and control, management reviews and other activities that support the system, helps to keep system lively and develop it." (221/Finland/salads, meat products/40 employees/certification < 2 years/ISO 9001)

The introduction of a Quality Standard System was decided by the Board of Directors, being fixed, in advance, a short term for purposes of obtaining the Certification. *"Even today, we suffer the consequences deriving from the fact that the process have not begun from down upward, being, thus, the Certification, the highest point of a collective display of organisation. As referred to above, the way of introducing the System had negative effects which remain nowadays in the adoption of "Quality" idea by the employees in general. To give an example, there was no concern on the adaptation of the language used in the procedural instructions to the normal vocabulary of the employees and, as a consequence, these ones learn it by heart instead of understanding it." (521/Portugal/milk products/281 employees/certification > 2 years/ISO 9002)*

"The difficulties mainly concern the lack of proper organisation of the company. The training is necessary and helps to overcome those problems, but it is not sufficient without the proper organisational structure. Further problems are generally caused by improvisation, amateurism and Greek mentality as well as by the pressure of work or by new employees who have not been trained yet. Bureaucracy is one of the most serious problems a company faces after the implementation of ISO standards. The employees become more responsible through the Quality Assurance System and all the documents help them to accomplish their tasks successfully. The problem of bureaucracy is dealt with the help of computerisation of the procedures. At any time one can check the PC and see which employee has a specific document, what's its edition etc." The enterprise tries to simplify the forms

and revise the instructions where this can be done (recently three forms were combined in one). *(321/Greece/ice-creams, fresh juices/437 employees/certification < 2 years/ISO 9002)*

"Because there's a lot of departments within production because of the various products we make, there does tend to be - I don't know if that's common to all factories - but you do tend to get 'that's not my job' sort of thing." (724/United Kingdom/edible cake decorations, sugar and chocolate confectionery, popcorn/160 employees/certification > 2 years/ISO 9002)

"Some staff members resisted the changes. This was particularly the case for staff member who had more than 10 years service in the company. They believed that up to the implementation of ISO no one had complained about the way they did their work, so why change now? The unions also had to be convinced. There was suspicion that the changes might bring about rationalisation. In the previous 5-7 years this had taken place. They had to be assured that the success of the company meant securing the employment for the existing staff. A move was also taking place from a culture of 'secrecy' to a culture of 'information sharing'. Previously, very little communication took place between management and staff. It was usually a case of carrying out the instructions dictated by management. Staff were never afforted the opportunity to discuss issues and to put forward solutions." (424/Ireland/full range of milk products/343 employees/certification < 2 years/ISO 9002)

"It was also the view of the existing management that many of the production and distribution staff were hithertofore, hired for their "brawn, and not their brain". At first, it was difficult to convince this workforce to change. Rationalisation had also taken place 7/10 years previously and many of the remaining staff had seen some of their colleagues leave the company. They feared that this was going to happen to them. Also, there was an initial difficulty when certain members of staff claimed to have understood the new procedures. However, it soon became apparent that they did not. Many of them did not want 'to be seen as being slow at learning the new methods'. Indeed, some even claimed to not having been consulted in the first place. As a result they demonstrated an unwillingness to undertake the new procedures. There was a concern that when writing up work procedures, there was an inclination on the part of staff to describe their job in terms of what they should be doing, rather than what they were actually doing. Caution was exercised with this task. This necessitated the need to explain in detail to staff the importance of

*accurately reflecting their jobs as they are currently carried out."
(425/Ireland/canning of food and vegetables, beverages, packing dry
pulses/295 employees/aspiring certification/ISO 9002)*

*"Process control cannot be carried out with static indices. Stable final
products from by nature varying raw material cannot be achieved through
standardised indices, experience is indispensable here. It doesn't work like
for instance mixing chemical pure basic material in the plastics industry."
(121/Germany/spices, spice mixtures/160 employees/certification > 2
years/ISO 9001)*

Critical analysis of the ISO system

As the expert interviews prove, a critical analysis of the establishment of the ISO
system in market relationships, as well as of this system itself as a new standard of
quality management, takes place in the SMEs of the food industry. Particularly
with companies being in the midst of the certification process criticism focuses on
the bureaucratic expenditure. But also company experts with longer ISO
experiences reported some points of criticism. The following line of criticisms can
thus be generalised:

- **Pressure for formal system conformity instead of assurance of concrete
  quality aims in the customer-supplier relationships:**

  With the ISO system becoming generally accepted as a competitive standard,
  the concrete dealing with product and process specifics of the particular
  company fall behind the demand of big customers of the trade, corporate
  parents and customers on SMEs to obtain the certificate. The transfer of know-
  how and the consulting between customers and suppliers about product
  requirements and good production practice are neglected. The SMEs are
  actually pushed into a merely formal compliance with the ISO standards.
  Critical comments about external consultants the companies had called in
  during the certification process pointed into the same direction.

- **Over-estimation of standardisable and measurable quality features:**
  The ISO system leads to a concentration of the quality efforts on production
  processes which have already been assured by technical modernisation and on
  nonconformities which are formally detectable concerning for instance the
  stability of the product features and complaints. The ISO system does not
  sufficiently promote the identification of the causes for complaints, it does not
  support the typical quality tasks of the food industry such as the identification
  of product requirements deriving from the processing specifications of the
  customers and from the consumer interests as well as the responsible handling
  of agricultural primary products and the mastering of their natural variations.

- **Sector-unrelated elements and element structure instead of process structure:**With some ISO elements - e.g. "maintenance" - it is quite obvious that they originate from the "dead" industry, with others the chapter classification - e.g. "preservation" as an element of distribution shows the same. In general, setting up a quality system along process steps would be more appropriate particularly in the food industry.

The focus of criticism is clearly on the "insufficient relation to the sector" and less on the inadequacies of the ISO system for structures of SMEs. This criticism is a productive scepticism as long as it does not reduce the quality system to a sort of small version for small enterprises but leads to a concrete adaptation to quality-deciding processes and internal and external interfaces. Those companies of the sample could be exemplary which explicitly extended their ISO system to company functions which are not necessarily relevant to certification or which have developed similar procedures of their own. The demand of SMEs particularly on big customers and external consultants to more strongly acknowledge and support their concrete quality policy by information flow and know-how transfer seems to be legitimate.

Despite the presented criticism the company experts localised in the very standardisation and formalism of the ISO system the usefulness for their companies' quality management.

- Particularly in small enterprises operations are now recorded objectively and continuingly for the first time. The effects are higher planning security of the management, clear work tasks and a higher job satisfaction of the operatives. Some companies point out savings in time and money.

- The documentation of organisational knowledge which has previously been linked to particular persons allows the standardisation of the best solutions. The formalised documentation of department-specific organisational knowledge allows communication beyond departmental borders about function-specific requirements and procedures and makes collaboration more efficient.

- The documentation makes the exact identification of specific critical points and critical interfaces in the food processing of the company easier. As an instrument of target-performance comparisons it allows the exact localisation of actual performance weaknesses, but also of potential strengths which are to be documented as an improvement of the standard processes. As an economic effect some companies especially point out savings in energy and supplies.

- It is particularly in the formal structure of the ISO system that some experts see a suitable instrument to sort external quality demands by the legislator and society and the specific quality demands of the customers and consumers and allocate them to specific company functions or processes as a precise task.

- Some interview partners emphasised the compatibility with other quality-related systems (HACCP; environmental management) so that the established ISO system makes a company-specific adaptation of these systems easier.

Some of the above criticism on the ISO system seems to have already been covered by the guidelines of the standards commission for the long-term revision of the ISO 9000 standards:

- enhanced suitability for SMEs

- relocation of the quality focus on the product quality and more emphasis on customer orientation and co-operation with the suppliers

- process-oriented organisation

It seems that other points of criticism can be covered less by better standards than by internal improvements of a tailor-cut quality system as well as by enhanced co-operation among the companies in quality issues, anyway.

Case examples and statements

"I find the ISO 9000 system as being exaggerated. It seems unnecessary to involve parts that you are not even affected by." (622/Sweden/ice-cream & frozen desserts/91 employees/certification < 2 years/ISO 9001)

"Nowadays each customer asks about the ISO system and HACCP. If you inundate them with papers, they'll be satisfied. If you don't have the system, big customers have a questionnaire which is like an audit." (123/Germany/egg products/100 employees/certification < 2 years/ISO 9002)

"Big companies obviously don't want to know unless you've got quality systems in place - whether they of certification or not." (724/United Kingdom/edible cake decorations, sugar and chocolate confectionery, popcorn/160 employees/certification > 2 years/ISO 9002)

"Most of the consultants have one –ism that they promote. They have no ability and they are not willing to make synthesis of different managerial approaches and apply them to acute situation of the organisation." (222/Finland/ice-cream/250 employees/certification > 2 years/ISO 9001)

"ISO 9000 and the quality notion deduced from it does not have an undisputed reputation any more. The reason being that the formal fulfilment of the system does not at all guarantee the actual quality of the product. Our company wants competent inspection by the customers and gives them all the documents. We ourselves carry out competent inspections at our suppliers." (125/Germany/frozen products/688 employees/certification < 2 years/ISO 9001)

There is a concern that ISO systems can focus too much on the number of complaints rather than on why the complaints exist. Instead, the focus should concentrate on the following: *"what are the reasons for the complaints; are the same customers making the complaints, are there trends emerging?". (424/Ireland/full range of milk products/343 employees/certification < 2 years/ISO 9002)*

"Quality is not related enough to the marketing and sales functions, it is very oriented towards production. We don't really know what happens with the merchandise when they have left the factory." (621/Sweden/wheat and rye flour, rice, peas, beans/95 employees/certification < 2 years/ISO 9002)

"Seen from the marketing point of view it is difficult to identify with ISO. The emphasis should be on the aim of the activities. An integrated system would benefit us much more". (623/Sweden/potato chips and other snack products/330 employees/certification > 2 years/ISO 9001)

"We can already see now that we cannot keep up a static quality management, that we need to move more towards process orientation. The ISO standard is organised in 20 chapters. This means that you have to describe, on the one hand, delimited work areas, on the other hand however, you have to describe in them clearly cross-departmental tasks. Somebody who for instance does design control does not only do just that, he or she also has to deal with production engineering and inspections, purchasing and transportation issues. So there is no thinking and acting according to chapters. You have to define the overall process of the task, the responsibilities and particularly the points where somebody has to take part in tasks of other departments. There must be regulations for the contact persons who are to make their contributions. This is the only way to make sure that a new product is manufacturable. So I must hold people responsible for the overall process, only then you get the final product and

also reliable scheduling." (121/Germany/spices, spice mixtures/160 employees/certification > 2 years/ISO 9001).

ISO system as a means and a way

In general, the certificate was important as a decisive goal only for those surveyed companies which were still in the process of implementing the ISO system. Apart from that most of the interviewed experts claimed to use the ISO system as a working basis for company-specific quality goals. However, the stated goals and focuses, the volume and the intensity of these improvement programmes are as diverse as the degree of strategic procedures and of suitable institutionalisation of the improvement process. The following procedures can be generalised as examples of good practice:

• using the initial certification process and the re-audit cycle as opportunity for an analysis and assessment of company weaknesses and strengths

• on-going adjustment and simplification of the quality documents with regard to the practical operations in the company

• making use of the system as an instrument of organisational development

• implementation of additional methods and systems of internal quality assurance such as statistical methods which are based on the systematic recording of operations and their formalised documentation as well as suitable sector or product-related procedures such as HACCP and environmental management systems

• extension of the internal ISO system to a working basis for a deeper quality co-operation with suppliers and customers or within a holding company

• change in the goals of the quality management from an optimisation of the internal processes to the optimisation of the external relations.

Special strategies and institutions of improvement will be dealt with under the headline "Corporate culture and organisation of improvement".

Case examples and statements

"As the company did not possess a strong tradition concerning the existence of written procedures - for instance, the Production Direction did not even dispose of an office of its own -, the opportunity of the certification process and working up of the Quality Manual was seized to put everything in question, and so restructuring and reformulating all those practices that were considered not so correct or susceptible of being improved." (523/Portugal/coffee/ 297 employees/certification < 2 years/ISO 9002)

"1994 when the company was separated from the mother company, there were hard pressures to survive and get the share of the market. In that situation quality system seem as a very good tool to promote those goals and aims that the company has. We have just got the contract with a partner in the European level. We believe that we have not got the contract or agreement without quality system." (223/Finland/milk products/289 employees/certification > 2 years/ISO 9002)

"The investment in Quality system is profitable, therefore the company didn't content itself with the implementation of the ISO 9002 standards but went even further into the implementation of ISO 9001 standards, even though ISO 9002 was sufficient for advertising purposes." (325/Greece/cooked pork meat/226 employees/certification < 2 years/ISO 9001/2)

"We made a strategic decision to involve the department of administration and finance in the certification process. Since ISO did not include these parts we decided to make a "company specific" adjustment. The department of administration and finance have written their instructions according to their activities". (622/Sweden/ice-cream & frozen desserts/91 employees/ certification < 2 years/ISO 9001)

The quality system according to ISO 9001 was implemented comprising all units of the company group and supported the restructuring of previously more independent and locally-oriented companies for the new company group. The ISO project was and the established system is being used as an instrument for the organisation development of the company group and for its strategy as a producer of brands. *"In the beginning there was the question: what is really new? Each company is in fact trying to adjust to current demands. The trigger here with us clearly was that the structures, which were strictly locally oriented in the production companies, were to be put under one common roof. The ISO project was also used as an instrument for the organisation development. Before, each factory had its own computer systems, its own quality department and inspection scheduling. If you want to be a producer of a brand you need well trained people, on the one hand, and a system, on the other hand, that makes sure that a product is produced at each location meeting the quality demands of the brand." (125/Germany/frozen products/688 employees/certification < 2 years/ISO 9001)*

SMEs of the food industry and their adaptation and implementation of quality management

Sector-specific aims and effects

The qualitative expert interviews and case studies show some sector-specific aims and effects of quality management which lead to specific features and emphasis of quality elements.

Improvement of internal operations, traceability, proactive and comprehensive in-process quality assurance

Despite the often mentioned external pressure to implement a certified quality system, many of the surveyed companies put the improvement of their internal operations as an aim to the fore. The experts particularly pointed out transparency, standardisation and documentation of the operations. First of all, these requirements are to serve the traceability of the products. The sector-specific aspect of this emphasis becomes most obvious in the ambitious objective of a surveyed company to assure the safety and integrity of "the food chain from the farm to the consumer". Here lies the crucial motive for the food industry to overcome a concept of subsequent quality assurance by way of inspections. Other experts also indicated the conflict between final inspections and the objective of fresh products. Consequentially, there is a concept of in-process and proactive quality assurance which is not only effective at the end or during the production process but already in purchasing. This ambitious objective also means that it cannot be confined within the company borders but that particularly the food industry needs to strive towards quality systems in the entire suppliers-customer chain which key in with one another.

Automation and computerisation; quality control of integrated processes

Many of the surveyed SMEs have only survived in the tight competition with stagnating demand in the European food industry because they were able to modernise and automate material flow and manufacturing. This has often lead to cross-functional technologically integrated operations of purchasing, storage, production, preservation and packaging. Particularly computer-based continuous processes also turn out for the companies as the "friendly" technological basis of the quality management and rationalise the "bureaucratic expenditure" feared in other sectors. In this respect quality management seems to be a part of and a contribution to rationalisation.

Quality costs, cost reductions, environmental management

Cost reductions were explicitly named as a targeted and completed effect of quality management by some interviewed experts. Here, quality expenses in the narrow sense were not to the fore. Much rather the systematic recording of the processes and particularly the involvement of staff into the critical examination of the processes allowed the identification of possibilities to reduce process costs and expenses for supplies. Linking such cost reductions with environmental aims of the companies seems to be sector-specific.

Customer and consumer satisfaction; brand policy; customer flexibility

Particularly in companies of the food industry the standardisation and formalisation of (primary) product characteristics and procedures are considered to be an important instrument to achieve better customer and consumer satisfaction. Product stability - essential for every brand policy - and product safety are guaranteed to consumers, a guarantee which holds also as product information against an increasingly critical awareness and in this respect substitutes or supports the advertising expenditure. Towards the customers of the distribution trade or of the processing industry standardisation and formalisation on the basis of the sector-specific mass production allow more reliable and faster co-ordination. Some surveyed companies use this quality knowledge in an extended consulting of their customers, that is, as a basis for extended customer services. In the opposite direction changing customer demands and consumer wishes can be translated much faster into precisely limited product and procedure changes increasing the market flexibility of the companies. It is true that in most cases modern technology is the backbone of reliable products and processes as well as their changes but quality management is considered to be an adequate supporting control system.

In summary, standardisation and formalisation of product specifics and procedures through a quality system is the basis for the achievement of these sector-specific quality aims and company effects. However, it is also quite obvious that these instruments can only be effective if they are used within a reliable flow of information and interdepartmental co-operation in the company.

Case examples and statements

"Quality management is connected with technical changes and it has influenced to changes. The traceability of products has improved in production." (222/Finland/ice-cream/250 employees/certification > 2 years/ISO 9001)

Food safety and traceability are important management priorities for the company. The company had to been seen as taking every measure to ensure they meet these requirements. Their focus was *"to develop systems to assure food safety and the integrity of the food chain from farm gate to market". (423/Ireland/full range of fresh dairy products/246 employees/certification > 2 years/ISO 9002)*

The toast that the company produces is a well-known product for more than 20 years, so its quality concerning its taste can't be changed. All the customers who buy it trust its taste which has been stable throughout the course of time. The better organisation that is achieved in many departments such as in the production, purchasing and stock department is significant even for the product itself. *(322/Greece/toast/258 employees/certification > 2 years/ISO 9002)*

The production has been up-dated to state-of-the-art technology over the past few years. The changeover to a vertical process technology ensures short ways of the product and the minimisation of oxygen exposure. This serves particularly to prevent the oxidation of flavours. The most important motives for the implementation of a quality system were and still are the improvement of internal processes and the management structures. Clear work instructions are to support particularly the big investments into the up-dating of the process technology and assure their optimum use by the staff. *"The people are very important for quality. But you must have the right technology if a good product is to come out. Otherwise staff can try however hard. The staff have always done a good job, but they used to come up against the limitations of technology. This has improved considerably. Now the right response of staff has to come in for optimum control of the technology." (124/Germany/roasted ground coffee/70 employees/certification < 2 years/ISO 9002)*

"A group of workers were able to save the company money by suggesting a use for the steam that was being emitted during the production process. This is just one example of the savings accrued by the company." (422/Ireland/butter/49 employees/certification > 2 years/ISO 9002)

"Each functional area actively look at ways of saving money. Energy is a high cost for the company. A recent initiative resulted in a substantial cut in the electricity bill. There were losses with pallets. These were being returned either damaged or not belonging to the plant. This meant a

considerable financial loss each year. A control system has been implemented. This ensures that pallets are returned in the order in which they left the plant. While there was an initial cost, the payback was good i.e. reduction in milling loss and return of pallets in good condition." (421/Ireland/animal feeds/39-44 employees/certification > 2 years/ISO 9001/2)

"The company avoids investing in advertising and prefers investing those implications in improving more the quality of its products." (321/Greece/ice-creams, fresh juices/437 employees/certification < 2 years/ISO 9002)

"The company have been quite successful in ensuring the quality of their products. In fact, it has been a consumer driven business. The particular branded products developed from a consumer driven environment. It has been marketing led from its very inception. Other businesses in the dairy industry have come from a co-operative led market i.e. milk supply came about as a result of farmers having cows which produced a milk yield. The demand was not necessarily as a result of the customers demanding the product. The opposite was the case with the yogurt product. It was by far a new entity. It was entirely customer driven. It was upon this factor that the brand was built. The fact that the product was consumer driven made it easier for the company to adopt quality systems and to have a greater appreciation of consumer requirements." (423/Ireland/full range of fresh dairy products/246 employees/certification > 2 years/ISO 9002)

A "Customers First" group was set up. Their task was to liaise closely with the customers. More recently a survey of major customers was conducted over an 8 month period. Recommendations from this resulted in the occurrence of four health safety checks being carried out quarterly. *(422/Ireland/butter/49 employees/certification > 2 years/ISO 9002)*

The customer base is geographically dispersed across the country. Branches were set up to serve the customers in each of the key areas. From these branches the customers place their orders. These are forwarded directly to the mill for processing using a sophisticated computer ordering system. The company also provides technical and marketing support to their customers. A feed co-ordinators' group has been established. A representative from each of the branches meets with members of the production and the laboratory teams to discuss customer requirements.

These meetings also safeguard against branches offering feeds to a customer which the mill are not in a position to produce. While the laboratory's purpose is to provide the company by providing a testing facility for quality control, it also allows the company to offer its customers a service which gauges the quality of their forage and grass. This also means that the sales representatives can bring valuable information and recommendations to customers to enhance the quality of their own feeding regime, and as such providing total diet management as part of that service. *(421/Ireland/animal feeds/39-44 employees/certification > 2 years/ISO 9001/2)*

Company-specific conditions and modifications

The implementation of quality management meets with an almost homogenous condition in the surveyed SMEs of the food industry. All companies have mostly continuous mass production with predominantly mechanical and increasingly automated procedures. This restricts the complexity and the variations of steps of the performance process which need to be integrated into the quality system. In this respect the specifics of the quality management are therefore relatively similar in the surveyed companies.

Yet, company-specific modifications of the quality system, the main points of the quality concept and the decision for the implementation of particular means and methods of quality assurance cannot be represented on a one-dimensional progressive line. They trace back to special conditions. The following conditions in the surveyed companies are typical, in individual cases they are partly overlapping.

Customer structure:

When it comes to customer-oriented quality tasks the companies differ considerably depending on whether they supply to the distributing trade, to companies or directly to consumer households. This decides e.g. on the amount of marketing functions (e.g. networking of the sales representatives) which are to be integrated into the quality system. The same is true for the differences in the demands on product variation and on flexibility despite underlying mass production.

Product and product line:

Depending on the product the company has to meet varying complex and critical requirements frequently supported by more or less dense public law standards (e.g. baby -, dietetic food etc.). This leads to differentiated verification requirements in the quality system and to special measures of quality assurance in the company. The company-specific complexity of the quality system is also influenced by the product range and possibly by different production methods.

The influence of nature and the position of the company within the processing chain:

The influence of varying qualitative and qualitative harvests and specific critical natural characteristics of the primary products and products affects companies quite differently depending also very much on their position within the processing chain. Quality management faces tasks of mastering hardly standardisable work tasks and processes and the decision to implement effective quality techniques. Moreover, nature-induced seasonal fluctuation in capacity utilisation and particularly seasonal work presents the quality system and its maintenance with special tasks.

The type of company:

Significant variations in the quality systems of the companies, expressed only very roughly in the different demonstration degrees of ISO 9001 and 9002, are based on the type of company. The company-specific tasks of quality management widely differ particularly at the external interfaces purchasing and marketing/distribution depending on whether it is an independent company with a full functional structure or a company operating independently within a group or a holding or as a supplier of a big customer. In the second case only logistic tasks need to be mastered whereas in the first case quality management also has to address strategic aims.

Effects of quality management on the organisation and process structure

Overall, in terms of quality management-related effects on the organisation, process structure, work forms and job profiles, the following points can be retained:

1. The implementation of quality management has mainly effects on the management structures, tasks and patterns. Reorganisation of quality-improving forms of work is currently centred on management, development and quality assurance laboratories.

2. At the operative level the companies do not see quality management as a decisive reason for a direct re-organisation of work structures and state little changes. Work organisation is determined by technological modernisation. Quality management is based on this modernisation or supports it. It is the main impact at the operative-productive level that the technologically modernised work organisation is being formalised, including new technology-based inspection tasks.

3. This is in accordance with the fact that quality-related measures of re-organisation, if in place, have an effect predominantly outside the direct

performance processes. There are internal improvement circles and new forms of quality co-operation with suppliers and customers.

Management

Modern quality management makes quality a management task. The ISO standards confront all surveyed companies with the tasks of defining the responsibility for quality, co-ordinating it with other management tasks, defining and organising management-delegation relationships, determining responsibilities and implementing them into the management structures or re-organising management structures and, if need be, employing more managerial staff. From the point of view of the interviewed experts, these tasks were accomplished by organisational changes in almost all surveyed companies. Most companies stated that beyond the definition of tasks and the embedding of the position of a quality manager quality management had hardly any effects on the management structure.

The organisational imperative of "flatter hierarchies", implied particularly by the TQM philosophy, meets with scepticism in most of the surveyed companies. While small enterprises operate with lean leadership anyway and being - often informally - deeply involved in the company operations, most of the medium-sized enterprises already have lean management structures for economic reasons.

While the implementation of quality management in the surveyed companies has obviously had little effect on the organisational structure of management, many of the interviewed managers highlight the new demands on the co-operation, the work and the leadership patterns of the management. Here implementation barriers have revealed weak points and quality management has induced improvement.

- Not so much hierarchical levels but rather hierarchical barriers were identified as a barrier in implementing a uniform and clear quality management. A strict separation between the administrative-commercial upper management and the operative management was pointed out. Special forms of this problem occurred with the centralisation of administrative-commercial functions in a holding as opposed to   mainly operative company units or with the centralisation of administrative-commercial functions of a company as opposed to the different production lines.

- Sometimes the basically correct division of responsibility for the quality system between the senior management and the quality manager is a barrier. Here, the problem was particularly indicated that the senior management defines the quality goals of the company, however, their support in the implementation - also institutionally - is not sufficiently guaranteed. There were special varieties of this problem in cases where there was a lack of understanding of the senior management for the new quality system in that they oriented their quality goals towards more traditional quality notions and formulated predominately economic specifications without regarding how they could be implemented in the system.

- Remarkably often differences between the marketing/sales management and the production management were barriers for a continuous quality system. They concerned the involvement of very different work procedures into a homogeneous formalised system, the integration of function-specific quality goals and notions (customer orientation & flexibility vs. standardisation and process stability), the - also institutional - assurance of quality-decisive communication.

Examples of good practice and improvement of the company management brought about by quality management were found in companies

- institutionalising the quality department as an interface between the senior management and the operative management

- ensuring and maintaining an open interaction between the senior management and the operative management

- establishing interdepartmental teamwork structures particularly for a customer-oriented design and change of products and product lines as well as for the implementation and maintenance of the quality system

- applying quality assurance to the work of the management and leading by example

Case examples and statements

"Quality Management is a tool for managers." (223/Finland/milk products/289 employees/certification > 2 years/ISO 9002)

The company is characterised - not only in the relation foreign daughter to company - by a relatively strict division of the commercial administrative functions of the senior management and the operative level of the production company. The senior management formulates the quality policy each year consisting of a few principles only and focusing on energy and water savings. The development and maintenance of the quality system and the implementation of quality management into the everyday processes is essentially the task of the middle management, the heads of departments and the responsible supervisors of the production. The main burden clearly rests with the person responsible for quality. Some communication problems between the senior management and the middle and operative level of the management were obvious. Some critical statements on unclear customer demands and unjustified complaints indicate an insufficient co-ordination at order acceptance. The fact that commercial specifications of the senior management are sometimes hardly comprehensible for the operative level also points to deficiencies in the communication between the general management and the operative management. Spoilage rates required by the department of accounts, which is part of the senior management, are not always harmonised with production and laboratory. The same is true for capacity utilisation plans. The company works off customer orders but it must balance variations in capacity utilisation. The calculations are done by the senior management and are not always in optimum accordance with product and production requirements. *"This is also about unit cost, the margin is always narrow. But I don't do the calculations." (123/Germany/egg products/100 employees/certification < 2 years/ISO 9002)*

The company consists of two main departments, the administration department and the production department. Due to the fact that the administration department functions out of the Quality System (except from one part), there have been some problems. *(321/Greece/ice-creams, fresh juices/437 employees/certification < 2 years/ISO 9002)*

Difficulties have been in the interdepartmental communication between the production and sales departments. The production understands the increased profit in a production of larger series. This requires larger quantities of primary products in the stock which is difficult today. The sales department do not understand the difficulties we have today with keeping primary products in stock. *"We made a strategic decision to involve the department of administration and finance in the certification process. Since ISO did not include these parts we decided to do make a "company specific" adjustment. The department of administration and finance have written their instructions according to their activities. (622/Sweden/ice-cream & frozen desserts/91 employees/certification < 2 years/ISO 9001)*

"The implementation process into manufacturing has been very hard. They have difficulties in understanding the customer demands. An example; we had customers that wanted another kind of package which the manufacturing could not understand. An endless discussion started which finally forced us - several months too late - into the change since our competitors already had adapted this demand. We were very close in loosing valuable market shares." (621/Sweden/wheat and rye flour, rice, peas, beans/95 employees/certification < 2 years/ISO 9002)

Customer-oriented product innovation sets new requirements for the production and the company organisation has to take this into account. *"This will always be a problem. You have to understand the production. If a process runs well they want to keep it that way. But this is not how business runs today. A customer wants a new product and we have to get it to the customer. That's what we're trying, also using computer support, with adjusting the production logistics so that changeovers can be carried out   swiftly   without   breaks." (125/Germany/frozen   products/688 employees/certification < 2 years/ISO 9001)*

The directors have regular contact with senior managers.... *"It's not a formal structure where, if you want to see one of the directors, you've got to get permission from somebody first. There's a lot of interaction between directors and other people - especially since we transferred the offices to open plan from enclosed offices - individual offices. All the offices are here. When they were built, we were individual offices so people had their own separate area. When we went open-plan, that really broken down a lot of the barriers between departments." (721/United Kingdom/tea/500 employees/certification > 2 years/ISO 9001)*

Management works on principles of target-oriented management. *"We have no job descriptions but result areas, that is, the target is defined and as the guideline for its achievement there is the management handbook. But we will have to go further on our way towards teamwork in the management. The result areas are still individualised but of course there are always teams   behind   them." (125/Germany/frozen   products/688 employees/certification < 2 years/ISO 9001)*

A management by objective performance appraisal system was put in place. This means that quality issues are linked to performance. Also, a bonus system is in operation. *(421/Ireland/animal feeds/39-44 employees/ certification > 2 years/ISO 9001/2)*

Quality manager

There are basically two ways the surveyed companies take when appointing somebody to the new function as quality manager: external recruitment of a trained quality manager or the internal appointment or redefinition of the task area of a manager most of the time involving external further training. There is a middle way in merged companies where quality managers rotate. It is interesting that in cases of an external recruitment there is often a quality expert from a completely different sector appointed particularly from the metal working sector, presumably resulting from time differences in the implementation of modern quality systems in the various sectors. In the cases of an internal appointment staff is predominantly recruited from the laboratory area who are already experienced in inspection methods and product design.

The statements of the experts show strengths and weaknesses of both ways. Externally recruited quality managers very often bring in very good management know-how and a modern leading pattern to the company. The quality approach of the new manager brings about a redefinition of other management functions as well. External staff are however not very familiar with the company-specific product aims, with external and internal - partly still informal - customer-supplier relationships and processes and with not yet systematically developed human resources. In comparison, experience and a grown trust of staff is the asset of an internally appointed quality manager. However, insufficient modern management know-how can also lead to "sticking to" old routines including traditional quality control with the result that optimisation potentials of the quality system might be "overlooked".

The *position and role* of the quality manager in the surveyed companies basically varies in the following types:

- full-time quality manager versus quality manager with other management tasks (product design & lab, personnel)

- general, equal or subordinate function of the quality manager within the management hierarchy. The significance of the formal organisational role of the quality manager is qualified in the company practice by the institutions of the information flow within the management, the organisation of the decision-making process and the involvement of the quality management in the general management.

Particularly relevant for the perspective of this survey is the finding that the new tasks of quality management stimulates in some companies the reorganisation of the task of personnel management. There is more often impetus for personnel development from the quality manager than there is from the more administrating personnel department. In some companies personnel development falls completely into the responsibility of the quality manager.

Normally, the surveyed companies do not define the tasks and the role of the quality manager with the traditional understanding as the leader of the quality department any more. Quality managers have cross-departmental authority. A growing public awareness of the safety of food production, customer expectations, cost pressures and competition force companies to administer comprehensive quality precautions and, therefore, require an efficiently organised influence of the quality manager on all company functions. In companies implementing and carrying out environmental management apart from quality management the quality manager is normally also in charge of this task.

Examples of good experiences can be particularly found in companies

* institutionalising the quality department as an interface function between the senior management and the operative management. This ensures, on the one hand, the support of the senior management in the maintenance and improvement of the quality system and, on the other hand, there is a feed back into the decision-making of the management on the practical implementation and implementation difficulties of the company's quality aims.

* ensuring the presence and accessibility of the quality department on the operative level of all departments. Interestingly enough, the surveyed companies take two opposite ways. One way is that the quality department regularly discusses quality issues with staff on site; sometimes its scope of responsibility is deliberately extended to personnel tasks such as work safety, health and further training. The other way makes a point in delegating the discussion about current quality issues to the supervisors and staff of the operative teams so that quality is no longer treated as the special responsibility of the quality department.

Case examples and statements

A "champion" was nominated to lead the team and drive the process. This person had previously worked with quality systems and was highly respected by staff. *(422/Ireland/butter/49 employees/certification > 2 years/ISO 9002)*

"Some of us are people who have been here - who came in as sort of ordinary operators - like myself, I just came in as a QA person doing checks on the shopfloor - and worked our way up and haven't got the managerial background. I mean you work up through a company and you're not always treated the same as someone who comes in as a manager or as a supervisor so it is difficult." (724/United Kingdom/edible cake decorations, sugar and chocolate confectionery, popcorn/160 employees/certification > 2 years/ISO 9002)

"Before dealing with quality management according to ISO 9000 thoughts in the company were rather more marketing-oriented. The way how an order was handled was not of much concern, the most important thing was that it was completed. The quality manager was and still is the business consultant in the company so to speak." (121/Germany/spices, spice mixtures/160 employees/certification > 2 years/ISO 9001)

"There were many organisational changes that were linked to the implementation of the Quality System. The most important was the creation of the quality assurance department which deals directly with the management of the enterprise. Another significant change that took place recently was the merge of the department of Quality Control with the department of Quality Assurance and the creation of a new independent department which also includes the R&D department." (321/Greece/ice-creams, fresh juices/437 employees/certification < 2 years/ISO 9002)

"We constantly ask ourselves: can we cut down on interfaces, can't we join departments also physically, make the organisation easier. We have already organised quality assurance and product design in one area. The area is now called product service." (125/Germany/frozen products/688 employees/certification < 2 years/ISO 9001)

A Quality Assurance Manager was appointed. He is also charged with the responsibility of all environmental issues. The quality function which was part of the production area was separated and made part of the laboratory function. *(421/Ireland/animal feeds/39-44 employees/certification > 2 years/ISO 9001/2)*

The County Labour Board in the region offered a number of companies a resource person for free to initiate the quality work within the company. By this the authorities in the region made an investment in the food-processing industry to accelerate the process with the introduction of quality management. This was also the introduction of the quality manager at the enterprise. 70% of the resource persons were employed as quality managers within the food-processing industry. *(622/Sweden/ice-cream & frozen desserts/91 employees/certification < 2 years/ISO 9001)*

Not surprisingly, the introduction of quality management had led to significant increases in the workload and responsibilities of the Quality Manager. He has overall responsibility for the operation of the ISO system. A small team of quality inspectors (15) assist him. Since the company achieved ISO certification, a Health and Safety Officer has been appointed. Previously the Quality Manager also had this responsibility and so this appointment has eased his workload somewhat. *(722/United Kingdom/children's sugar confectionery/610 employees/certification > 2 years/ISO 9002)*

The appointment of a BS co-ordinator within the Quality Department is seen as an important step towards maintaining quality standards. *"Her job is to liaise with supervisors and to explain, and guide them through, any changes to procedures that occur. She also helps supervisors to put changes in themselves if they feel these are needed and to produce the necessary documents. She also goes into the various factory areas and trains the staff. This job was created as a direct result of quality management."* *(724/United Kingdom/edible cake decorations, sugar and chocolate confectionery, popcorn/160 employees/certification > 2 years/ISO 9002)*

During the introduction training for the ISO system proficient and committed people were called into the team of internal auditors. Auditor training - with external support was carried out with them. A team of 10 internal auditors came out of this involving a steering group of three at management level. *(124/Germany/roasted ground coffee/70 employees/certification < 2 years/ISO 9002)*

The company is seeking to convey the message that each operative is responsible for quality management and this does seem to be becoming accepted: *"Most of the factory floor operatives are very conscientious in that way and quick to alert us to problems. There is always the temptation for the Quality Manager to be seen as responsible. My own boss has just re-defined our team's role. I used to be the Quality Manager and now I'm the Scientific and Technical Manager. Quality is everyone's responsibility and he's trying to get this across."* (725/United Kingdom/peanut butter, gales honey, tablet jelly/300 employees/certification > 2 years/ISO 9002)

Management teams

Quality management-oriented leadership of the company implies interdepartmental teamwork of the management as an organisational imperative.

Specific requirements in the food industry have led, to a certain extend, to such structures and work methods even before the implementation of a quality system in the surveyed companies. The following requirements were named:

- assurance of product stability with varying raw materials
- product development under the condition of naturally varying raw materials and as regards manufacturability
- Accelerating product development

- production, purchasing and storage planning with the aim of optimal capacity utilisation

On the other hand, several companies indicated that the complex task of developing a comprehensive quality system for the company was only possible within a quality management team and that permanent new forms and task fields of cross-hierarchical and interdepartmental co-operation have opened up from this "embryo". Mentioned were in particular:

- The documentation of expert knowledge in the management makes it more widely available.

- By teamwork in the management the production, purchasing and storage planning became more flexible with regard to the market and more efficient with regard to cost cutting.

- In the team the staff responsible for customers and suppliers ensure a customer-oriented product design.

- Enhanced co-operation within the management improves the information flow of company know-how to customers and suppliers and from the external relations into the company.

- The allocation of central and decentralised management tasks is optimised, especially in structures of holdings.

There were comparatively little attempts to open up the management organisation directly for the involvement of staff competency into the decision-making process.

Case examples and statements

"When we were building the quality systems - when we were putting the systems together - we used smaller teams within the departments to get the systems together and to get work instructions together. So that, if you like, was an embryo." (722/United Kingdom/children's sugar confectionery/610 employees/certification > 2 years/ISO 9002)

The organisation within the company is divided in three different divisions. The process and work organisation is today not yet organised cross-departmentally. The amount of co-operation between the division is limited to meetings between the supervisors and the managers. The implementation of quality management has so far induced some minor organisational changes. This applies particularly to the interfunctional teamworking in design for manufacturability. The change was initiated by the quality manager and is mainly about the product development within the enterprise. *(625/Sweden/soft drinks, beer, mineral water/100 employees/certification > 2 years/ISO 9001)*

"A good example of cross-departmental team formation is the possibility to produce personalised sugar packages for our best customers. That possibility appeared in result of a more extended search aiming at the satisfaction of our customers' needs. To make it possible, it is necessary to adjust the will of the commercial structure to the production planning and to the strict management of by-products, in order to reduce to the minimum the additional costs this service involves." (523/Portugal/coffee/ 297 employees/certification < 2 years/ISO 9002)

Interfunctional teamworking takes place in contract acceptance. The departments which co-operate are the production, the general management and the marketing. A prediction of sales is made and that is translated in production programme and finally in supply programme. The departments of work scheduling and production are co-operating on a daily basis. *(322/ Greece/toast/258 employees/certification > 2 years/ISO 9002)*

The enterprise is today in the middle of a mayor organisational change which could to a certain extent be referred to the implementation of the quality system. This is at least a factor that has speed up the process. The new concept is based on a process oriented organisation which is a contrast to the former hierarchical. *"The most significant change will be the integration of the seven divisions into the three different production lines. This will be done by forming competence teams which will have the total responsibility from specifications to the distribution. More precisely this means that the executive level remains as well as the middle management with the departments of technical- and administrative service."* The enterprise prepares itself for the new organisation by forming workgroups and by choosing staff for the competence teams. The aim is to introduce the new organisation in the beginning of next year. *(624/Sweden/fruit preparations and chocolate products/130 employees/certification > 2 years/ISO 9001)*

Process-oriented cross-departmental co-operation is indispensable as the following example shows. Based on market research new products such as spice mixtures can be designed, their realisation, however, depends on whether the quality of primary products presupposed in the design is available at all. For example, the colour of paprika varies year after year. *"We had a very nice product idea, a mixture based on deep red paprika. But the purchasing said: You can't get it from this year's harvest."*

(121/Germany/spices, spice mixtures/160 employees/certification > 2 years/ISO 9001)

A feed co-ordinators' group has been established. A representative from each of the branches meets with members of the production and the laboratory teams to discuss customer requirements. These meetings also safeguard against branches offering feeds to a customer which the mill are not in a position to produce. *(421/Ireland/animal feeds/39-44 employees/certification > 2 years/ISO 9001/2)*

"Even the departments that are not directly related to Quality, such as the finance department, have to communicate more directly with departments such as the Quality control and the production ones. At this point there have been and still are some difficulties, that can be overcome by identifying and correcting the mistakes." (324/Greece/pasta, tomato products/336 employees/certification > 2 years/ISO 9002)

The interaction between central marketing and product service, on the one hand, and the production in the production companies, on the other hand, is considered as being crucial for the achievement of the market and quality aims of the company. *"The visions for new products come from marketing. But it has to "take hurdles". In a briefing the marketing has to prove that the new product is sustainable for a long time and possibly justify the necessary investment. Only then the idea is handed on to the product design which itself is divided in developing steps. At a certain step the production comes in finally taking over the responsibility for the first production. With the opening of the first production the operating manager has taken on the responsibility that performance and costs can be kept and also the responsibility for the quality. If they decide that it is not possible the product is given back to the product design. That's what we call internal customer-supplier-relation including cost responsibility." (125/Germany/frozen products/688 employees/certification < 2 years/ISO 9001)*

Middle management

In accordance with the theoretical imperatives of quality management several interviewed experts highlighted the key position of the middle management for the implementation of the quality system. Others reported that the implementation of quality management meets, at least temporarily, with the greatest barriers in the middle management.

In most of the surveyed companies the technological transition in the food industry has considerably changed the traditional work tasks and role of the middle management. Technological process control is increasingly taking the place of long trained sensory capability and craftsmanship. Person-related competency which is based on this can even turn out to be a wrong interference with the automated processes. The loss of traditional authority based on craftsmanship towards collaborators is experienced as a threat to status at least temporarily. Many of the barriers in the implementation of quality management which occur with the middle management in the surveyed companies correlate with this field of problems. This particularly shows in traditional rural companies where the middle management has very often "grown up" from the level of the operatives.

The companies have to cope with a movement into two opposite directions:

1. The formalisation and documentation of quality-assuring procedures particularly concerns this group of staff. Some of the interviewed companies set up procedure instructions documented in writing only up to this level. The formalisation of work tasks is considered in some cases - at least temporarily - as a disclosure of master craftsman knowledge and as a restriction of former decision-making and instruction authority.

2. On the other hand, the interviewed experts point out that quality management allows and even requires the responsible involvement of the "intermediate level" in new and extended competencies:

    - upgrading product-specific and job-related expert knowledge to company-wide know-how

    - imparting the company's quality goals, of customer demands and product requirements to the staff as a guideline for job-related quality demands

    - promoting a proactive quality awareness of staff for the identification of nonconformities and process weaknesses

    - justifying quality requirements of the own work area to the closely-related departments and justifying suggestions for improvement in the decision-making of the company

    - identifying skill needs of staff, the provision of work-accompanying training and the promotion of practical implementation of competencies of staff.

Examples of good practice are found in companies

- promoting the training of the middle management in new specialist and management skills

- reliably organising the top-down multiplier task and the bottom-up moderator role of the middle management in the company
- deliberately promoting a new relationship between supervisors and staff.

Case examples and statements

Respondents felt that there should be changes made to break down this strong departmental culture but there was a feeling that 'old habits die hard'. Many of the staff had been with the company for a long time and were often resistant to change. Some of the supervisors and managers had worked their way up from the shopfloor without adequate management training: *"Some of us are people who have been here - who came in as sort of ordinary operators - like myself, I just came in as a QA person doing checks on the shopfloor - and worked our way up and haven't got the managerial background. I mean you work up through a company and you're not always treated the same as someone who comes in as a manager or as a supervisor so it is difficult. So I think there could be a definite improvement made there on secondary management, really, rather than top management level. Because some of them aren't real management material really and they're very much 'it's not my job, it's your job' and this is where we get everybody working for themselves rather than all working together as a company." (724/United Kingdom/edible cake decorations, sugar and chocolate confectionery, popcorn/160 employees/certification > 2 years/ISO 9002)*

"Our understanding of a manager: everybody responsible for processes". Being in charge of processes includes the responsibility for staff and requires a different behaviour of executives: *"Before there was the principle of the three Cs: calculation - command - control. Now there is pressure in the opposite direction. The people complain about tasks which are not practicable. Every now and then there are employees who have a problem with responsibility. But on average we have a type of employee today who wants to take responsibility and also wants to be measured by it. The employees also initial. That has caused problems. Today employees do not like taking responsibility for trash. These are gestures which are very efficient. The executives used to have different tasks than they have today. They have to master techniques other than placing orders. They are more of a moderator and a coach." (125/Germany/frozen products/688 employees/certification < 2 years/ISO 9001)*

Hierarchies became flatter when rationalisation took place. As a result managers' jobs have been broadened. In addition, the personnel section was disbanded and the responsibility for personnel rests with each manager. Previously when staff experienced problems with their manager they went straight to personnel instead of speaking with their line manager. This was viewed as being corrosive and did not lend itself to creating good working relations between management and staff. Since the personnel department was disbanded an Industrial Relations Officer was appointed. He reports directly to the General Manager. He mediates between management and staff if and when the need arises. *(425/Ireland/canning of food and vegetables, beverages, packing dry pulses/295 employees/aspiring certification/ISO 9002)*

There was a drive to adopt a team based approach to work. This put on onus on management to be *"seen to be leading by example"*. Job responsibilities associated with quality management were delegated to managers across the different functional areas across the company. *(422/Ireland/butter/49 employees/certification > 2 years/ISO 9002)*

Work organisation

In most of the interviewed SMEs the implementation of quality management meets with a work organisation which is characterised by technological modernisation:

- automation of the production process
- technical merging of production with distribution functions (portioning, preservation, packaging) and increasing networking with purchasing, storage and material flow
- computer-based production planning and process control and an increasing networking with distribution and purchasing.

Many interviewed companies use particularly the computerisation also as a technical basis of their quality management. This minimises the administrative expenditure of documentation and the flow of documents, assures crucial quality elements such as traceability and facilitates the use of statistical methods. The automation of the production procedures minimises hygiene risks and allows in some cases the technically integrated inspection of critical process points, also as a basis of operator self-inspection.

The biggest challenge for the implementation of quality management is mostly the quality promoting organisation of the work of staff. Clearly documented procedure and work instructions make an improvement in comparison to person-related instructions with sometimes blurred responsibilities.

However, they are first of all only instructions for quality-assuring work and need to be complemented by orientation knowledge. Because, if quality is focused on technical parameters and process stability, the technical logic of the process quality does not show staff the benefit of product quality and customer satisfaction. Insufficient understanding of customer expectations, of product features, of manufacturing processes and of the quality system prevents staff from internalising the apparently "simple" and, due to documentation, apparently "clear" tasks. The restriction to technical process quality can also be a barrier for contributions of the operatives to the execution of quality tasks of other departments.

Case examples and statements

"Quality management has had to take into account the effects of technical change within the company rather than vice versa." (721/United Kingdom/tea/500 employees/certification > 2 years/ISO 9001)

"Technical changes are not connected with implementation of quality management. Automation and the control of processes and changes of processes are part of the technical development and people act in that process." (223/Finland/milk products/289 employees/certification > 2 years/ISO 9002)

"The company tailored the quality system to suit the technology that was in place. Quality management did not influence technical changes. Instead, technology influenced quality management." (422/Ireland/butter/49 employees/certification > 2 years/ISO 9002)

The production has been up-dated to state-of-the-art technology over the past few years. The changeover to a vertical process technology ensures short ways of the product and the minimisation of oxygen exposure. This serves particularly to prevent the oxidation of flavours. Clear work instructions are to support particularly the big investments into the up-dating of the process technology and assure their optimum use by the staff. *"The people are very important for quality. But you must have the right technology if a good product is to come out. Otherwise staff can try however hard. The staff have always done a good job, but they used to come up against the limitations of technology. This has improved considerably. Now the right response of staff has to come in for optimum control of the technology." (124/Germany/roasted ground coffee/70 employees/certification < 2 years/ISO 9002)*

The Quality System control was adjusted to computerisation so that there are no major differences from the ISO standards. Significant computer support of the System already exists and the goal is that 90% of the controls be done from there. Computerisation is considered to be the centre of the enterprise. *(323/Greece/puff pastry, strudel leaves, frozen vegetable, pizza/231 employees/aspiring certification/ISO 9001)*

Computer-aided evaluation of elements is introduced and there are thoughts that concern installation of a specialised software system. That system will support Quality Assurance procedures and will even reach production planning. *(324/Greece/pasta, tomato products/336 employees/certification > 2 years/ISO 9002)*

"With the newer technology much of the 'by chance' decision making has been removed. In all, the changes in technology have led to higher quality production methods and in turn higher quality products." (425/Ireland/canning of food and vegetables, beverages, packing dry pulses/295 employees/aspiring certification/ISO 9002)

"New technologies help quality management, because they make the process easier and control operations essential in perfectly defined stages, and, at the same time, they provide more data for specific processing." (523/Portugal/coffee/ 297 employees/certification < 2 years/ISO 9002)

"We are building our quality system documentation into intranet. That would help us to control and maintain our documentation system." (224/Finland/biscuits/250 employees/aspiring certification/ISO 9001)

The enterprise has a totally integrated computerised administrative system. The quality handbook is integrated in the system and all the changes are done directly in the system. This reduces and minimises the amount of administration every time an instruction has to be altered. *(624/Sweden/fruit preparations and chocolate products/130 employees/certification > 2 years/ISO 9001)*

Purchase, storage and material management

It is typical for the sector that the surveyed companies pay high attention to purchasing and material flow not only as regards quality management but also for other economic reasons. Systems like First-In-First-Out were often in place. An optimal utilisation of capacities is the result of careful planning ensuring a continuous provision of raw materials. Streamlining storage and material flow is instrumental in cost efficiency. The purchasing policy and materials management is therefore not only crucial for the quality of the products but also for the efficiency.

Therefore, many of the interviewed experts attribute, on the other hand, efficiency-increasing effects to quality management particularly in this area which goes beyond the optimisation of quality costs. The systematic recording of internal processes does not only allow the identification of quality-related risks and weak points but, at the same time, the identification of efficiency potentials. Quality management of external relations, supplier evaluation, quality agreements or mutual quality management appears for many interviewed companies to be imperative also for economic reasons. Apart from clear product specifications quality management includes commercial agreements. In normal cases, computerisation is considered to be necessary by the interviewed experts with a different degree of implementation in their companies.

In the surveyed companies, the quality management concepts for purchasing differ basically according to the following cases:

- For operative companies within a holding purchasing is often centralised, the company itself handles mainly logistical technical tasks.

- Medium-sized traditional companies especially those close to the producer in rural areas often keep on operating on a long term basis of confidence which is only partly formalised.

- Extremely extensive tasks for the quality management of purchasing arise above all in independent companies operating within a large and partly international context.

According to the statements of the experts quality-deciding factors, in a narrow sense, are in purchasing particularly the exact recording of the properties of the primary products in order to assure stable product quality even with primary products varying by nature and to assure processable quality of the primary products. In both cases it is obvious that these tasks are of interdepartmental nature.

Examples of good practice are found particularly in companies

- complementing quality agreements with suppliers by a system a mutual information flow and consulting service

- building external customer-supplier relationships into co-operation relations. (see also "customer-supplier; company co-operation")

According to the statements of the experts quality critical tasks, in the narrow sense, are in storage and material flow first of all the perishability and damage above all impairment of hygiene in in-company transport. Apart from inspections and precautions crucial improvements in quality assurance are achieved in an effective planning of the overall process. So here as well the interdepartmental nature of the tasks shows.

Case examples and statements

"In purchasing there are activities become more precisely and the contract has become more specific and also traceability. Purchasing specifications are more precise." (223/Finland/milk products/289 employees/certification > 2 years/ISO 9002)

"We have very demanding customers who consider us as suppliers as being part of their organisation. If they accept trash they have huge expenditures to make something usable of it at all. However, if I strongly involve the partner I have an efficient situation for both partners. That's how we feel as well. We are transparent and audit-friendly." (125/Germany/frozen products/688 employees/certification < 2 years/ISO 9001)

"The implementation of quality management in our company have induced some organisational changes. This applies especially to:

interfunctional teamworking in contract acceptance; in contract acceptance/writing, demand on the suppliers to be ISO certified

networking of functional areas; example: when receiving material to the production the need of control of delivery is needless when the supplier is certified

purchasing, stock, material flow are linked to the contract acceptance. No business with suppliers without certification." Quality raw materials and a careful handling of the potatoes is important. The enterprise has developed a unique system for the transport, storage and processing of potatoes. The potato storage centre is located a few miles from the factory close to most of their contract growers. When the potatoes are needed for production, they are transported in a special closed truck where a constant temperature is maintained from the warehouse to the factory. (623/Sweden/potato chips and other snack products/330 employees/certification > 2 years/ISO 9001)

"A clear example of cross-departmental changes occurred in the Purchase Department where before the implementation of a Quality System "each one purchased according to its wishes" for reasons connected with the lack of analysis capacity in most cases. To give examples, purchase of covers to yoghurt to be used during many years of production/packages not

according to the needs of the Marketing Department. Accurate rules for the management of stocks, which were established when the Quality System was implemented, excluded this kind of situations and prevents now more serious ones to occur, such as the cases where there is a "non-healthy" approaching between the purchaser and the seller." (522/Portugal/milk/ 406 employees/aspiring certification/certification > 2 years/ISO 9002)

"There has been an increased improvement in the relationship with the main importers of raw materials. There is a mutual objective to ensure consistency of quality. Many of the local suppliers of raw materials are also the customers. Therefore, it is of mutual benefit to comply with each other's specifications." (421/Ireland/animal feeds/39-44 employees/certification > 2 years/ISO 9001/2)

Production

Several interviewed experts consider production to be the core area of the implementation of quality management and the production manager as the driving force. On the other hand, relatively little change in the manufacturing operations and the work organisation for the implementation of quality management are stated. Much more frequently it is the case that the foregoing modernisation of the production processes provides a "friendly" technical basis for the systemisation and formalisation of work and quality tasks.

The technical innovation comprises above all automation and computerisation of the production process. The introduction of computer-based production lines allows shorter production times, greater flexibility, better capability to respond to market demand and product freshness. The automation of the production process causes a stronger specialisation of the work force since work consists basically in controlling the production cycle. Restricting manual operation to a minimum facilitates keeping hygiene standards. Market and competitive requirements, on the one hand, the potentials of modernisation, on the other hand, have also in SMEs of the food industry eliminated the separation between the actual production process and the up- and down-stream processes. Sector and product-specific portioning and packaging - in other sectors rather more distribution functions - as preservation of delicate products have in many cases been an integral part of production for quite some time. Now the border to material flow and storage is increasingly abolished by an integrated technology. Essential demands on a quality system are regarded to be solved technically.

However, some statements of the experts at this point reveal a possibly sector-specific "trap" for the comprehensive implementation of quality management: External or internal "ISO specialists" develop the quality system along the technical flow processes. Quality is focused on technical parameters and process stability. The technical logic of the process quality does not show staff the benefit of product quality and customer satisfaction. Some complaints of the interviewed experts about hardly routinisable hygiene standards, measuring and documentation tasks of staff, on the one hand, and about well-meant but wrong interventions of staff into the procedures, on the other hand, are considered by other experts as resulting from the fact that the "human factor" has been neglected. Insufficient understanding of customer expectations, of product features, of manufacturing processes and of the quality system prevents staff from internalising the apparently "simple" and, due to documentation apparently, "clear" work tasks. In some cases the apparently direct connection of technical streamlining and quality management gave also rise to some resentment with staff who feared a devaluation of former specialist knowledge and a lack of job security. This obstructs the newly opened participation of staff who could contribute with their competence and work experience to incorporating the best manufacturing practice of the company into the quality system. The restriction to technical process quality can also be a barrier for contributions of the operatives to the execution of quality tasks of other departments, for example, when it comes to clarifying the manufacturability of customer wishes.

Examples of good practice are found in companies

- ensuring information and knowledge about product and customer goals of quality requirements

- developing procedure and work instructions of the quality system strictly with staff involvement and setting free staff competency and experience for the improvement and practicability of the system.

- establishing teamwork at least in quality-critical production tasks

- treating technically assured processes only as a basis for the identification of weak points and for process optimisation by staff.

Case examples and statements

"It is easy enough to document a system, but you then have to implement it." (422/Ireland/butter/49 employees/certification > 2 years/ISO 9002)

While ISO is seen as a generally broad management standard it tends to focus on the manufacturing unit of a company. As a result it would have impacted on the production manufacturing unit. In particular, it affects the day to day operations. Quality control at the operator level has been significantly increased. In many respects, with the exception of production, there is a perception that all other functional areas in the company are considered to be peripheral to the quality system. *(422/Ireland/butter/49 employees/certification > 2 years/ISO 9002)*

"Technology that is implemented is very modern, with up-to-date machines, functional spaces where the hygiene standards are kept. Hygiene is an important part of the Quality System. All those helped to the practical implementation of the System." (325/Greece/cooked pork meat/226 employees/certification < 2 years/ISO 9001/2)

"From a production perspective it might be easier to produce a few products in larger volumes. It would involve easier processing and achieve efficient runs. However, the customer does not want that. Therefore, the company has to become more flexible form a manufacturing point of view. Technology allows more flexibility. Flexibility can be designed into manufacturing, thus allowing a quick response to customer requirements. The plant must run efficiently and have a quicker changeover time when required. A wider range of products can be produced with greater variations formulations and packaging. This comes down to a teamwork approach, with staff working together and knowing what the customer requirements are." (423/Ireland/full range of fresh dairy products/246 employees/certification > 2 years/ISO 9002)

Difficulties arose from the outset of the company's involvement with quality management as the management wrote the procedures and put them in place without checking first what shopfloor workers actually did. Some of the procedures have, according to the production manager: *"tend to have been written with a bias towards quality management and are not always practical or applicable to production. They have been long-winded and difficult to follow and this has tended to lead to some resentment which has increased the negative resistance that always seems to occur in the factory when any changes are made. There were then a lot of instances where the shopfloor said 'well we don't do it like this'. And they were told 'well, this is what your manager said you do'. And then they'd say 'well, he's never made chocolate raisins'".* Fortunately, this is now changing with the introduction of a combined HACCP and working procedures which are more precise and 'user-friendly'. *(724/United Kingdom/edible cake decorations, sugar and chocolate confectionery, popcorn/160 employees/certification > 2 years/ISO 9002)*

"There are some difficulties with attitudes towards documentation and frustration to write down all activities done before without such activity." (221/Finland/salads, meat products/40 employees/certification < 2 years/ISO 9001)

While the company was partially successful in getting the workforce to take on board the quality systems, they found it difficult to maintain consistent work practices among staff. This was particularly relevant when it came to the repetitive task of form filling and signing off documentation. This change took some time to achieve. However, it was facilitated by the younger members of staff who were more positively disposed to the changes. *(425/Ireland/canning of food and vegetables, beverages, packing dry pulses/295 employees/aspiring certification/ISO 9002)*

"The biggest problems in the implementation of quality management with employees has been the attitude toward documentation. The major barriers do not occur in identifying independently quality problems insisting on elimination or developing and advancing solutions but to document them." (223/Finland/milk products/289 employees/certification > 2 years/ISO 9002)

The motivation of staff for quality-oriented work is predominantly extrinsic. *"That is an instruction which is given. The people know that there is the requirement of a big customer behind it and that they would probably lose their job if we lost this customer. The people are quite aware of how much we supply to this customer."* Because of the simple supplier-relations with some large scale customers the company does not see any need for extended customer orientation and product knowledge of staff. *"There is no position where people should give further thought to this. This is the job of the administration. It would be an issue if the system were transferred to the other companies of the group which have a more differentiated customer structure and produce more complex products."..."Hygiene always slackens after a while. You can tell from the consumption of disinfectant which increases after the training and then slowly decreases again. You have to remind people regularly." (122/Germany/tinned fish/12 employees/certification <2 years/ISO 9002)*

Differences in the view of the division managers exist in regard to the qualifications needed for the staff. The marketing manager considers the knowledge of customer demands / company's products market oriented skills as necessary while for the production manager the knowledge of quality control and the use of new equipment are most important. *(321/Greece/ice - creams, fresh juices/437 employees/certification < 2 years/ISO 9002)*

Quality is considered to be a matter that concerns everybody in the company and that can only be achieved by team-work . *"The production includes a stage of sorting out which is done by the employees without the intervention of machines. At that point   co-operation between the supervisors and the staff is needed so that the sorting out procedure is done properly." (322/Greece/toast/258 employees/certification > 2 years/ISO 9002)*

Distribution

In the food industry, distribution is a strategic task with a crucial significance. Crucial competitive strategies of the sector in Europe concern distribution. Their results have structural effects on the companies. Significant investments of the sector serve and decisive costs arise in this function.

From the perspective of quality management distribution in the food industry is a decisive interface. In the direction from the companies to the consumers it is not only decided here that the product reaches the consumer flawlessly, the product utility is supplemented by services oriented to customer wishes, buying habits and consumption patterns. This task is also subject to comprehensive and close public-law standardisation (labelling, packaging etc.). In the opposite direction distribution especially of SMEs with rather lean marketing structures is to be treated as "the ear on the market" that lets crucial quality demands of customers flow back to all upstream company functions. This task as an interface of quality management shows many points of contact with marketing tasks in the food industry particularly with the brand policy important in this sector.

The surveyed SMEs differ strongly or even structurally in the shape of the internal distribution function as to what and how many external distribution steps there are between the company and the consumer, for one thing, and as to which distribution-logical tasks arise from the properties of the company products, for the other. The establishment of modern information technology with its revolutionary possibilities, also for quality management, of cross-departmental networking with a different level of development can be seen in the companies.

In a simplified way the sample of the interviewed companies can be differentiated according to three types:

- operative companies whose distribution is centralised in a holding or group

- companies selling to distribution companies and being subject very often to sector-specific high and dense quality demands and high pricing pressure

- companies with their own distributive channel to the consumers among which some companies are seeking innovative ways to changing buying and consumption patterns.

As a whole, the tendency in the European food industry in which the distribution is increasingly losing its character as an independent company function has also been shown in the sample of companies surveyed. Two reasons are responsible for it. For one thing, ever more strategic distributive functions go from the mainly productive small and medium-sized enterprises over to the large commercial enterprises or higher company structures such as holdings etc.. From the point of view of a comprehensive quality management this occasionally entails the risk that small and medium-sized enterprises loose touch with the customer and his requirements. For another thing, the rather logistic distributive functions remaining in the production units are increasingly integrated in the production process.

Significantly more of the interviewed experts set the effects of the implementation of a quality system on the work organisation of the distribution department in the management level. Their focus is on a reliably formalised and efficient involvement of the distribution manager in the company internal decision-making and the information flow from and to the companies. It is particularly in this area that companies show examples of good practice.

At the level of operatives the increasing technical rationalisation and integration of performance processes are the determinants of the work organisation in the distribution. Work in distribution is considered by the interviewed companies as a particularly simple work which can be assured - on a modern technical basis - by "simple, clear instructions". A particularly large proportion of unskilled staff work in this area. Occurring barriers, however, show a similar picture as in the production and are indicating an analogous need for quality-promoting re-organisation. Technology and mere instructions do not convey to staff the quality relevance of their actions although the management level is well aware of the significance of distribution. Examples of good practice of companies show that quality-promoting work organisation and quality awareness of staff can also lead to favourable cost effects.

Case examples and statements

In distribution the activities have not been formalised but quality aims of the distribution and the inspections of their fulfilment have. Regular meetings of the district managers serve the evaluation of formalised documented experiences of the sales representatives. Action plans are developed identifying which areas of the companies need to react: e.g. marketing, transport. *"As an independent company we stood directly before the consumer as our customer. The company made direct marketing. Once a year we had a consumers' day, marketing staff asked consumers in the shops about their assessment of the products. In the future, these tasks will be carried out by the holding "* (121/Germany/spices, spice mixtures/160 employees/certification > 2 years/ISO 9001)

One product only (pigmeal) is sold   directly from the plant. All other products are sold in the company's branches. Branches are located on a regional basis. They are managed by Branch Managers, all of whom are Agricultural Science graduates. The appointment of Agricultural Science graduates to the position of Branch Manager was a departure from previous company practice.   The company considered it vital to have highly educated and personnel with expertise to deal with the clients.   These managers know the technical specifications of the products. They can assist the customer is selecting the right product for their animals. The Marketing section has the responsibility for marketing all of the company's products. This requires on-going contact with the branches who must be kept informed at all times about product changes. Over the past few years a considerable effort has been made to modernise the branches. *(421/Ireland/animal feeds/39-44 employees/certification > 2 years/ISO 9001/2)*

The enterprise has an integrated computerised administrative system. An incoming order is registered and sent to the production. The storage of the products are at four different depots in the country where the enterprise has district staff responsible for the activity. The surveillance and penetration of the market, is done by contacts with different customer categories and by the sales organisation in their contacts with the market. The sales organisation is divided in two different areas, the retail trade and restaurant- and service trade. They are represented at seventeen different locations in the country and they are the most important link that the enterprise has to the market. All the vital information on the need of new products on the market is delivered by the sales organisation. *(622/Sweden/ice-cream & frozen desserts/91 employees/certification < 2 years/ISO 9001)*

Quality control and operator self-inspection

A crucial change of the work processes in production by the implementation of modern quality management consists of shifting quality inspection back to the manufacturing process. The solution of the conflict between the time needed for final inspections and product freshness for the customer is an additional sector-specific motive. This always requires a systemisation and documentation of procedures and work steps for a clear definition of the inspection points and inspection parameters.

It is striking that only a minority of the interviewed experts point out that quality management in their companies has led to increased efforts to introduce operator inspection. Two reasons were identified.

1. On the one hand, it has to be differentiated between shifting the quality inspection up-stream and replacing quality inspection and final inspections by specialist staff by reintegrating quality responsibility into the work of the operators and, along with this, an extension of their work profiles.

   - Normally the surveyed companies do not replace inspections through a special department (e.g. laboratory) by manufacturing-integrated operator inspections but organise it in a complementary way.

   - Quality demands particularly external ones by legal requirements and by customers make it necessary that manufacturing-integrated quality inspections are carried out by inspectors - partly with certified special qualification - and not by the operatives themselves.

2. On the other hand, inspection of primary products and products as well as measuring and control activities of the processes have always been an essential integral part of the work tasks in the food industry, which have been formalised and re-organised at best but not only just introduced.

Some interviewed experts see an important task of quality management in the quality-related handling of the technology-induced process of change.

- Traditionally sensory inspection plays a big role involving person-related capabilities and experiences. The respective staff has great decision-making and intervention authority. This role subsists in small companies of the survey and in traditional production. In some companies it remains indispensable at some process points such as at the receiving inspection of various raw materials and at final inspections. But with the modernisation of the procedures technical measurement, inspection and process control on the whole dominate.

- Modern process-integrated inspection technology does not only provide a technological basis for quality inspections which take effect early on. It also results in broadening the range of control activities of staff. However, a barrier can occur that staff cannot "see, smell and taste" this quality responsibility. Here, some experts pointed out implementation problems in the documentation tasks of staff. Also, often comparatively little direct decision-making and intervention authority is attached to the new inspection responsibility. Well-meant interventions also of well-trained and experienced food experts can even lead to contra-productive effects on the process and product quality.

Examples of good practice can be found in companies

- setting free traditional workplace competency of staff for the product design, improvement of processes and the quality system and for knowledge-based quality motivation of staff

- clearly regulating and documenting largest possible intervention authority of staff on shortest possible ways

- detecting "hidden" experience and involving it in decision-making levels

Case examples and statements

To control varying raw material specifications the production staff themselves check the procedure parameters and the mixture ratios, adjust them within the framework of defined margins and document these measures. ... There is an awareness in the company that a quality concept of final inspections has its problems. Some laboratory inspections can only work as information since the inspection time and freshness regulations are contradictory. Here a product-specific critical point becomes obvious in a quality assurance which is exclusively based on final inspections. *"If quality problems occur here, you have to take action immediately." (123/Germany/egg products/100 employees/certification < 2 years/ISO 9002)*

"For 2-3 years we have worked with self-inspection, that is, staff at the line have the quality responsibility for their product. The quality department with their special knowledge - e.g. legal restrictions - prepares the measures as inspection orders including documentation tasks. The inspection results of the people at the line are evaluated by the quality department and depending on the process stability the inspection planning is adjusted or the process settings are optimised. So the quality department does the inspection planning but the line carries out the inspection." (125/Germany/frozen products/688 employees/certification < 2 years/ISO 9001)

*"Nowadays operatives have the power to stop a process if they believe that standards are not being achieved. This has resulted in increased worker motivation and satisfaction"....*The Plant Manager believes that *"while ISO provides a structure it does not cover the full story"*. He believes certain skills are instinctive to the skilled worker which are not easily documented, e.g. the worker knows by "the feel", or "the sight" of a feed component what is to be added to the process. Also, some workers have a "natural flair" about machines and can spot a problem before anyone else. He believes this experience is based on know-how. He also states that this is not always easy to quantify. *(421/Ireland/animal feeds/39-44 employees/certification > 2 years/ISO 9001/2)*

"The implementation of quality management in our company has induced some organisational changes. Particularly delegation of jobs:

all the personnel are responsible for the quality within the enterprise

anyone has the authority to stop the production in case of nonconformities

the quality groups within each production unit meet weekly with staff from the laboratory." (624/Sweden/fruit preparations and chocolate products/130 employees/certification > 2 years/ISO 9001)

"The operator inspection continuously came along with the progress of analysis techniques and significantly improved handling of inspection equipment. We have not only just introduced this with ISO." Many operative tasks of quality control are delegated to the production and are carried out by the production staff in self-responsible inspection as part of their job. *" We have no strict division here. The shift-accompanying inspection on site in roasting and also in the packing area is largely carried out by staff themselves. The quality department has only a checking function because quality has to be produced and not inspected." (124/Germany/roasted ground coffee/70 employees/certification < 2 years/ISO 9002)*

For employees, quality management has led to significant new demands. The onus for checking products is slowly shifting from being the sole responsibility of the Quality Department to becoming that of the operatives themselves - a process that has not been completely painless! *"We get them to do their own checks - we did start off with one person doing the checks but now we've got all the people trained up so they can all do them. And all the production operators who make the sweets have various checks that they do - they tend to be weight checks and colour checks. So they all trained to do the various checks rather than as it was before. It started out with us doing them all but we felt the way forward was to get QA onto the shopfloor and it seems to work quite well. There still tends to be a little bit of secrecy where if somebody's made something wrong they're a bit reluctant to highlight it." (724/United Kingdom/edible cake decorations, sugar and chocolate confectionery, popcorn/160 employees/certification > 2 years/ISO 9002)*

Teamwork & Interdepartmental work

Teamwork and interdepartmental co-operation as the work organisational implementation of imperatives of the quality system can be found in the surveyed companies predominantly at the management level (see "management teams"). At the operative level the departmental networking and work organisation is much stronger determined by technology than by direct work organisational measures for an improved completion of quality tasks. Exceptions to this general finding apply mostly to work scheduling and work-accompanying activities such as maintenance.

The qualitative analysis of the expert interviews shows that abstract work organisational imperatives of the theory of quality management are only suitable - from case to case - critically scrutinised for the description of the individual practice of SMEs of the food industry. This is particularly true for the term "teamwork".

- In some cases interviewed executive staff already call work division which is planned and therefore co-ordinated by the management "teamwork".

- It is very common that teamwork does not mean practical organisational changes of work forms and contents, division of responsibility and decision-making but efforts for a more conflict and friction-free co-operation among the different groups of staff in the company.

- Some managers associate teamwork less with the direct working relationship but much more with the social relationship among the hierarchical levels and the social behaviour of the status groups. Particularly traditional family enterprises with social relationships which go beyond working relationships call themselves "a team".

The following findings belong closer to the issue of quality-related reorganisation measures of the work:

- Particularly in small companies there is scepticism against a normative deduction of teamwork in the process organisation from quality management. They see no need to change their transparent processes and divisional structures for quality management.

- With the predominant continuous mass production the food manufacturers see as regards direct work tasks too little room for disposition and too little on-going co-ordination and planning needs at the operative level in order to justify the reorganisation and possible time expenditure for team structures.

- In the companies initiating interdepartmental work and teamwork structures this does not result solely from quality management. The aim of a more quality-aware work of staff by extended knowledge of the company, its quality goals, products and customers is normally linked with the aim to be able to employ staff more flexibly. Close to quality this serves the capability of the company to respond in a more flexible way above all with product variations and innovations to customer wishes. Rather more economic motives require more flexibly employable staff to counterbalance seasonal utilisation variations with different product lines or as regular staff as opposed to seasonal workers. Some experts identify also in these cases the quality effect, that is, extended know-how of staff as quality assurance with changing work requirements.

Case examples and statements

"Teamwork is not implemented in our company as it is mentioned many times in this kind of contexts. The management group is working like that. We have clear production processes." (223/Finland/milk products/289 employees/certification > 2 years/ISO 9002)

TPM – total production maintenance has been introduced. There is close co-operation between the operators of the equipment, the maintenance personnel and the quality control staff. This has helped staff to focus on the product and machine performance. Formal and informal meetings are held on- and off-site to discuss pertinent issues. TPM is seen as a separate initiative to ISO, but one that is considered to be a natural progression from it. *"Firstly, you deal with the product and product quality. Then you move onto machine performance, efficiency and throughput". (422/Ireland/butter/49 employees/certification > 2 years/ISO 9002)*

"All the staff working at the production line work on the basis of job rotation. This means that the work operations vary for the employees from the handling of the potato delivery to the final packaging..." This enterprise is characterised by a dedicated workforce. The enterprise made a strategic decision already in the 60s in the placement of the plant. This was built in an area with a high rate of immigration. The strategy was to recruit personnel to the production from this area to enable them to identify with the enterprise. This is a fact today which has had many positive social consequences among the many different categories of immigrants. Investments have been made to provide the staff with well equipped facilities during brakes and lunches. *(623/Sweden/potato chips and other snack products/330 employees/certification > 2 years/ISO 9001)*

Although the company organisation is divided in departments, the processes and the work organisation are to a large extent organised cross-departmentally . The work profiles are enriched and enlarged. If some person is needed in different apartment that he or she mainly works this is possible. The cross-departmental work organisation is based on the fact that this enterprise concentrates itself completely on the production of system approach, working with people who has worked there a long time together. The management considers this being the reason that the employees have no reservations against quality management in that they fear new forms of personal performance control although it is question of mass production. *(221/Finland/salads, meat products/40 employees/certification < 2 years/ISO 9001)*

"The difficulties we have experienced is in the interdepartmental communication between the market- production - work place. It has been difficult to translate the information into something more understandable and to find more concrete ways to measure. This is essential in the product development within the company." "Today we have a system where personnel from the production are involved in some of the market activities. It is of vital importance to 'confront' them with the customers to make them more receptive to the customer demands." (624/Sweden/fruit preparations and chocolate products/130 employees/certification > 2 years/ISO 9001)

"The 'Know-How' contract with the Dutch firm highlighted the importance of strong teamwork. They also cautioned against changing a process in one area without considering the impact it had on other area. The company realised that the way to move forward was to take a team-based approach. The quality changes forced the management team and the staff to work as a team." (421/Ireland/animal feeds/39-44 employees/certification > 2 years/ISO 9001/2)

The intention is to bring in teamwork so that all employees will feel more of a sense of responsibility for the work that they do. This will also, it is hoped, improve communications within the company. The idea for introducing teamwork arose when building the quality systems. Smaller teams within the departments were set up to get the systems and work instructions together and this acted as a spur to introduce teamworking on a larger scale. *(722/United Kingdom/children's sugar confectionery/610 employees/certification > 2 years/ISO 9002)*

"TQM is not just a matter of management's commitment but has to do with the general philosophy of the company including all employees, from the office cleaner to the general manager. Top executives are considering the possibility of TQM implementation as a long-term goal." (321/Greece/ice-creams, fresh juices/437 employees/certification < 2 years/ISO 9002)

Customer-supplier, company co-operation

Almost all interviewed managers agreed that especially the quality of food cannot be guaranteed solely internally, that good internal manufacturing practice and even an internal quality system are not enough. Here, concerning the issue of external customer-supplier relations, two not always conflict-free development tendencies emerge in the surveyed SMEs.

1. On the one hand, the awareness in the companies for a comprehensive responsibility for the food chain is growing not only because of the modern quality concept and the explicit requirements of the ISO standards but predominantly because of the demands of the well-informed consumers, the public and the "sector's code of honour". Also, food scandals prove the crucial economic significance.

2. On the other hand, many SMEs, in particular, are forced by cost pressures and competition and concentration processes in the food industry and trade to transfer essential outside function and thus responsibilities out of the company or to the trade or holding and corporate structures. Within these relationships there are normally high quality demands on the SMEs not least the demand for a certified quality system as a condition for marketability, but not always does this quality co-operation run smoothly and not always do the strong external partners give quality support which is adequate to their high quality demands.

From the expert interviews and above all from the examples of good practice the assurance of a comprehensive information and know-how transfer as an additional service of the companies crystallises as a crucial quality task. Reasons given for this are that the improvement of the quality of food and its production is driven by two forces which are not always immediately in accordance: the wishes and the lifestyle of consumers on the one hand, and the scientific-technological progress of the food sciences and the process technology on the other hand.

Case examples and statements

"Develop systems to assure food safety and the integrity of the food chain from farm gate to market". (423/Ireland/full range of fresh dairy products/246 employees/certification > 2 years/ISO 9002)

As the company is so large (the international Head Office is in Switzerland), management can seem very remote: *"People that far from the sharp end can't really appreciate what's going on here. We'd be far better off if it was more de-centralised and more decisions were taken locally." (725/United Kingdom/peanut butter, gales honey, tablet jelly/300 employees/certification > 2 years/ISO 9002)*

Pressure from big customers, particularly multinational groups of the food industry, was the predominant motive for establishing a certified quality system. *"They say: Our customers want us to purchase only from A-suppliers. And A-suppliers are only certified suppliers."* The external pressure for the fulfilment of quality assurance is also viewed critically in the company. With some customers there is a lack of knowledge about the production procedures in the company, and the concrete quality tasks of their products are neglected. This also limits the know-how transfer into the company. *"Nowadays each customer asks about the ISO system and HACCP. If you inundate them with papers, they'll be satisfied. If you don't have the system, big customers have a questionnaire which is like an audit."* (123/Germany/egg products/100 employees/certification < 2 years/ISO 9002)

"The whole system has changed. When we start to think investments, we try to find places where to visit and make some benchmarking. Nowadays it is more difficult than before . Companies want to keep the technical knowledge themselves, particularly if they consider to have some advantage of it." (221/Finland/salads, meat products/40 employees/certification < 2 years/ISO 9001)

In purchasing, the company works with systematic incoming lot inspections and with auditing the suppliers from all over the world on site. Harvest contracts are to assure the quality of fruit and vegetables in advance at the same time the geographic dispersion of the purchasing is a safeguard of satisfactory quality against the risks of local bad harvests. The company itself is open to auditing by customers. And the ISO system is considered to be the basis not a substitute. *"We have very demanding customers who consider us as suppliers as part of their organisation. If they accept trash they have huge expenditures to make something usable of it at all. However, if I strongly involve the partner I have an efficient situation for both partners. That's how we feel as well. We are transparent and audit-friendly."* (125/Germany/frozen products/688 employees/certification < 2 years/ISO 9001)

"Most of what we have as a quality system we have learnt from our suppliers. We have ISO certified suppliers who invited us and showed us the system on site. These suppliers continue to be our suppliers. Because we could see how well their quality philosophy works. This doesn't mean that we give up checks. But it is a different kind of collaboration, if you

know what clear structures the others work with." (124/Germany/roasted ground coffee/70 employees/certification < 2 years/ISO 9002)

"The replacement of equipment to gather milk samples from each farm allowed the implementation of a system of milk quality evaluation in all aspects, regarding, for instance the speed and accuracy of the conclusions deriving from the analysis to be delivered to the milk producer." (522/Portugal/milk/ 406 employees/aspiring certification/certification > 2 years/ISO 9002)

"Customers are invited into the mill to see how the products are manufactured. Many of the suppliers to this company are also its customers i.e. farmers supplying grain, who in turn buy feed for their animals. Therefore, the company, the supplier and the customer are aware of the need to ensure quality of the products, whether they are raw materials or the end products....There are times when the customer wants a particular product which he has heard about/or read in a farming journal. But, the Branch Manager knows that it is not the best product for the farmer's needs. The Marketing section is consulted and a feed co-ordinator (agricultural science graduate) agrees to meet with the Branch Manager and the farmer to discuss his needs. There is also a responsibility on the branches to ensure that they do not offer a product to the customer which the mill cannot produce. Therefore, they must be kept informed of the raw materials and products being produced. This was not the case prior to ISO." A feed co-ordinator works closely with the branches and the customers establishing new customer requirements. Communication and information processing play a very important role in the company.... The Company is now able to offer an advisory service to its customers on the nutritional value of certain feeds and advise on diet management. Its customers' forage and grass can be tested at the company's laboratory. This provides added value to the customer as the sales representatives are in a position to provide valuable information and recommendation to customers which allows them to evaluate the quality of their own feed regime. *(421/Ireland/animal feeds/39-44 employees/certification > 2 years/ ISO 9001/2)*

Corporate culture and organisation of improvement

Some interviewed managers use the buzzword "cultural change" when summarising the changes relating to the implementation of quality management in their companies.

One aspect of this term calls for scepticism. It embraces in a strikingly undifferentiated way the quality philosophy and the process practice, changes of the external and internal company relations, practical changes of the company organisation and subjective motivational changes. It does not show what the staff levels are for which something has changed.

On the other hand, this term puts the focus on the social and subject-related dimension of quality management: quality as an organisation aim and the role of the employee within the company.

As a general summary concerning the quality concepts of the surveyed companies it can be said: Direct reorganisation of work particularly at the operative level for the implementation of quality management and for continuous quality promotion was hardly found in the surveyed companies. Typical for the sector, the decisive reasons for this appear to be the widespread mass production, and the technological modernisation of increasingly automated processes as determinants of the work organisation.

On the other hand, explicit efforts of companies for quality-promoting staff participation and for interdepartmental communication and co-operation in quality issues could be noticed. Wherever companies undertake this it is organised predominantly outside the direct production of goods and services in quality circles and improvement groups. The clear preference of quality circles and improvement groups outside the direct work organisation appears to be sector-specific in the above sense. Judging from the statements of the interviewed managers, this also characterises the tasks of these work groups. Their members tackle not so much workplace-related quality issues but much more from the start comprehensive quality issues in the overall process, especially customer-oriented product issues and process weaknesses.

The starting point are often cross-hierarchical and interdepartmental work groups for the preparation for the ISO certification. With a healthy self-critical attitude some company management's simply discover in the expenditure for the documentation their own lack of practice-orientation and the qualification and work experience of staff as an indispensable support for the establishment of quality management. Also the confrontation with insufficiently tailored external consulting provision at no low costs leads to this decision.

With a lot of the surveyed companies, however, a break can be identified between the re-discovery of existing qualifications and the practical involvement of staff after a successful certification. This is legitimate as long as it is about the necessary next stage of making the new system a routine. It becomes problematic, on the other hand, if the company loses the awareness that the qualifications and the concrete work experiences, also the ones concerning the quality system, is an indispensable internal source for the proactive development of concrete steps for the maintenance, continuation and improvement of the company-specific quality system, proactive as opposed to external assessments and demands by customer complaints or the reaudit.

A second line of change in the corporate culture shows in new fields of relations to customers and suppliers and above all new forms of their involvement in the development of knowledge and decisions in the company.

Case examples and statements

"The suggestion of the simple worker can't be worse than the one of the manager who is not there (in production) and doesn't know the specific procedure functions." (323/Greece/puff pastry, strudel leaves, frozen vegetable, pizza/231 employees/aspiring certification/ISO 9001)

"Before there was the principle of the three Cs: calculation - command - control. Now there is pressure in the opposite direction. The people complain about tasks which are not practicable. Every now and then there are employees who have a problem with responsibility. But on average we have a type of employee today who wants to take responsibility and also wants to be measured by it. The employees also initial. That has caused problems. Today employees do not like taking responsibility for trash. These are gestures which are very efficient. The executives used to have different tasks than they have today. They have to master techniques other than placing orders. They are more of a moderator and a coach." (125/Germany/frozen products/688 employees/certification < 2 years/ISO 9001)

"A quality system is nothing, if not a continuous improvement programme" (424/Ireland/full range of milk products/343 employees/certification < 2 years/ISO 9002)

"In this kind of organisation it is usual to occur a barrier between management and workers, being also very often the existence of ties of family and personal relationship between the workers. Of course, this renders easy the existence of different treatments not grounded on objective reasons, which can increase the conflicts in the organisation. The existence of a high percentage of old workers, with low levels of scholarship and having power privileges transferred from the foreground to a secondary one the younger and more qualified workers, who, thus, cannot show all their potentialities. This framework evidences, in a deep way, the needs of training both from a technical and a behaviour standpoint. Thus training plan must be general and long and take into consideration the described differences to be able to change the general framework of the existing

*relationship."   (522/Portugal/milk/   406   employees/aspiring
certification/certification > 2 years/ISO 9002)*

*"We went down to the level of staff, because those who sit at the desk do
not know precisely enough how the job is really done. You have to involve
the experiences and ideas of the people who are actually doing the job and
are supposed to do it systematically in the future. They are the ones who
have the experience of what can be done and how to act most efficiently. It
takes, of course, some effort to find an agreement with almost 200 people.
But then you have created something which is accepted by everybody. The
second step that logically followed quality management was introducing a
continuous improvement process. The people had learned that they could
take part in the work, they could develop and implement something
themselves. You're dealing with the work processes then and, by the way,
not only with quality issues. There are CIP groups meeting regularly. They
have their documentation, recording the actual state of the work and what
to do. This works very well." (121/Germany/spices, spice mixtures/160
employees/ certification > 2 years/ISO 9001)*

Through a process of continuous improvement and training workers are
more responsive to changes in the company's operations. They are kept up
to-date on the company's business goals and any changes that take place.
This is achieved through company bulletin reports which appear fortnightly
on the notice boards around the plant. *(423/Ireland/full range of fresh dairy
products/246 employees/certification > 2 years/ISO 9002)*

The company operates a suggestion scheme. This is part of a continuous
improvement process.   Safety, personnel welfare, production, etc. are
some of the areas where suggestions have been made. All suggestions are
passed to a Steering Committee, which consists of management and staff.
An award is made for the best suggestion. The company award
money/trophy   when   a   team/group   come   up   with
suggestions/recommendations on saving the company money. One such
group in the Boiler House won an award for saving the company
considerable money last year by using steam in a more effective and
efficient manner. In addition, a "Recognition Evening" is hold for cross-
functional teams who have collaborated and produced "the best cost saving
idea". These suggestion schemes also are a positive move towards fostering
the culture of teamwork. *(422/Ireland/butter/49 employees/certification >
2 years/ISO 9002)*

Personnel-related concepts of food-processing SMEs

Quantitative findings

The interviewees were allowed to rate multiple criterions. The scale of 0 - 300 results from the rating scale of 0 - 3 and from the fact that the survey results based on different quantities of respondents have been extrapolated to a number of companies of 100 in order to obtain data that are comparable between the staff groups and between the sectors.

Quality-related demands on the staff and staff groups

It was an essential aim of the survey to get an insight into the personnel-related implementation of quality management in the quality loop of the departments and more specifically in the work of different staff groups. The surveyed companies were asked to point out quality-related work requirements for the following departments and personnel groups:

Development (R&D):	Supervisors	Skilled staff	Semi/unskilled staff
Purchasing/stock/ material flow:	Supervisors	Skilled staff	Semi/unskilled staff
Production:	Supervisors	Skilled staff	Semi/unskilled staff
Distribution/service:	Supervisors	Skilled staff	Semi/unskilled staff

They were given the following standardised questions, the criteria of which are deliberately in accordance with terms of the ISO standard and/or internationally established terms of quality management:

Question: In order to achieve the quality demands of the company, to what extent do you consider it necessary to know, understand, master or ignore the following (**Rating according to following key:** 0 = ignore (unimportant), 1 = know (be informed), 2 = understand (skilfully follow), 3 = master (plan, carry out)):

- Proper handling of means of production
- Handling of products
- Document use (job and procedure instructions)
- Workplace safety & Hygiene
- Nonconformity identification and documentation
- Test equipment
- Quality inspections
- Document control
- Control of nonconforming products
- Quality demands of related departments
- Inspection planning
- Nonconformity analysis and assessment
- Corrective action
- Composition of the company products
- Quality aims of the company
- Quality-related costs
- Legal standards
- Data collection & statistical methods e.g. 7 QC tools, SPC (statistical process control) etc.
- Preventive QM methods e.g. QFD (quality function deployment), HACCP (Hazard Analysis Critical Control Point) etc.
- Teamwork
- Structuring of operations of the company
- External customer-supplier relations
- Internal customer-supplier relations
- Co-operation techniques e.g. communication tools, problem analysis techniques, creativity techniques, team building, conflict settlement etc.

Not all of the interviewed companies saw themselves in the position to make such detailed assessments. Different sets of reference of the companies with the evaluated occupational groups are based on the fact that the respective departments and hierarchical groups of staff are not represented in all companies of the sample. A quantitative evaluation of the hierarchical level semi/unskilled staff in the departments purchasing and R&D was refrained from since not enough of the interviewed companies gave details about this and/or since in R&D there are hardly any semi/unskilled workers.

Quality-related demands on development supervisors

For this group of staff the following profile was identified:

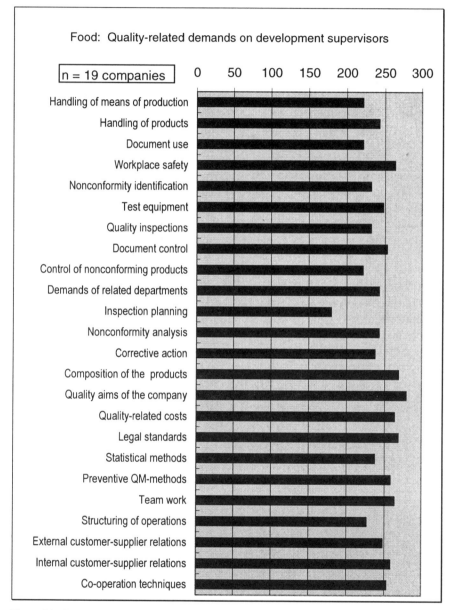

Figure 28: Quality-related demands on development supervisors in the food industry

The interviewed companies expect above all supervisors to master the "quality aims of the company", the "composition of the company products" and the "legal standards". This corresponds with the functional work profile of the R&D department in the food industry and the high degree of legal regulations for this sector. Already the next highly rated requirements - "workplace safety"[1] and "quality-related costs" - describe a cross-departmental responsibility profile of design supervisors as regards the decision and implementation of quality aims in the entire company. Emphasising the responsibility for safe production and work conditions including the definition of hygiene standards, on the one hand, and for the commercial cost implications of quality, on the other, which are rated identically, this group of staff obviously has a strategic role in the quality system of the company. This is in keeping with two findings from the qualitative expert interviews. On the one hand, many interviewed companies try to assure these decision-making tasks of designing products through the establishment of cross-functional project teams at the management level across the departments and processes. In so far, the highly rated demand "teamwork" on staff responsible development is not only directed towards their leading patterns and their work methods in the R&D department. On the other hand, the expert interviews showed that many quality managers or employees quality responsible in the interviewed companies are recruited from the personnel group of development managers. Striking, that is divergent from the findings on the other occupational groups, is the relatively high rating of "preventive quality management methods" (7) as a requirement for supervisors of the R&D department. This occupational group is obviously entrusted with the responsibility for the implementation of preventive quality management. This applies particularly to the definition of critical process and control points and the determination of adequate measures of quality assurance.

Requirements which are considered as more operative tasks not only of production but also of quality assurance get low ratings and are delegated to other functional areas. This also becomes apparent in the relatively strict functional division between the planning-developing and the operative levels in the food industry.

---

[1]   "Workplace safety" is in all surveyed staff groups a high rated quality-related requirement in the interviewed companies of the food industry since it includes the basic requirement of the sector for hygiene. Therefore it is not specifically commented on with the following groups.

Quality-related demands on development skilled staff

For this group of staff the following profile was identified:

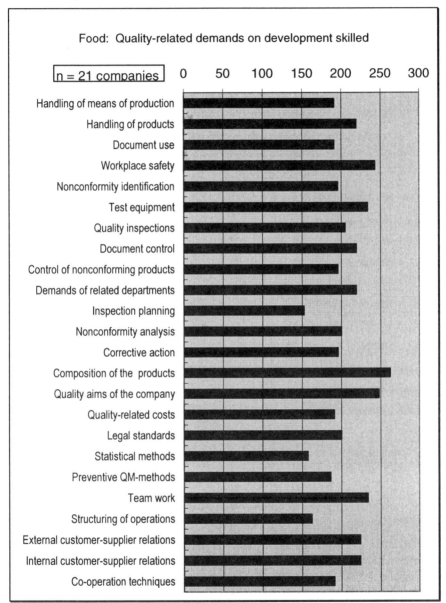

Figure 29: Quality-related demands on development skilled in the food industry

Skilled staff of the development department are expected to be first and foremost experts on the "composition of the company products" and are to be guided by the "quality aims of the company". The interviewed companies place the eminent quality responsibility first in the direct occupational area of this group of staff. But, particularly the highly rated task fields "work place safety" and "test equipment" as well as "external customer relations" and "internal customer-supplier relations" clearly define a cross-functional requirement profile. In the interviewed companies, skilled staff of the development department are obviously responsible for the process and inspection-technological conditions for the execution and are therefore supposed to consider the entire external and internal chain of the quality relations as their field of tasks.

The low rated requirements correspond, on the one hand, to those of the supervisors of the development department and, on the other hand, they indicate a division of competencies in this department.

Comparison: development

Extrapolating a hierarchy of the seven best rated quality-related job requirements from the occupational group-specific ratings, the following picture emerges:

Table 12: Best rated quality-related job requirements in the development department (Food industry)

Development supervisors	Development skilled staff
1. Quality aims of the company	1. Composition of the company products
2. Composition of the company products	2. Quality aims of the company
3. Legal standards	3. Workplace safety
4. Workplace safety	4. Test equipment
5. Quality-related costs	5. Teamwork
6. Teamwork	6. External customer-supplier relations
7. Preventive QM methods	7. Internal customer-supplier relations

Some department-specific as well as hierarchy-specific statements can be deduced from this picture.

The development department in small and medium-sized enterprises of the food industry is obviously attributed a cross-departmental responsibility for the quality aims in the entire company. In this department product and procedure decisions are developed involving economic aims, this department is also expected to make specifications for the required inspection points and technologies for the quality assurance of the entire process.

From a hierarchy-specific point of view a certain up-keeping of the pattern "target definition versus execution" can be observed. Development supervisors are more responsible for strategic decisions of product quality and its possibly preventive assurance involving also responsibility for the legal regulations and the economic efficiency of the company. Skilled staff in the development department have above all the responsibility for the material conditions and means for the execution of quality production in the entire external and internal process chain. This division of responsibilities in the development department is confirmed by a comparison with the lowest rated requirements: "preventive quality management methods" and "quality-related costs" do not fall into the scope of tasks of skilled staff but are tasks of the supervisors of the development department.

Extrapolating a hierarchy of the seven lowest rated quality-related job requirements from the occupational group-specific ratings, the following picture emerges:

Table 13: Lowest rated quality-related job requirements in the development department (Food industry)

Development supervisors	Development skilled staff
• Inspection planning	• Inspection planning
• Proper handling of means of production	• Data collection & statistical methods
• Document use (job and procedure instructions)	• Structuring of operations of the company
• Control of nonconforming products	• Preventive QM methods
• Structuring of operations of the company	• Proper handling of means of production
• Nonconformity identification and documentation	• Document use (job and procedure instructions)
• Quality inspections	• Quality-related costs

Not only production-specific requirements such as "proper handling of means of production" hardly come in as tasks for the development staff. This staff group is also not expected to take on operative activities of quality assurance. This rather belongs to the field of tasks of a special quality department or the production staff on the basis of modern technology and documented instructions.

Quality-related demands on purchasing supervisors

For this group of staff the following profile was identified:

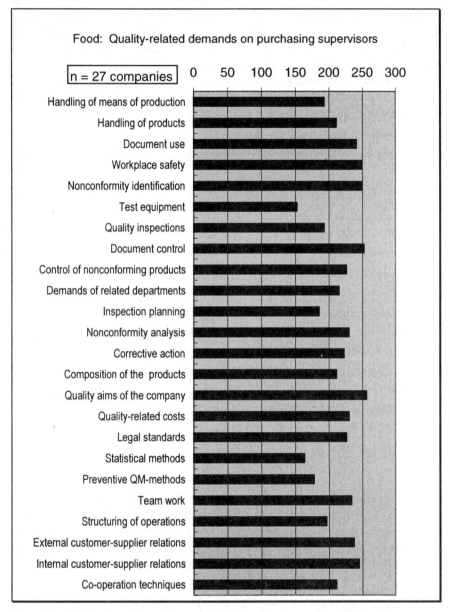

Figure 30: Quality-related demands on purchasing supervisors in the food industry

Supervisors of the purchasing department are first of all supposed to master the "quality aims of the company". The high rate of "document control" stands for a quality-critical responsibility of purchasing supervisors in the food industry: small and medium-sized enterprises of this sector attach crucial importance to comprehensive specification, marking and retraceability of primary products for the quality assurance of their own products. Also the highlighted requirements "nonconformity identification and documentation" shows that purchasing supervisors are supposed to guarantee that only faultless and manufacturable primary products find their way into the company and the processing.

The combination of the requirements "document control", "internal customer-supplier relations" and "document use" defines the interface function in the quality system which the interviewed companies assign to this staff group: Not only does this group carry the responsibility for the incoming of faultless and manufacturable primary products but their clear specification of primary products are the basis for quality-decisive specifications for the correct processing in the company. To ensure this - particularly with primary products varying by nature - is the most important task of the purchasing supervisor.

The interviewed companies give priority to this interface responsibility for the internal quality assurance from the incoming of merchandise to the processing above the mastering of "external customer-supplier relations". In the latter requirement traditional functional tasks of purchasing are identical with the requirements of the quality system. In the external relation to its suppliers the purchasing supervisors represent the quality demands of the company on primary products and materials. In the qualitative expert interviews, initiatives of the company could be identified to extend the tasks of the purchasing supervisors in supplier relations. They are entrusted with the tasks of preventive quality co-operation with suppliers and producers of primary products.

The interviewed companies make low demands on the purchasing supervisors as regards the rather more production-specific criteria such as "proper handling of means of production". The same is true for the planning, technology and operative execution of process-related quality assurance.

Quality-related demands on purchasing skilled staff

For this group of staff, the following profile was identified:

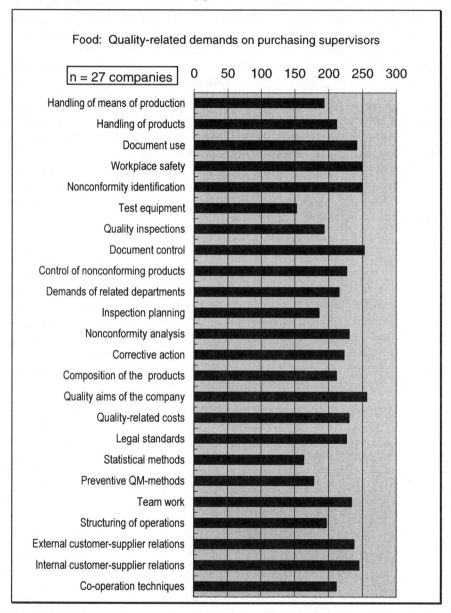

Figure 31: Quality-related demands on purchasing skilled in the food industry

In their contents the primarily quality-related demands of the companies on the skilled staff of the purchasing department largely correspond to those which are made on supervisors in this function, however in a different ranking. The stronger emphasis on "document use (work, procedure instructions)" and the requirement "teamwork" seem to reflect that these employees are bound by instructions. The high ratings for "nonconformity identification and documentation", "internal customer-supplier relations" and "document control" also characterise the job profile of the purchasing skilled staff[2] as an interface within the quality system.

Comparison: Purchasing

Extrapolating a hierarchy of the seven best rated quality-related job requirements from the occupational group-specific ratings, the following picture emerges:

Table 14: Best rated quality-related job requirements in the purchasing department (Food industry)

Purchasing supervisors	Purchasing skilled staff
1. Quality aims of the company	1. Workplace safety
2. Document control	2. Quality aims of the company
3. Workplace safety	3. Document use (job and procedure instructions)
4. Nonconformity identification and documentation	4. Teamwork
5. Internal customer-supplier relations	5. Nonconformity identification and documentation
6. Document use (job and procedure instructions)	6. Internal customer-supplier relations
7. External customer-supplier relations	7. Document control

Mainly department-specific statements can be deduced from this.

With this requirement profile the surveyed companies attach an interface function between external and internal customer-supplier relations to the purchasing department clearly emphasising internal quality tasks. Across the hierarchies, the job profiles in this department comprise cross-departmental quality tasks, critical elements of preventive quality assurance and above all a high responsibility for

---

[2]   The methodological difficulty of this survey to homogeneously delimit the occupational group " skilled purchasing staff" in the surveyed companies must be pointed out. Several of the interviewed companies do not allocate especially logistical functions of the primary product input such as "storage" and "material flow" to the purchasing department but to production, not least on the basis of modern process-technological integration, on the one hand, and outsourcing of storage tasks, on the other.

reliably documented quality specifications for the down-stream process steps in the company. An essential reason for this could well lie in the sector-specifics of working with primary products which, due to nature, are not standardised.

Extrapolating a hierarchy of the seven lowest rated quality-related job requirements from the occupational group-specific ratings, the following picture emerges:

Table 15: Lowest rated quality-related job requirements in the purchasing department: (Food industry)

Purchasing supervisors	Purchasing skilled staff
• Test equipment	• Data collection & statistical methods
• Data collection & statistical methods	• Preventive QM methods
• Preventive QM methods	• Inspection planning
• Inspection planning	• Structuring of operations of the company
• Proper handling of means of production	• Legal standards
• Quality inspections	• Test equipment
• Structuring of operations of the company	• Proper handling of means of production

Low demands on the purchasing staff are made by the interviewed companies with regard to rather production-specific criteria, to process-related quality assurance, quality techniques and technologies, as well as external framework conditions - "legal standards" . Small and medium-sized enterprises of the food industry delegate these tasks mostly to the quality planing of the development department or the quality-responsible staff of the production. In the face of the fact that the companies clearly recognise the interface function and clearly give prominence to the task of employees in the purchasing department to provide for faultless and processable intermediate products, it is surprising that the companies make low demands on "data collection & statistical methods" and "preventive quality management methods" and that they apparently also attach rather little relevance to knowledge of "structuring of operations of the company".

Quality-related demands on production supervisors

For this group of staff, the following profile was identified:

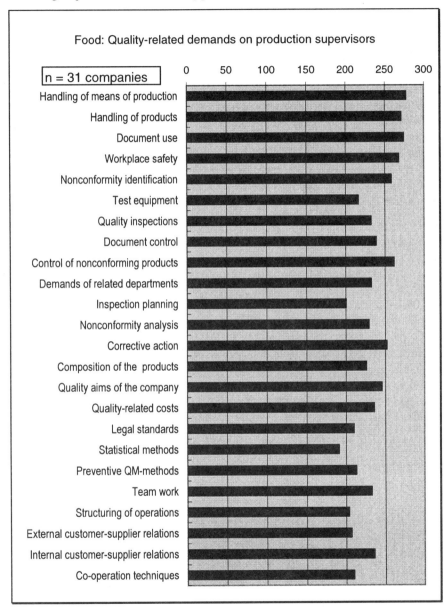

Figure 32: Quality-related demands on production supervisors in the food industry

With the priority of "proper handling of means of production", "document use" and "handling of products" as quality-related demands on production supervisors, for this occupational group quality tasks coincide largely with the functional job profile of technical and personal control of the production process.

The tasks "control of nonconforming products", "nonconformity identification and documentation" and "corrective action" indicate that the interviewed companies have refrained from a final quality inspection by a special department and have shifted parts of product- and process-related quality assurance to the production and have integrated them into the tasks of the staff responsible for the production. These demands on production supervisors might be interpreted as responsible decision-making tasks. This applies to the decision on which nonconforming products are not to be further processed in order to avoid that they reach the customer. This particularly applies for the task "corrective action" which includes, with the modern process technology of the food industry, the decision about interventions which, due to their far-reaching consequences, require of the responsible staff a high degree of process competence as the basis for the decision.

Strikingly low ratings were given to "data collection & statistical methods", "inspection planning" and "structuring of operations of the company". This suggests that in the interviewed companies the tasks for production supervisors, also with regard to their quality responsibility, are defined predominantly department-specifically and oriented towards the technology. The quality planning and decisions on its inspection technical implementation as well as the evaluation of quality data for the control of quality assuring measures belong predominantly to the field of tasks of the laboratory or a special quality department. This is in keeping with the finding from the expert interviews that there is generally a relatively strict division between the administrative-planning level and the operative-productive level in the companies of the food industry. It also becomes obvious, however, that production supervisors are involved in the planning process at the management level in many companies.

Quality-related demands on production skilled staff

For this group of staff the following profile was identified:

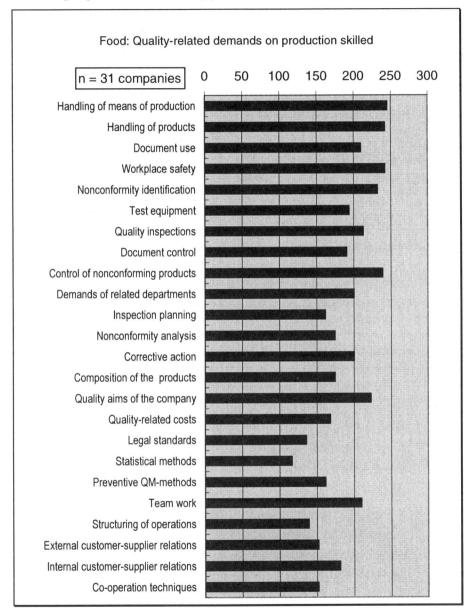

Figure 33: Quality-related demands on production skilled in the food industry

The priority of "proper handling of means of production", "workplace safety" and "handling of products" as quality-related demands on skilled staff of the production corresponds to traditional job profiles of production staff. Striking, however, is the nearly equally high rating of "control of nonconforming products" and "nonconformity identification and documentation". This shows the tendency that at least operative tasks of quality control and quality assurance are transferred back to manufacturing and extend the work tasks of the production staff. This is particularly represented by the relatively highly rated task "quality inspection". In the expert interviews the finding was substantiated that self-responsible inspection activities make an increasing part of the activities at the line and that for this reason the handling of inspection instruments and techniques increasingly belong to the required qualification profile of skilled production staff in the food industry. The tendency to implement self-inspection into the production also explains that the companies expect production staff to be aware of the "quality aims of the company". This should be the point of reference in the extended quality responsibility.

As with the production supervisors the rather low rated demands on skilled production staff that their quality-related tasks are focused on the operative-productive functions within the boundaries of their own department.

Quality-related demands on production semi/unskilled staff

The profile of demands on the semiskilled and unskilled production staff is almost the same as those on the skilled staff in this department except for a less emphasised responsibility for "quality inspections". Strikingly high is the rating of the requirements "control of nonconforming products" and "nonconformity identification and documentation". This shows that across hierarchies it is the first and foremost quality task of the production to prevent nonconforming products from being further processed or even from reaching the customer.

For this group of staff the following profile was identified:

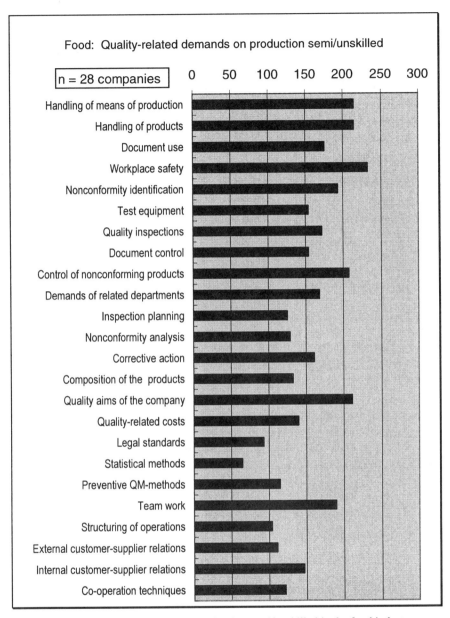

Figure 34: Quality-related demands on production semi/unskilled in the food industry

Comparison: production

Extrapolating a hierarchy of the seven best rated quality-related job requirements from the occupational group-specific ratings, the following picture emerges:

Table 16: Best rated quality-related job requirements in the production (Food industry)

Production supervisors	Production skilled staff	Production semi/unskilled staff
1. Proper handling of means of production	1. Proper handling of means of production	1. Workplace safety
2. Document use (job and procedure instructions)	2. Workplace safety	2. Proper handling of means of production
3. Handling of products	3. Handling of products	3. Handling of products
4. Workplace safety	4. Control of nonconforming products	4. Quality aims of the company
5. Control of nonconforming products	5. Nonconformity identification and documentation	5. Control of nonconforming products
6. Nonconformity identification and documentation	6. Quality aims of the company	6. Nonconformity identification and documentation
7. Corrective action	7. Quality inspections	7. Teamwork

Some department-specific as well as hierarchy-specific statements can be deduced from this picture.

The surveyed small and medium-sized enterprises of the food industry expect their production staff first to carry out the operative-productive tasks in the production. Also extended quality-related self-responsibilities focus on product and process in the production. The execution of cross-departmental quality-related tasks are obviously not considered to be priority responsibility of production staff.

From a hierarchy-specific point of view a certain maintenance of the pattern decision-making competence versus execution can be observed.

Extrapolating a hierarchy of the seven lowest rated quality-related job requirements from the occupational group-specific ratings the following picture emerges:

Table 17: Lowest rated quality-related job requirements in the production (Food industry)

Production supervisors	Production skilled staff	Production semi/unskilled staff
• Data collection & statistical methods	• Data collection & statistical methods	• Data collection & statistical methods
• Inspection planning	• Legal standards	• Legal standards
• Structuring of operations of the company	• Structuring of operations of the company	• Structuring of operations of the company
• External customer-supplier relations	• External customer-supplier relations	• External customer-supplier relations
• Legal standards	• Co-operation techniques	• Preventive QM methods
• Co-operation techniques	• Inspection planning	• Co-operation techniques
• Preventive QM methods	• Preventive QM methods	• Inspection planning

Across the hierarchy, on the one hand, tasks of quality planning and the use of quality methods get low ratings. On the other hand, low ratings for e.g. "structuring of operations of the company" and "external customer-supplier relations" suggest that the interviewed companies consider it rather less necessary that production staff takes on tasks outside their own department.

Quality-related demands on distribution supervisors

For this group of staff, the following profile was identified:

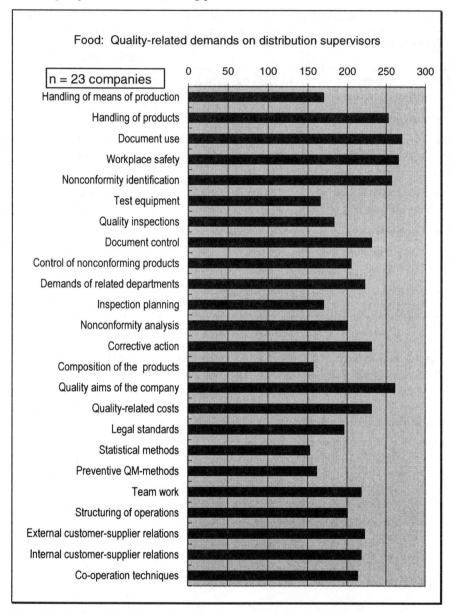

Figure 35: Quality-related demands on distribution supervisors in the food industry

The reason for the fact that "document use" is the best rated demand on supervisors of the distribution is that in general the distribution department in small and medium-sized enterprises of the food industry has mostly executing tasks if it does still exist as an independent department[3] at all. In this sense the highly rated "handling of products" and "document control" might be understood. The proper handling of the finished products and assurance of continuos marking and feedback is priority. However, the requirements "nonconformity identification and documentation" and "corrective action" show that supervisors of the distribution are also entrusted with the responsibility for a final inspection.

Quality-related demands on distribution skilled staff

The profile of demands on skilled staff of the distribution coincides with the one on the supervisors of this department except for the responsibility for "corrective action".

For this group of staff, the following profile was identified:

---

[3]   The relatively small number of companies which made statements on quality-related demands on the distribution goes back to two factors. Firstly, in many companies the material distribution activities such as packaging are integrated into the production. Secondly, the products of the food industry are mostly distributed by independent trade companies.

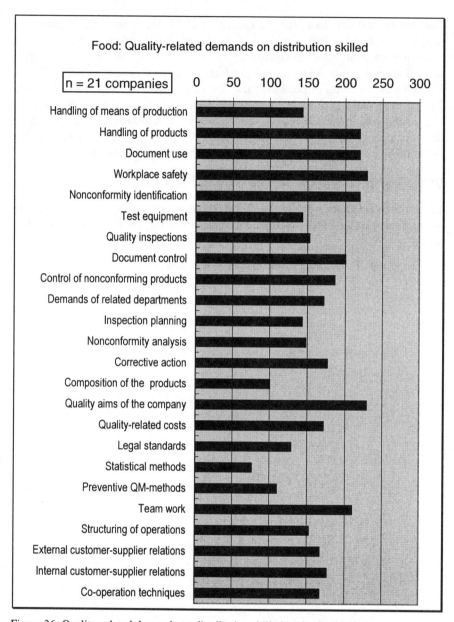

Figure 36: Quality-related demands on distribution skilled in the food industry

Quality-related demands on distribution semi/unskilled staff

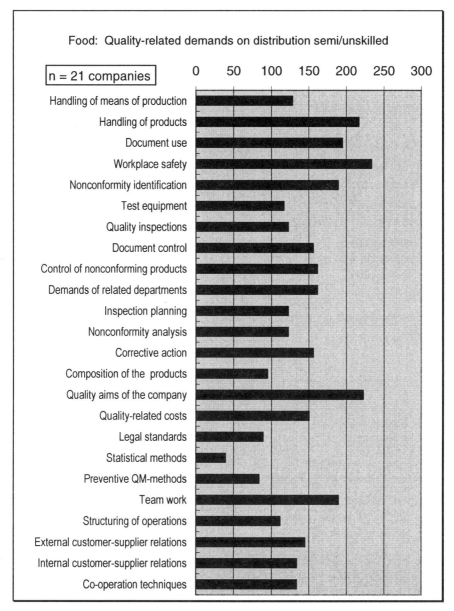

Figure 37: Quality-related demands on distribution semi/unskilled in the food industry

The profile of demands on semi/unskilled staff of the distribution coincides with the one on the skilled staff of this department.

Comparison: distribution

Extrapolating a hierarchy of the seven best rated quality-related job requirements from the occupational group-specific ratings, the following picture emerges:

Table 18: Best rated quality-related job requirements in distribution (Food industry)

Distribution supervisors	Distribution skilled staff	Distribution semi/unskilled staff
1. Document use (job and procedure instructions) 2. Workplace safety 3. Quality aims of the company 4. Nonconformity identification and documentation 5. Handling of products 6. Document control 7. Corrective action	1. Workplace safety 2. Quality aims of the company 3. Handling of products 4. Document use (job and procedure instructions) 5. Nonconformity identification and documentation 6. Teamwork 7. Document control	1. Workplace safety 2. Quality aims of the company 3. Handling of products 4. Document use (job and procedure instructions) 5. Nonconformity identification and documentation 6. Teamwork 7. Control of nonconforming products

Some department-specific as well as hierarchy-specific statements can be deduced from this picture.

Across the hierarchical levels proper handling of the company products and the execution of marking and documentation activities is expected.

There is hardly any hierarchy-specific division of tasks except for the responsibility of the supervisors for corrective action.

Extrapolating a hierarchy of the seven lowest rated quality-related job requirements from the occupational group-specific ratings, the following picture emerges:

Table 19: Lowest rated quality-related job requirements in distribution (Food industry)

Distribution supervisors	Distribution skilled staff	Distribution semi/unskilled staff
• Data collection & statistical methods	• Data collection & statistical methods	• Data collection & statistical methods
• Composition of the company products	• Preventive QM methods	• Preventive QM methods
• Preventive QM methods	• Legal standards	• Legal standards
• Test equipment	• Composition of the company products	• Composition of the company products
• Proper handling of means of production	• Structuring of operations of the company	• Structuring of operations of the company
• Inspection planning	• Test equipment	• Test equipment
• Quality inspections	• Quality inspections	• Quality inspections

Quality-related demands on the staff

Summarising the quality-related job requirements for the different staff groups across the departments, the following profile emerges:

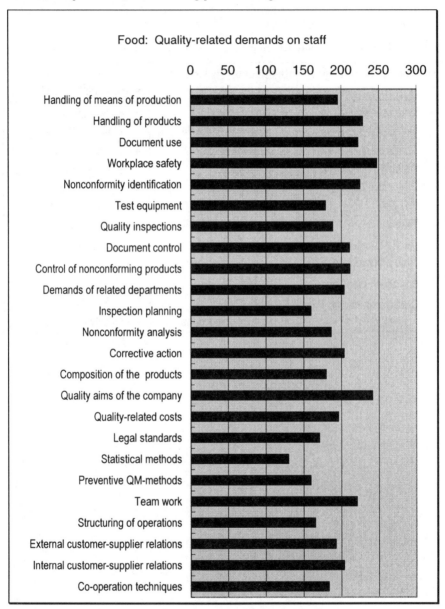

Figure 38: Quality-related demands on staff in the food industry

"Workplace safety" is the priority quality-related demand on staff across the departments. The reason for this is that for the food industry it includes the basic requirement for hygiene. The interviewed companies attach particular significance to the requirement for staff across the departments to be guided by the "quality aims of the company".

The emphasis of the quality tasks "nonconformity identification and documentation" and "control of nonconforming products" focuses the quality responsibility of staff on the aim to prevent nonconforming products from reaching the customer. Together with insisting on "document use", the quality related demands on staff correspond to the average state of developments of quality management in the surveyed small and medium-sized enterprises which are still essentially oriented towards the ISO system on the basis of reliable work and procedure instructions but which does not transfer the task "quality" to a special department alone but delegates elements of quality control broader.

Table 20: Rated quality-related job requirements on the staff (Food industry)

Best rated quality-related job requirements	Lowest rated quality-related job requirements
1. Workplace safety	• Data collection & statistical methods
2. Quality aims of the company	• Preventive QM methods
3. Handling of products	• Inspection planning
4. Nonconformity identification and documentation	• Structuring of operations of the company
5. Document use (job and procedure instructions)	• Legal standards
6. Teamwork	• Test equipment
7. Control of nonconforming products	• Composition of the company products

To the assessment of an implementation of quality management essentially still remaining within the framework of the ISO system corresponds the focusing of staff's tasks on internal quality assurance. The external customer-supplier relations, that is customer orientation and quality responsibility within the food-processing chain, do not make particular cross-departmental demands on staff. The low rating of statistical and preventive methods, the "structuring of operations of the company" and especially the "composition of the company products" is striking. It has already come out that for these elements of the quality system in the surveyed small and medium-sized enterprises of the food industry mostly special departments, particularly the development department and the executives of the purchasing department, are responsible. Particularly the quality-related responsibilities of production staff are clearly restricted to the operative-productive functions within the department boundaries. This also becomes apparent in the following comparison of the best and the lowest rated requirements between the departments.

Comparison: cross-departmental

Table 21: Best rated quality-related job requirements across the departments (Food industry)

Development supervisors	Development skilled staff
1. Quality aims of the company	1. Composition of the company products
2. Composition of the company products	2. Quality aims of the company
3. Legal standards	3. Workplace safety
4. Workplace safety	4. Test equipment
5. Quality-related costs	5. Teamwork
Purchasing supervisors	**Purchasing skilled staff**
1. Quality aims of the company	1. Workplace safety
2. Document control	2. Quality aims of the company
3. Workplace safety	3. Document use (job and procedure instructions)
4. Nonconformity identification and documentation	4. Teamwork
5. Internal customer-supplier relations	5. Nonconformity identification and documentation
Production supervisors	**Production skilled staff**
1. Proper handling of means of production	1. Proper handling of means of production
2. Document use (job and procedure instructions)	2. Workplace safety
3. Handling of products	3. Handling of products
4. Workplace safety	4. Control of nonconforming products
5. Control of nonconforming products	5. Nonconformity identification and documentation
Distribution supervisors	
1. Document use (job and procedure instructions)	
2. Workplace safety	
3. Quality aims of the company	
4. Nonconformity identification and documentation	
5. Handling of products	

Table 22: Lowest rated quality-related job requirements across the departments (Food industry)

Development supervisors	Development skilled staff
• Inspection planning	• Inspection planning
• Proper handling of means of production	• Data collection & statistical methods
• Document use (job and procedure instructions)	• Structuring of operations of the company
• Control of nonconforming products	• Preventive QM methods
• Structuring of operations of the company	• Proper handling of means of production
Purchasing supervisors	**Purchasing skilled staff**
• Test equipment	• Data collection & statistical methods
• Data collection & statistical methods	• Preventive QM methods
• Preventive QM methods	• Inspection planning
• Inspection planning	• Structuring of operations of the company
• Proper handling of means of production	• Legal standards
Production supervisors	**Production skilled staff**
• Data collection & statistical methods	• Data collection & statistical methods
• Inspection planning	• Legal standards
• Structuring of operations of the company	• Structuring of operations of the company
• External customer-supplier relations	• External customer-supplier relations
• Legal standards	• Co-operation techniques
Distribution supervisors	
• Data collection & statistical methods	
• Composition of the company products	
• Preventive QM methods	
• Test equipment	
• Proper handling of means of production	

Customer orientation demands on staff

Does the customer orientation proclaimed especially by small and medium-sized enterprises result in extended quality demands on the work of staff? The marketing executives in the surveyed companies were asked the following semi-standardised question:

Question: "The satisfaction of the customer is the crucial measure of quality!" - Does this statement imply new demands on your employees? If so, what are the implications for training? Is training required to meet gaps in knowledge? **Rate answers according to following key:** 0 = unimportant, 1 = plays a role 2 = important, 3 = very important

Company experts for customer contact consider improved knowledge of staff necessary mainly with regard to "customers' demands on the company" and "the company products".

These expectations on the entire staff from the point of view of marketing are in strong contrast to the statements of the company about the current quality-related demands on staff clearly focusing on the internal quality assurance according to the formalised instructions in the ISO system.

The quantitative evaluation identified the following picture:

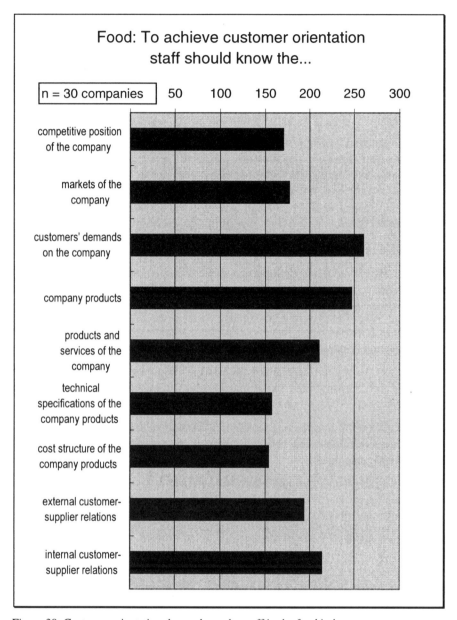

Figure 39: Customer orientation demands on the staff in the food industry

Quality-related actual training issues

The survey intended to identify the actual state of the companies' training efforts and examine whether or how these training efforts correlate with the indicated quality-related demands of the companies on their staff in general and on certain staff groups.

But those standardised questions met with greatest difficulties in the companies which, broken down to departments and staff groups, asked about training programmes and courses relevant to quality management. It was particularly hard to obtain quantitative statements on thematic and participant-specific training volume.

Due to this data situation, only the statements of personnel managers are evaluated for a generalised question in the following.

Question: Where are the most important areas of training for the quality management system of your company at the moment? **Rate answers according to following key:** 0 = unimportant, 1 = plays a role, 2 = important, 3 = very important

---

The evaluation is shown by the following picture.

Training in "vocational specialised knowledge" and "knowledge of the quality system of the company" are clearly priority. Many companies are still in the phase of the personnel consolidation of their quality system.

Training efforts in "co-operation techniques" also get a high rating. The qualitative expert interviews identified here a training focus especially for executives and middle management staff.

Training efforts in "product knowledge" and "knowledge of inspection techniques" point to efforts of the companies to improve the qualification basis of staff to take on extended quality responsibility.

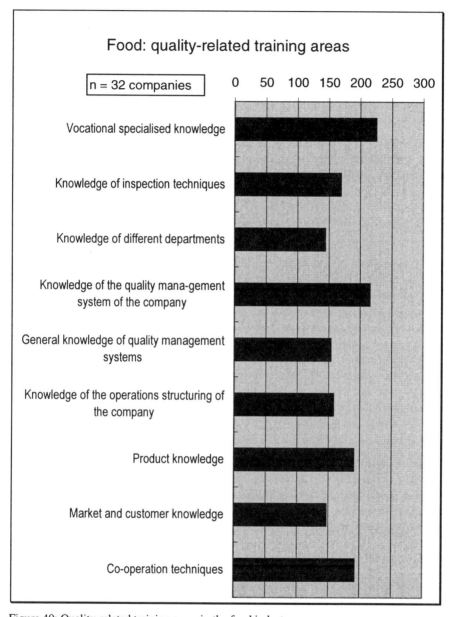

Figure 40: Quality-related training areas in the food industry

Qualitative findings: Barriers, critical points, examples of good practice

The following description deals with expert interviews concerning the question of what personnel-related tasks food-producing SMEs in Europe face when introducing and implementing quality management and what conclusions they draw.

To come straight to one finding: In the surveyed companies quality management leads, particularly at the management level and in the product designing and traditionally quality assuring laboratory area, to a reconsideration of staff competencies, practical competencies to act as well as to a redefinition of required qualifications. At the operative level, employees experience quality management in the immediate performance process predominantly as technological changes and as new formalised job instructions.

The presentation of identified barriers, critical points and examples of good practice in the quality-related personnel policy of the surveyed companies is to open up the "experiments" of the individual companies for an overall discussion. The presentation is based, on the one hand, on a thematically organised summary of details given by the company experts about identified implementation problems and problem solving experiences which will in parts be documented by "statements" and "case examples", and, on the other hand, it is based on meta-analyses of generalisable personnel-related implementation problems of quality management and already recognisable tendencies of personal-related concepts in the surveyed companies.

Personnel and qualification structures

For the identification of new skill needs arising from the implementation of quality management in the companies the existing personnel and qualification structures were recorded in the surveyed companies as reference points. Analytically, three main characteristics can be indicated for the surveyed food-producing SMEs which represent relevant frame conditions for a personnel-related implementation of quality management:

- strict separation between the business-administrative and planning functions and the operative-productive functions in the organisation structure of the companies

- strongly graded qualification levels

- high proportion of part-time and seasonal work

On average, the surveyed companies are organised in departments. A relatively strict separation of the commercial and planning functions from the operative-productive functions can be found. The majority of staff is involved in production which very often integrates storage and material flow as well as substantive distribution functions. On average the second largest department is the laboratory section comprising very often research & development and quality assurance.

More substantial modifications of this organisation and personnel structure at the surveyed companies can be traced back to the following factors:

- Companies with highly diversified production lines combine these production lines with purchasing and distribution functions in the sense of a divisional organisation.

- The more directly companies sell their products to the consumers the more developed are the marketing and distribution functions which then very often include a sales force network.

- The competitive and concentration strategies in the European food industry add to the separation of commercial-planning and R&D functions from the operative-productive functions. Many interviewed companies have become predominantly producing units, the main commercial, planning functions are now with the marketing companies or are centralised in higher corporate structures such as holdings.

It follows from a significant number of expert statements that the relatively strict separation of functions are a barrier and/or the integration of market-related and operative-productive quality demands are a crucial challenge for the implementation of a cross-departmental comprehensive quality system in SMEs of the food industry.

On average, the qualification structure of staff is strongly graded in the surveyed companies. High, very often academic professional qualifications, can be found in the management and particularly in the laboratory. Here, legal restrictions also play a role. At the operative level in production and particularly distribution there is a high percentage of staff without formal qualifications. Rather an exception are companies in the sample which employ staff in production who are appropriately qualified for traditional close-to-the-trade production methods. The high percentage of staff who are, at least in a formal sense, unskilled can be attributed to the following factors:

- Traditionally, but also according to modern locational decisions, some food manufacturers are situated close to the producers of agricultural primary products in rural areas. These companies recruit a large number of their staff from the rural population with agricultural careers.

- Many companies consider company-specific learning and work experience as more important staff qualifications for their industrialised and highly specialised manufacturing procedures than a formal broader training. Some surveyed companies focus their personnel strategy on the maintenance of such an internally developed regular staff with little fluctuation. This is particularly true for tasks requiring a sensory capability which has been developed over many years of experience.

- The increasing automation of procedures in the food industry makes it easier and the competition-induced cost pressures in the sector forces companies to employ cheaper unskilled staff.

Some counter tendencies can also be observed in the surveyed companies.

- The modernisation of the equipment and above all the modern information and control systems require a higher industrial know-how of the operative staff.

- A market- and customer-oriented product diversification and a faster product innovation also for a better utilisation capacities require flexibly employable staff with a broader basic understanding of products and processes of the food industry.

- The broad range of increasing quality demands of the public and the consumers on the companies of the food industry leads some of the surveyed companies to diagnose that in spite of - and sometimes also because of - the extensive technological quality assurance and formalised and documented quality instructions, only sufficiently qualified staff can implement the demanding quality goals of the companies in a responsible way.

The improvement groups promoted in some companies can be considered as examples of good practice for a quality-oriented overcoming of the function and qualification barriers.

A main characteristic of the personnel structure in the surveyed companies is in a sectoral comparison the high percentage of part-time and seasonal employment. Seasonal employment is induced by two factors:

- On the one hand, the natural growing cycles of agricultural primary products lead to seasonal changes in capacity utilisation in the companies of the primary processing steps. This is, however, counteracted by the international purchasing of primary products and the modernisation in the agricultural technology.

- On the other hand, some products of the food industry are subject to seasonal changes of the consumer demand. This is counteracted by the companies by product diversification and by changes in the consumer behaviour.

However, part-time and seasonal employment remains to be a crucial challenge for the personnel-related implementation of quality management and its qualification implications. Given the financial and time restrictions for quality-oriented employee training indicated by many companies, the efforts of some companies to deliberately utilise the period with less orders for improvement projects of the quality system as well as for employee training can be considered as examples of good practice. This is also true for scheduled preparation of training of seasonal staff during this period.

Case examples and statements

"A broad range of tasks which require very high qualifications and simple activities which can be carried out by semiskilled staff is typical for the food sector." Academic qualifications are required particularly in the laboratory area. In the production there are industrial workers for whose tasks the original occupational qualifications are less important than the knowledge and work experiences gained in the company itself. This however requires personnel development knowledge at the management level. *"Know-how for the sector-related handling of personnel development and training would also be necessary. How do you deal best with the wide range of personnel qualifications, how do you reliably identify personnel development needs."* *(121/Germany/spices, spice mixtures/160 employees/certification > 2 years/ ISO 9001)*

"Biscuit consumption differs a lot month by month, so there is a list of 150 employees, who work occasionally or when they are called and they have time to come. This gives flexibility to company in their personnel structure." *(224/Finland/biscuits/250 employees/aspiring certification/ISO 9001)*

The seasonal personnel exists in the tomato industry and is trained before it starts working but also throughout the first two weeks next to an experienced person (on job training). The evaluation of the training of the employees is also very important because it shows the knowledge gaps that the employees still have and helps the planning of the training that will follow. *(324/Greece/pasta, tomato products/336 employees/certification > 2 years/ ISO 9002)*

Because of the seasonal nature of the products the company works fully during the summer period whereas in the winter it passes to a stage of maintenance with reduced production. The standard number of employees is 137 throughout the year , 54 (40%) of them are semi- or unskilled personnel. During the summer the number of employees increases to 437 by the addition of 300 seasonal workers. From the 300 seasonal workers 280 are unskilled and work mainly in the production and stock departments.... *"A special training programme exists for the seasonal staff. They are called in during winter to attend some training sessions in production, so when they start working they are all well-informed about the important issues of the company." (321/Greece/ice-creams, fresh juices/437 employees/ certification <2 years/ ISO 9002)*

The company is a family owned enterprise with roots in the mill business and with a history within the same family that goes back thirteen generations. The enterprise received a honourable mention by Veckans Affärer (Weekly Business in Sweden) in 1993 as being the "Best family business" by the motivation: "A family enterprise in its 13th generation and its fifth century is unique"... The culture within the enterprise is characterised by very old traditions and a family history which dominates the whole company. Each staff member is highly valued and a concern for the family situation of every employee is also a concern for the company. One of the characteristics at the enterprise is a history of succession from middle management to management and a low staff turnover... The enterprise as a whole is characterised by a low degree of education. The traditions within the enterprise is to find the right person for the job, mostly locally recruited, since it is important to support the local trade. The specific skill demands within the enterprise requires training at site (in house) of new recruitments. *"Specialised training for different demands within the food-processing industry is hard to find." (622/Sweden/ice-cream & frozen desserts/91 employees/certification <2 years/ISO 9001)*

Personnel policy and company strategy

The ISO 9000 standards require of companies the execution and documentation of a systematic training needs identification and training of personnel. The surveyed companies comply with this requirement for the certificate.

In the formal organisational execution of this task, the fact that the majority of the companies in the sample have a regular personnel department plays a role. Moreover, the predominantly clear functional structure and the industrial mass production methods of the food industry generate relatively clear long-term work profiles of staff. The organisation of the employee training required by quality management falls in most cases into the responsibility of the personnel department. The tendency is, however, obvious in most of the surveyed companies that in comparison with the rather more personnel-administrative function of this department, essential impetus with regard to contents for the personnel development comes from the quality manager.

In spite of a formal organisational and predominantly systematic personnel and training policy of the surveyed companies, analytical findings of the survey and statements of the interviewed managers show that a documentation according to a quality system is not always based on a quality-oriented strategy of the identification and development of human resources.

In the interviews, those standardised questions met the biggest problems with the interviewed experts which inquired after quality management-induced new qualification demands on staff and after the respective company-specific training programmes and measures in relation to the different departments and staff groups. It was particularly difficult to get quantitative information on subject- and participant-specific training expenses. In order to avoid possible terminological problems, mostly standardised terms of the ISO standards and/or generally accepted terms of the quality management theory were deliberately used for these subjects in the survey instrument.

In answers to open questions some of the interviewed managers indicated that in order to fulfil the ISO requirements very often only the personnel development measures were documented which are undertaken not so much to promote quality but rather to comply with the legal requirements or to support internal restructuring.

Based on the explanations of the experts, some barriers for the implementation of the ISO demands on a systematic employee training into the company-specific personnel development can be characterised in more detail:

- Due to the competitive and cost pressures in the food industry and due to the variations in the orders position and operating rate many companies consider the expenditures of money and time for personnel development as a predominant flexible quantity. (see "Training methods and training conditions")

- Particularly in some companies seeking ISO certification, it becomes obvious that a more systematic identification of the company's human resources and a more strategic planning of their skill development is initiated only by the ISO process.

- Traditional companies of the food industry, particularly in rural areas, rely on the long term company experience of the staff as the best informal personnel development and do not see any necessity for modern methods of the human resource management. On the other hand, however, there are complaints that these long-term members of staff trained in this very way - especially those who have advanced to the middle management - find it particularly hard to deal with the new requirements of quality management.

- Further training is most of the time the privilege of the already higher qualified specialised personnel in many interviewed companies. Many companies consider the operative tasks in their modern production procedures as being "simple" and the ISO documentation of job instructions as a "simplification", so that efforts in personnel development could rather be reduced instead of extended.

- In a considerable number of companies the individual interest of employees in further training is given decisive weight for the planning of training. Appreciated as this participation of staff is in principle, it also encourages that personnel development focuses on those with already higher qualifications. The complaint of some interviewed experts on operatives lacking motivation for development must be viewed critically. Because a self-responsible identification of skill shortages and interest in further training presupposes an already developed know-how. Often the difficulties of the new *personnel development skills* which the company requires of the middle management are underestimated and very often the middle management is, therefore, not sufficiently supported. Here, managerial staff is expected to advise and support employees in their training planning – but managers have too little contact with employees to identify their training needs, which is a weak point. The analysis reveals weaknesses both in the ISO system and the personnel development of the surveyed food-processing SMEs.

1. It is a strength of the ISO standards that they insist on employee training, their systematisation and planning. But, at the same time, the ISO system is not suitable for many surveyed companies as an adequate planning instrument. However, the system has to be fulfilled.. It is a weakness that very few guidelines or even standards for a quality-oriented personnel policy and personnel development have been developed so far.

2. It is a weakness of the personnel strategy of the surveyed companies that it is oriented towards the organisational division of functions and range of qualifications and that it, on average, reacts to external requirements and internal notification of an already critical need. A systematic identification of existing human resources and a more proactive personnel development strategy is on average not very common. For the organisational implementation of quality management, management teams are becoming common – but there is no analogue development in the staff-related implementation of quality management, in the management of human resources. Company-specific needs profiles based on long-term company aims are most likely used in recruitment. Also a systematic evaluation of personnel development measures has not been very common so far. In cases where such arrangements could be identified they were mainly reserved for cost intensive external training programmes

As a whole, the internal-company personnel policies, but also the external training provisions (see "External training") do not yet keep pace with the structural change of the food industry in Europe: with the technological modernisation and the resulting change of skill profiles, the changes of the work division between companies, in particular within the framework of concentration processes and of new product and quality requirements. This represents a challenge not only for managers of small and medium-sized enterprises but also for sectoral organisations and particularly for the strong customer companies, for example in commerce in form of a know-how transfer.

Examples of good practice were found in companies

- responding with training to nonconformities in the work of staff. A critical comment has to be made as to the fact that sanctions are not always replaced by support.

- using and evaluating external and above all internal audits also for the identification of personnel development needs.

- delegating skill needs analysis to the middle management and at the same time providing appropriate social competencies for this staff group and institutionalising reliable methods for systematisation throughout the company.

- developing personnel development implications within the framework of improvement projects and improvement groups.

- implementing requirements of market and customer orientation in the personnel development as well.

- translating externally or internally induced company restructuring via quality management into supporting personnel development.

A closer analysis of theses cases suggests the conclusion that the establishment of quality management for acquiring the certificate alone is seldom reason enough for a re-organisation of the company towards a more strategic and more proactive personnel policy. Instead, in most cases of good practice it shows that in these companies the implementation of quality management itself is an integral part of a more comprehensive company strategy in which quality management supports the realisation of other company aims. Within this framework, however, quality management proves to be a decisive catalyst for the identification of personnel development tasks. The examples for a more proactive personnel policy within the framework of comprehensive company strategies can be typified according to the following aspects:

- quality management to support a technological modernisation strategy

- expansion of the customer service within the framework of a market exploration strategy

- company reorganisation within the framework of combinations and mergers with simultaneous transfer of management know-how

- comprehensive strategy for the integrated implementation of quality management, HACCP and environmental management

- benchmarking in product quality particularly within the framework of an internationalisation strategy

- reorientation of the company in a europeanisation and internationalisation strategy (partly supported by national and European funding programmes)

The two latter framework strategies, in particular, allow view that the strategic potentials of quality management are not fully utilised in companies which stick to a reactive personnel policy. Whenever training for the ISO system occur predominantly as a formal additional requirement of the personnel development for the certificate, the companies did not fully succeed in transferring the system into a company-specific quality policy which at the same time provides with periodical quality aims a framework for a strategic personnel development.

Case examples and statements

"The Human Resource Management is in the centre of the Quality Management." There is a strong belief that the quality goals of the company can be achieved through extensive training of the personnel. *"Quality should emanate from the employees. If the employees don't understand completely the ISO standards, Quality won't be reached. Thus the employees should have a main role in the System. They participated quite enough to the documentation of the whole System. There is also a relevant document which encourages staff to put forward suggestions for the improvement of the System, if any weaknesses are spotted."* ... Every year, beginning of September, when the cycle of production is completed, due to the fact that the goods produced are seasonal, the supervisors of production units or the employees themselves submit proposals that concern the products and how they can be improved. After those proposals have been taken into consideration, an integrated training programme for the company is made. *(321/Greece/ice-creams, fresh juices/ 437 employees/certification < 2 years/ISO 9002)*

The weakest point is undoubtedly connected with the identification of training needs and with the elaboration of a training scheme aiming the improvement of the quality of the work, not only of a few of the employees, but of the greatest number of them. Statement of the Director of Human Resources: *"There isn't an annual budget for training, which unfortunately means that the research of the said needs is assumed as a mere formal proceeding in the scope of the Quality System..."* *(522/Portugal/milk/ 406 employees/aspiring certification/certification > 2 years/ISO 9002)*

The decisive reason for the company certification is deeper and centred in its charismatic leader: "... *the company philosophy and cultural values are based on the example of its founder...*" It is possible that the professional training intended to give the employees the know-how necessary to the new organisational reality has been more superficial than the process demanded. On the other hand, the outstandingly family-type management, allowing a close relationship between the workers and the management staff, made it easier to balance the insufficiency of the training through the support and teachings of that staff. *(523/Portugal/coffee/ 297 employees/certification < 2 years/ISO 9002)*

There is a planning and schedule made for two years to give training for different groups of people from different substances depending on what an employee needs in his or her work. It is made by asking for employees what the training needs is from the perspective of them. The whole programme is tailored for this company. *(223/Finland/milk products/289 employees/ certification > 2 years/ISO 9002)*

The needs for training are judged at any time and are materialised directly. *"Everybody has the ability to express their thoughts about training and what they think necessary to be done and to which group of employees. Training depends on the needs but also on the time available." (323/Greece/puff pastry, strudel leaves, frozen vegetable, pizza/231 employees/aspiring certification/ISO 9001)*

Training is geared as much to individual needs as to the needs of the company. *"It's really how well people perform and how generally interested they are in progressing . In the factory again, it's mainly based on people's aspirations or what future we see for people i.e. succession plan". (723/United Kingdom/infant and dietetic foods/280 employees/certification > 2 years/ISO 9002)*

"We reinforce it with the operators that they are responsible for the product coming off their layouts and if they have any deficiencies in the product that they have not identified, then unless they've got a fairly good explanation and they've just failed to find it because of lack of discipline, they can go to a disciplinary action. But that is the last stage - we make sure that they fully understand what their responsibilities are and what their requirements are before we go there. ..... It's slowly getting there - that people are realising that everybody has this impact on quality and not

just quality control inspectors or quality assurance managers."... "There's no defined policy for training - it's really down to individuals or departmental areas to identify training. But I think if there is a need for training - if an individual does require training - then the company is not against that. For instance our factory manager wanted to do an Open University course and the company sponsored him for that." In theory, managers are expected to hold regular six-monthly meetings with employees to discuss their training requirements but this rarely happens in practice because of the lack of a clearly defined training policy. Although the quality system requires training to be maintained and training needs identified on a regular basis, there is no coherent system in place for doing this: *"so individual departments will maintain their training records as they think appropriate. There may be two or three different styles of training records - people might do a matrix, people might do individual records ... So it's not a formal system saying that 'this is what your training records should look like'...So really, a structured system of reviewing and identifying training needs is not in place." (721/United Kingdom/tea/500 employees/certification > 2 years/ISO 9001)*

The enterprise has today a strategic plan for all the training required within the enterprise. This is thanks to the financial contribution which they have received from the European Social Fund, objective 4 programme. The aim of the contribution was a mapping of the total training needs for each individual within the company. The mapping has speed up the work with the training system for the employees in maintaining and in the introduction of the quality system. The system is recently being introduced and is characterised by the following:

introduction programme for new employees and apprentices in the quality system

training programme for sales personnel in the quality demands at the production

a system for transfer in experiences for the quality management group usage of suppliers in the training. *(622/Sweden/ice-cream & frozen desserts/91 employees/certification < 2 years/ISO 9001)*

The company lays special emphasis on the quality of its products, therefore it didn't content itself with the implementation of the ISO 9002 standard, which was sufficient for advertising purposes, but went further into the implementation of ISO 9001 standards, while a HACCP system has also been adopted. A training programme based on a funded EU programme lasted for 2 to 3 months and included the basic training concerning the

Quality system. After the certification the main target of the enterprise is the constant improvement of the system. The existing system is seen by the company as the first step towards TQM. The Quality manager considers that the meaning of TQM is realised but one more year is needed in order for the company to be able to move towards this direction... External-company training provisions are quantitatively sufficient available but they are too general and do not cover the company's needs of specialised knowledge on product quality. The company invites therefore foreign experts for the training of employees on special hygiene and quality issues. It also makes use of EU-funded seminars for improving the qualifications of the staff on basic as well as on quality and hygiene issues. *(325/Greece/cooked pork meat/226 employees/certification < 2 years/ISO 9001/2)*

The responsibility for the identification of needs and the planning of employee training is not with the personnel department but with the immediate supervisors. *"I cannot place somebody new at the line without enabling him to do the new job. If you have the responsibility for staff it is also your duty to ensure training. Also to the personnel department! This falls under our broad understanding of "responsibility of the management". Supervisors are then also in charge of controlling the employee training".* On the whole, the company still sees the need to improve its employee training system. This applies to the methods of a comprehensive identification of needs as well as to the extent of the training efforts. *"Supervisor interviews with staff may be conducted soon. But we have not yet achieved a 360-degree assessment everybody talks about today. Today we are ready to start with benchmarking. For example, how much time is spent for employee training at international leading companies: 80 hours/year for operatives, 120 hours/year for employees and management staff. In their acquisition strategies international groups compare the companies at each location. They also do benchmarking within the corporate group. We want to be a European brand and therefore we must be able to measure up to the best in Europe."* *(125/Germany/frozen products/688 employees/certification < 2 years/ISO 9001)*

The personnel department is now defunct. The reason given was that staff complaints were being taken directly to personnel, bypassing the line management. The present system is now seen as being far more effective and it pushes responsibility back to each department manager to ensure good staff relations. An Industrial Relations officer (reporting directly to the General Factory Manager) has been employed. His role is to assist staff and managers to deal with IR issues, if and when they arise. Each line manager has responsibility for the personnel function within his/her department. It is felt that this is far more conducive to better communications and interactions with staff. Also, issues are more readily discussed and addressed. In addition, the responsibility for training now rests with each manager. However, there is a concern that some managers are not 'pro training' and this could have a negative effect. Efforts are made by senior management to counter this by continually reinforcing the objective of having a better trained workforce. *(425/Ireland/canning of food and vegetables, beverages, packing dry pulses/295 employees/aspiring certification/ISO 9002)*

Qualification-relevant new demands by quality management

ISO certification and ISO process

According to the mostly concurrent opinion of the interviewed experts, the implementation of quality management for an ISO 9000 certification makes two general new skill-related demands on the companies:

- Identification, reorganisation and documentation of company processes set new comprehensive tasks first of all for the senior and the middle management. All interviewed companies identify skill needs of the management naturally in quality management know-how but most of the time also in general management know-how. In a restrictive case this only applies to the persons responsible for quality.

- For the entire personnel the implementation of the ISO system results in a formalised description of workplace requirements and thus at least in a basis of a more exact definition of the required skill profiles.

In the senior management and the management responsible for quality, not only an understanding of the systems of quality management must be ensured. The implementation requires the quality-oriented analysis and assessment of the company-specific performance processes and division of tasks. The question "How do we actually work?" requires apart from target-oriented management above all a management which critically analyses the performance. However, some company leaders, above all many managers who are responsible for the implementation of the system, rediscover with the expenditure for the documentation the qualification and work experience of staff as an indispensable support for the establishment of quality management. Self-critically several interviewed experts indicated that quality instruction originally designed at the management table were conforming with the system but not applicable. External consultants can help to break down the ISO standards and make them applicable to the company and its specific processes but they are cost intensive. Many of the interviewed managers point out in some cases critically, in other cases self-critically, that the benefit of external consultants was only limited to establishing a quality system tailored to the own company. In the task to screen the concrete processes of the company for strengths and weaknesses, systematise and document them, the employees are identified as the experts who know these processes from daily practice and know about the weaknesses. But the task to open up these staff experiences for the quality system of the company requires on the part of the responsible management new skills of a communicative and supporting personnel leadership.

In some companies these experiences lead to a re-discovery of the qualifications and work experiences of staff and to a reassessment of their significance for the company. Resorting to the knowledge and experience of staff for the establishment of a quality system is not only problem-adequate and target-oriented: Many quality assurance methods and techniques are themselves scientific generalisations of or scientific methods for the practical systematisation and analysis of experiences and experience knowledge of practical operations and performance processes. The exploitation and promotion of staff knowledge and clearly defined extension of their competencies and responsibilities have also an influence on the amount of "bureaucracy" and the applicability of the documented system: The higher the qualification-based responsibility of an employee, the less small stepped and extensive the job instruction have to be. Particularly those companies which have critically analysed this correlation show examples of good practice.

In general, however, the implementation of the ISO system results, as regards the work and skill profiles for the entire personnel, first of all only in a more formalised description of the job requirements but thus creates at least the basis of a more exact definition of the required skill profiles for the personnel policy and the personnel development. Also in this limited sense the expert interviews already prove positive effects. Many companies enter it as a benefit that they have significantly better instruments for the decision-making when it comes to recruitment. In many companies the job and procedure instructions of the quality management also provide the basis for the introductory training for new staff. Within the framework of this survey, this is particularly worth mentioning because it suggests the conclusion that in the food industry quality assuring tasks are congruent with the essential elements of the occupational profiles in industrial food processing.

In a lot of the surveyed companies, however, a break can be identified between the re-discovery of existing qualifications and the practical involvement of staff after a successful certification. This is legitimate as long as it is about the necessary next stage of making the new system a routine. The employees are concerned with the step that the clarified and determined processes, procedures and quality assuring techniques have to be learned, followed and mastered in everyday practice. Also interviewed experts from the companies with rather precise prospects for the implementation of TQM emphasise the indispensability of this phase. Only on this basis can the quality instructions become an instrument in the hands of staff to actively identify in target-performance comparisons weaknesses in the work and company processes as well as in the documented quality system. Some interviewed experts see a break-through point when external and internal audits are no more treated by staff as a well-prepared inspection of system conformity but as a system inspection which staff critically supports.

On the other hand, it becomes problematic if the company loses the awareness that the qualifications and the concrete work experiences, also those concerning the quality system, are an indispensable internal source for the preventive development of concrete steps for the maintenance, continuation and improvement of the company-specific quality system, preventive as opposed to external assessments and demands by customer complaints or the reaudit. Frequently, it has to be assessed as a sign of stagnation if basic hygiene, safety and documentation routines need to be frequently updated.

Case examples and statements

When operators are being recruited for the plant there is a desire to employ the more educated person. Prior to ISO implementation the level of education was never a consideration. *"It is very important to have a skilled workforce. There is a growing awareness of the need to have the 'quality worker' certified, i.e. a certificate to formally recognise the work achieved relating to quality, and hygiene." (423/Ireland/full range of fresh dairy products/246 employees/ certification > 2 years/ISO 9002)*

One of the main reasons for which the certification hasn't been completed yet is that the company doesn't want to write down some procedures that won't be kept by the employees. A basic principle is that nothing is done unless it is written down and that nothing is written down unless it is done. There is a project leader in every work team that is formed, who is responsible for the materialisation of the project and the rest of the employees have as their main task the part of the project that they undertook. There is flat hierarchy in those teams. The employees wrote down what they are doing and the changes that took place were aiming at the improvement of their work. The employees spotted the weaknesses by themselves and suggested changes. The ISO 9001 standards are treated as the first step taken for the materialisation of Total Quality Management. The certification could have taken place but the company wanted it to be passed on to all the departments and to all the activities of the enterprise (for instance, the services that are offered by the accounts department to the sales department, the production department to the sales department and vice versa). *"Everything has to be included in one System." (323/Greece/ puff pastry, strudel leaves, frozen vegetable, pizza/231 employees/aspiring certification/ISO 9001)*

"Hygiene always slackens after a while. You can tell from the consumption of disinfectant which increases after the training and then slowly decreases again. You have to remind people regularly."(122/Germany/tinned fish/12 employees/ certification < 2 years/ISO 9002)

When the Quality System was about to be introduced, there was an agreed, global approach to professional training. After reaching that goal, is looks as though the company had turned over the page of the maintenance of comprehensive training plans. *(521/Portugal/milk products/281 employees/ certification > 2 years/ISO 9002)*

"Every detail of the business and every part of its activities are documented. This has the added benefit when new staff are recruited into the company. As part of their induction they are given the relevant procedure manuals to read."   (422/Ireland/butter/49 employees/certification > 2 years/ISO 9002)

Internal audits are conducted regularly which serve as a reminder to everyone to keep the focus on quality and safety. The Mill Manager said *"previously, if you told staff there was to be an audit, they would want to shut down the place for a few days to get ready for it. It now happens as a matter of routine." (421/Ireland/animal feeds/39-44 employees/certification > 2 years/ISO 9001/2)*

"I think a major weak point is getting a uniform approach to training. We have a training procedure, obviously, but something we need to address is that people have got their own interpretations of that procedure. I think we probably need to re-write the training procedure to address it because different departments have different requirements for their training. And that's probably a weak area that we're behind with at the moment." Whilst quality management has not really affected qualifications to a great extent, it has affected the identification of training needs. An appraisal system which was already in place prior to ISO certification facilitated the identification of any training needs for staff at a more senior level: *"At supervisor level and above ... everyone is on an appraisal system. As part of that system everyone is given a training needs interview as part of that annual or 6-monthly appraisal. So peoples' requirements were really well-identified prior to ISO."* However, for staff below supervisory level, the identification of training needs - prior to ISO - was rather more 'hit-and-

miss'. The introduction of quality management has led to improvements in this area - *'now we've got the discipline of yearly training needs interviews'.* *(723/United Kingdom/infant and dietetic foods/ 280 employees/certification > 2 years/ISO 9002)*

Changes of the internal processes and the work organisation

The majority of the interviewed experts denies that in their companies the implementation of quality management has led to such changes in the processes and the work organisation which resulted in skill shortages of staff and the need for training programmes. Naturally, the methodological problems of expert interviews play a role in these statements that managers even in hindsight are reluctant to attest organisation weaknesses of their companies and qualification gaps of their personnel. More important, however, are the following explanations:

- Interviewed experts understand changes of the processes and the work organisation as obvious organisational or technological restructuring of the company. For such restructuring market-oriented changes of the product line, economically necessary procedure innovations and company-structural competitive strategies clearly have priority over the requirements of the quality system. Since quality management is from this perspective - particularly in the sense of the ISO system - not the decisive reason for comprehensive changes of processes and the work organisation, the interviewed managers do not identify from this perspective new job requirements and skill needs of staff.

- The interviewed food-producing SMEs implement quality management in the sense of the ISO system essentially in the existing work organisation and the existing process technology. This way, in relation to the direct performance process of the company, what takes place is less a reorganisation but rather a redefinition of the tasks of staff. On the one hand, this goes for the laboratory area whose tasks are extended from inspection to the management of quality aims. At the operative-productive level modern process technology defines the work organisation and the tasks which already prior to the implementation of quality management mostly comprise activities and behaviour which essentially are quality assuring: monitoring and controlling the process parameters, monitoring product specifications and sorting, hygiene and safety. Frequently, technological improvement of the process and product control come prior to the redefinition of tasks of the operatives by the quality management or are at least parallel to them.

Explicitly quality-promoting work reorganisation measures start in the surveyed companies predominantly outside of the internal performance processes which are primarily assured by the ISO system. So companies implement new organisation forms of collaboration between distribution/marketing, research and development and production planning for customer oriented market strategies. These new work procedures can be first found at the management level. The same is true for the effort for a thorough quality assurance within the external purchasing chain. Within the framework of customer-oriented market strategies some companies identify also the necessity to have flexibly deployable staff at the operative level at hand with a broad basic understanding of products and processes being able to handle within teamwork structures product diversification and fast product innovations.

Furthermore, is seems to be typical for companies of the food industry that new forms of collaboration of staff for the solution of quality issues can be more strongly established apart from the performance organisation which is determined by technology. The establishment of quality circles and improvement groups characterises rather the trailblazers in the implementation of quality management among the surveyed companies. The influence on the direct work organisation of such quality organisations is still in its beginnings.

Case examples and statements

"They did it before, they are doing it today. You don't have to watch it."
(122/Germany/tinned fish/12 employees/certification < 2 years/ISO 9002)

"The processes were set, nothing has really changed in the company. What used to be only in the heads of the production staff is now in writing. But now the people have clear product specifics and procedure instructions."
(123/Germany/egg products/100 employees/certification < 2 years/ISO 9002)

"It was easier at a management level to change procedures. But it was much more difficult to do this at the operative level." According to the Plant Manager *"when you get down to the second level of ISO documentation i.e. work procedures and operating procedures it is difficult to inform and train staff in recognising the need to change".*
(422/Ireland/butter/49 employees/certification > 2 years/ISO 9002)

"After a certain level, the improvement of the system becomes very difficult. In order for it to be achieved, there has to be an improvement of technological knowledge which is reached only through training."
(324/Greece/pasta, tomato products/336 employees/certification > 2 years/ISO 9002)

There is a growing awareness of the need to satisfy the ever changing customer requirements comes the recognition of the need to be more flexible. The technology has allowed for more flexibility. The Plant

Manager believes that *"flexibility can be designed into manufacturing, thus allowing for a quick response to customers' requirements"*. He proudly admits that *"the plant runs more efficiently and has a quicker changeover time when it is required"*. Also, a wider range of products can be produced with greater variations in formulations. There are no skill shortages. However, the company feel they should be using a teamwork approach. The Plant Manager hold the view that *"it is important to be more flexible; more responsive; able to rework certain products; and to produce a greater variety of formulations"*. This he believes *"comes down to a teamwork approach with staff working together and knowing what the customers requirements are"*. *(423/Ireland/full range of fresh dairy products/246 employees/certification > 2 years/ISO 9002)*

Changes of the external relations

There is a very distinct difference between the surveyed companies as to the extension of their quality management of external customer-supplier- relations.

However, this cannot be interpreted as an index for the state of the development of the individual company's quality system. Because the quality tasks which are to be managed independently by the companies vary depending on the position of the company within the processing and distribution chain, the division of tasks among the companies (outsourcing) and the degree of independence within the company context, the products and the performance penetration. Generally there is a growing sense of responsibility for the entire food-processing chain.

Quality-related new requirements for the execution of quality tasks in the external company relationships arise for skilled staff in purchasing and incoming merchandise particularly in those companies which complement quality agreements with suppliers with a system of mutual information flow and consulting services. The same is true for the specialist staff in marketing and distribution in companies offering as an additional benefit for the customers consulting services for the usage or further processing of the company products and customer-oriented product variations. Apart from a comprehensive know-how about the products and the performance potentials of the company, these employees need to have extensive knowledge of dietetics and process technology as well as management skills in order to integrate the external information and demands into the internal decision-making, planning and implementation.

Particularly the increasing auditing by customer companies has made many interviewed companies aware that from the external customer-supplier relationships new qualification-related requirements arise also for the internal operative staff. Staff have to not only follow the quality instructions for their workplaces but they need to be able to understand and demonstrate their own significance within the quality system of the company and for the customer benefit. Examples of good practice were found in companies which deliberately made an effort to change over from a reactive policy towards the public food monitoring authorities, on the one hand, and the complaints, demands and audits of customers, on the other, to proactively involving these authorities in quality-related training of staff. Some interviewed experts see the crucial advantage of those elements of quality training of staff not only in the know-how input into the company. In comparison with training measures by internal authorities staff get a much more tangible idea of how quality instructions of the company serve the expectations of the customers and the public.

Examples of good practice were also found in the transfer of quality know-how in some companies within holding structures. This happens particularly when an established quality system of a company is transferred and adapted to other companies in the group. In some cases critical comments of interview partners could be registered on the incongruity between the quality demands of the superior organisation units and their support of the quality efforts of the own company.

The co-operation of companies in consulting networks for the implementation of the ISO system, particularly those which have been supported by national and European funds, has proven beneficial to several of the interviewed companies as a communication structure for the exchange of quality knowledge, even after the successful certification. The trust grown in the collaboration and the awareness of the sector's responsibility for the quality of food play a very important role. This is opposed to experiences of some experts that companies which have been contacted without such a basis of trust are very reluctant with information on their quality experiences for competitive reasons.

Case examples and statements

The Quality Control Manager and the Plant manager delivered a programme on product quality, quality control, inspection, and safety. The emphasis throughout all the programmes was on the changing requirements of the customer and the importance of getting ISO for the company. Customers were also invited to deliver an input on some of the training session. *(422/Ireland/butter/49 employees/certification > 2 years/ISO 9002)*

The interviewed managers all agreed on the fact, that the implementation of quality management, had caused new demands on the personnel and in some ways resulted in skill shortages. This was characterised by the lack of understanding on the customer demands at the company. The group of employees that would benefit mostly of training in this regard is the personnel at the production. The strategy for solving the training needs, was to bring staff from production along in the meeting with the customers.... Today the external training with regard to quality management is quite extensive. The strategy at the enterprise is to engage the suppliers of the primary products in some parts of the training. *(624/Sweden/fruit preparations and chocolate products/130 employees/certification > 2 years/ISO 9001)*

The general opinion among the management regarding future training needs is that it is all issues regarding the further training of the management. There are mainly two areas which will be more important than others: 1. The management role of the supervisors and questions regarding how to delegate, 2. Language training, a quality issue for enterprises with export to other markets and organisations with foreign part-ownership. *"Since we are an enterprise with foreign part-ownership we have made a strategic decision; this is to integrate English speaking managers in the management group. The compulsory use of the English language will probably affect the meetings in the beginning, but in the long run we will certainly gain a lot". (623/Sweden/potato chips and other snack products/330 employees/certification > 2 years/ISO 9001)*

Cross-company training of main topics: The holding organises an internal further training system for the staff of all company units each year. The planning of the training contents for certain staff groups is co-ordinated with those who are responsible for the training in the different units. *(124/Germany/roasted ground coffee/70 employees/certification < 2 years/ISO 9002)*

The enterprise has already started the process, of the implementation of environmental quality management. The quality manager is participating as one of ten managers in the country in a national training programme in EMAS. The programme is financed by contribution from NUTEK - The Swedish National Board for Industrial and Technical Development - and the European Community and is part of a total European training programme for quality managers called - Euro Management Environment. Although the specific training given to the quality manger the management agreed unanimously to apply to an external consultant in the process. *(622/Sweden/ice-cream & frozen desserts/91 employees/certification < 2 years/ISO 9001)*

Training issues, areas and methods

Training issues and training areas

It has already been critically commented on that for the formal fulfilment of the ISO requirement of employee training some interviewed companies document training in specialist knowledge and generic knowledge as quality training that, however, this does not always correspond with a true integration of these training measures into a consistent concept of quality-oriented personnel development. This is exemplified by a methodological problem of the following presentation. In the interviewed companies a distinction was, on the one hand, made between quality-related and other occupation-specific and generic skill demands on staff and the respective training measures, and, on the other hand, according to very different criteria varying from company to company, and very often the interviewed experts pointed out that it was a problem to give clear allocations. This could be interpreted in such a way that in these companies these quality elements were not sufficiently identified in their interfaces. On the other hand, this problem is based on the fact that the standards for quality management require quality-related personnel development but that they offer little guidelines for a definition of which measures comply with this requirement. Together with a rather wide-spread opinion among the interviewed experts that the implementation of quality management has improved the organisation of the company processes, yet not reorganised them and has, therefore, not resulted in new job profiles and skill shortages, many interview partners do not attribute the training efforts of their companies to the aim of implementing quality management. On the other hand, it was emphasised that they are also always undertaken to achieve company-specific quality aims.

Specialist training

On average, in the interviewed companies the strong gradation of qualification levels is reproduced in the training programmes for occupational specialist knowledge.

Skilled staff of the laboratories for product design and quality assurance and skilled staff for purchasing and marketing need to continuously update their knowledge of international developments in dietetics, food and process technologies, the guidelines of "good production practice" and "good laboratory practice", legal standards etc. as well as of the sales and above all the purchasing markets first of all related to the specific products and procedures of the own company. The skill needs of these employees increase in companies which practice extended quality agreements with suppliers and consulting services and/or extend their services for the customers. It becomes increasingly significant that specialist staff in purchasing and distribution have, apart from commercial knowledge, the know-how in modern distribution and transport logistics systems including the information-technological basis thereof.

At the operative level specialist knowledge of the product structure and production technology are confined in may cases to the supervisors or foremen. The modernisation of control and process technologies increases the need of companies for higher skilled personnel, but very often specialist maintenance staff are trained for this or recruited.

In the vast majority of the interviewed companies the special handicraft skills, manual and sensory skills have become redundant through usage of modern technology. They are predominantly used for quality assurance of primary products in a partly preventive purchasing strategy and process control.

On the basis of their modern materials flow and process technology most of the companies identify for the majority of the operatives occupation-specific training needs predominately in the fields of hygiene and safety as well as machine and product handling. The occupational-specific training focuses in essence on quality-assuring behaviour and quality-controlling activities such as monitoring, measuring, control and documentation of process and product parameters. Technologically integrated and improved handling of control instruments facilitate the extension of inspection responsibilities of operatives. Increasing elements of self-inspection at the production line require training in handling inspection instruments and inspection methods, in systematic inspection routines and inspection documentation.

Examples of good training practice for operatives can be found particularly in companies deliberately identifying this quality dimension and for that reason do not restrict themselves to mere job instructions. With extended training programmes for quality-oriented process understanding they develop a vocational training approach for the industrial food processing adequate to the technological innovation whereas large parts of the institutionalised vocational training is still strongly oriented towards traditional craft vocational profiles. Rather an exception, however, were companies which are engaged in a better vocational basic training for their operatives and critically analyse their organisation.

Case examples and statements

"Measures and measurement. The pressure comes from the demands of customer satisfaction. All kinds of measurement. To find right ones, that there is reliability and measures should support the management system." (221/Finland/salads, meat products/40 employees/certification < 2 years/ISO 9001)

"On the skilled side - craft, fitters - we are looking to train people through NVQ to establish skills within their tasks. On the engineering side, we need HND/HNC as a pre-requisite. On the factory floor, we take people with all sorts of qualifications or none and train them as we consider appropriate. One thing that has changed is that anyone coming in to a managerial or team leader position has to have computer skills. Everything we do is now based on the computer. We used to have a few people who were computer specialists but now everyone has to be capable on them." (725/United Kingdom/peanut butter, gales honey, tablet jelly/300 employees/certification > 2 years/ISO 9002)

"The company needs future training in technology related to products that it produces. During the training, informing must be provided about all the last progresses in its branch and simultaneously about matters of hygiene, cleanness and new tools for the keeping up of the Quality System. Those issues concern all the production personnel. Training is needed not just for the person who makes salami but also for the one who controls it and the one who takes care of the hygiene standards." (325/Greece/cooked pork meat/226 employees/certification < 2 years/ISO 9001/2)

"ISO gives you a structure, but it does not cover the full story – particularly from the production perspective. While there are procedures in place some of the work is instinctual, it is based on know-how and experience and sometimes is difficult to quantify." (421/Ireland/animal feeds/39-44 employees/certification > 2 years/ISO 9001/2)

"The making of beer is a craftsmanship that should be based on proven knowledge and not a large scale industrial point of view which in the end becomes an artificial product." (625/Sweden/soft drinks, beer, mineral water/100 employees/certification > 2 years/ISO 9001)

Before the introduction of quality assurance procedures, production workers and packers 'just did their jobs mechanically'. Now it is thought that if they have more knowledge of the processes and products, their job performance will benefit: *"It's highlighted the training need to upskill the general operator/packer - to give them the knowledge to do the job properly. They will know more about it - they'll know why you boil sugar at such and such a temperature and not at another temperature."* Training in health and safety is another important issue in a factory such as this where the components for the products are processed at very high temperatures and, again, this has now been targeted as an area where more training is needed. Having a greater general knowledge of the composition and production of the products would, it is felt, improve the feeling of 'ownership' and responsibility for products which the company is keen to foster.   This is seen as essential to instil the feeling that quality management is everybody's concern.   The NVQs (National Vocational Qualification) which are being taken by everybody will, it is hoped, help to address this issue. The intention is to ensure that all employees will have achieved at least an NVQ level 1 by the end of this year: *"What we are doing at the moment means that everybody in the factory will have Level One NVQ by the end of the year and the key process operators - a lot of those will have Level Two by the end of the year and some will go on to Level Three. Some of the supervisors/managers are also doing Level Three and Four NVQs at the same time. We started looking at NVQs in September 96 and putting them together. Last year we got about 50 people through Level One and we were preparing for Level Two and that was doing it with part-time assessors. Now this year we've got 3 full-time assessors (and five part-time assessors) to take Level One through to everybody throughout the company by the end of the year. And they look like they will probably achieve that target. It's a tough target. It'll keep them busy! And Level Two's have started as well this year." (722/United Kingdom/children's sugar confectionery/610 employees/certification > 2 years/ISO 9002)*

"Every employee has an opportunity to take one-year programme at vocational school. There is quality knowledge integrated in vocational knowledge. We   are   supporting   the   vocational   development." (221/Finland/salads,   meat   products/40   employees/certification   <   2 years/ISO 9001)

Cross-occupational training

In most of the interviewed companies there is an awareness that for the internal implementation of quality management the collaboration of the departments of the company is crucial. The buzz-word of "internal customer-supplier-relations" is rather common.

Critical points and/or weak points of the quality management of their companies to be overcome were identified by the interviewed managers mostly in the communication and collaboration between the departments first of all at the management level. This is very often not only about quality but also about time and cost targets. This applied particularly to

• efficient collaboration between the superior and subordinate organisation units

- information flow and decision-making between the different quality aims of marketing - customer-oriented flexibility - and production - possibly continuos utilisation of possibly stable processes - including cost estimations.

- efficient co-ordination of different product lines with varied requirements of up- and down-stream departments

- harmonisation of commercial requirements with quality specifications and product requirements.

The companies first look for solutions in reorganisations of structures and methods of management. On average, the interviewed companies identify a main emphasis of their training needs in the qualification of the management in methods and techniques of teamwork and project management. This is very often in connection with training in interpersonal behaviour and personal leading patterns. Training of management personnel in integrated information technologies and company-specific software becomes more and more important.

At the operative level, sector-typical decisive quality tasks of staff are cross-occupational: i.e. hygiene and safety, handling and marking of primary, intermediate and final products in the internal transport. Quality inspections and documentation at the production line serve as job requirements for the up and downstream functions and for the control of the overall process. Most of the companies see solutions first in modern technological solutions for the flow processes and for the information flow as well as in reliably documented job instructions. On this basis, training of operatives is limited in several cases obviously to the instruction in the workplace-specific routines. As regards the implementation of new information technologies, the internal cross-departmental training of staff has so far been restricted very often to the immediate acquisition of strictly user-oriented computer knowledge.

Examples of good practice can be found in companies

- de-formalising the training in the routine tasks and imparting an understanding of their cross-departmental quality significance within the overall process, for example within the framework of training in the company's overall quality management.

- supporting cross-departmental groups for dealing with concrete problems in the internal customer-supplier-relations which also have an influence in the planning of the employee training.

Case examples and statements

"There will always be commercial decisions that are taken out of our hands. If a customer is screaming for an order, there's a big fine for not delivering on time - this sort of thing. Then occasionally what we would

feel is a sub-standard product may get through but it might be that the customer has agreed to take it. And on those instances we do try and explain to the staff why we still let something go because there's nothing worse than somebody spotting something and for us to say 'well, no actually I'm going to let that go'. There's always the chance that they'll think 'well, they sent that last time, I'll not tell them again'. So we try and explain why we do something if we do have to let it go and let them understand the reason behind it rather than just say, you know, let it go. Sometimes that decision's taken out of their hands." (724/United Kingdom/edible cake decorations, sugar and chocolate confectionery, popcorn/160 employees/certification > 2 years/ ISO 9002)

"The instance already mentioned of a greater interconnection between Maintenance and Production is a typical example of a growing functional interconnection. On the other hand, a great effort is presently being made in order to train all employees engaged in the introduction of the HACCP (Hazard Analysis Critical Control Point) system and provide the company with a methodology for the process study and analysis, as well as with preventive and corrective steps. A professional training plan is also in course, meant for the industrial maintenance area and quality audits." (521/Portugal/milk products/281 employees/certification > 2 years/ISO 9002)

"Example internal customer-supplier relations: There is this catch phrase in the management handbook: Don't hand on trash, don't accept trash. This i.e. applies to the supplier: product design. Without good specifications the product cannot be processes in such a way that we can achieve our aim - quick solutions for the customer. This is understood by everybody at the line." (125/Germany/frozen products/688 employees/certification < 2 years/ ISO 9001)

"As a result of the changes, operatives have to be computer literate. Also the new technology allows for each operator's activities to be tracked, particularly as the plant works a 24 hour shift and in peak season 7 days a week." (421/Ireland/animal feeds/39-44 employees/certification > 2 years/ ISO 9001/2)

Current main training topics are inspection techniques, cross-departmental knowledge of processes and safety issues. *"Training here with us is not just mere imparting of facts but more of an exchange. If you sit together you may as well gather and exchange everybody's know-how. An important multiplication platform are the CIP groups." (121/Germany/spices, spice mixtures/160 employees/certification > 2 years/ISO 9001)*

Training of quality system knowledge

The demand of the ISO standard for quality training of staff is understood in most of the surveyed companies as the challenge to make all members of staff understand the system of quality production of the company. The companies could be classified according to their practical training efforts to this end as those which cover this task merely formally by presenting the ISO system to the staff and those which instruct staff into workplace-related quality elements without any further reference to the system.

A closer analysis of many statements of the interviewed experts right across the companies shows, however, that almost all companies see themselves faced with a problem they so far have found only rudimentary solutions for:

- The management theory and/or the management philosophy behind quality systems is expert knowledge and is not congruent in its totality with the company-specific quality aims which are organised in the quality system of the own company.

- The latter is true particularly for the formal organisation methodology such as the elements structure of the ISO system but also for company-specific organigrams representing responsibilities and ways but also do so only formally.

- Quality aims of the company represent a company-specific orientation and can be expressed in terse terms but as general company aims they are no concrete orientation for action.

- The workplace-related procedure and job instructions contain only very narrow, operationalised references for an orientation within the overall system.

In this perspective most of the interviewed companies are struggling with a "gap" and are experimenting in their quality training with solutions for the following question:

> In how far does training in quality management and the quality policy of the company support the training of staff in detailed quality tasks of their specific work area, in how far, the other way round, does specialist workplace-related quality training underpin the understanding of staff for the quality system throughout the company and promote the commitment of staff to maintain it and support the improvement aims of the quality policy?

On the other hand, it was obvious that especially in the food industry training in the system or in elements of the system of quality management of the company covers essential parts of personnel qualifications and thus the training of operatives as such. This is based on the fact that in the sector-specific mass production operative job requirements and respective skill profiles remain relatively stable for a long time. Strongly varying requirements assuming a potential of differentiated special qualifications of operative staff are rather rare even if the need is increasing with a more flexible deployment of operatives. In most of the SMEs of the food industry there is a tendency that quality documents are at the same time personnel instruments.

• Many companies organise the settling-in of new employees as a quality training and combine at least the instruction in the company regulations and the workplace with an instruction in the quality system and the workplace-specific quality instructions.

• The instruction of staff in new tasks arising from product changes or procedure changes frequently coincides to a large extend with the instruction in changes in procedure and job instructions of the quality system.

This is in keeping with the finding of the survey as regards the vocational training efforts of the interviewed companies. On the basis of modern material flow and process technologies, vocational specialist knowledge essentially concentrates on quality-assuring behaviour and quality controlling activities such as monitoring, measuring, control and documentation of process and product parameters, technologically integrated control instruments extending the self-inspection responsibilities of operatives. This vocational profile of operatives in the industrial food processing increasingly replaces, at least at this level, the product-oriented craftsmanship.

Significant differences between the surveyed companies can be found, however, in how strategically they identify the system knowledge of their staff. Ambitious long-term planning for the qualification of staff to active supporters of the improvement of the system - partly oriented towards the milestones of the quality policy of the companies - contrast with rather narrow workplace-related instructions in the quality documents. In some companies there was also a contrast between the system orientation of staff training for the implementation of the ISO system and the practising and up-dating training after a successful certification. The required extent of such a training need is not to be underestimated. Occasionally critical statements of the interviewed managers on the frequent need and the unexpected lengthiness of such a training indicate also shortcomings of the training concept. The necessary comprehensive system knowledge, the awareness of the cross-functional relevance of the "own" quality elements is neglected for the practising training of workplace-specific elements and routines. For example, self-responsible techniques of quality inspection and documentation - the "what", "when", "how" - require the awareness of the why and for whom, the marking and documentation tasks get their intrinsic motivation only in their orientation towards the "why" and "for whom".

The survey on the training efforts of the interviewed companies which explicitly serve the maintenance and extension of the quality system leads to a second finding about the sector-specific effects of quality management on vocational and skill profiles. Several companies train internal auditors. The expert interviews at least suggest the hypothesis that with these internal auditors a new type of specially qualified skilled staff develops in the food industry. System control and problem identification and solution in co-operation with staff seems to increasingly replace traditional supervisor tasks such as monitoring output and work.

Case examples and statements

"You cannot expect employees to take on new demands without explaining to them why they are needed" (424/Ireland/full range of milk products/343 employees/certification < 2 years/ISO 9002)

"An important issue for quality-related training is ensuring that employees ask of the product they produce or pack 'would I buy it if I were the consumer?'" (724/United Kingdom/edible cake decorations, sugar and chocolate confectionery, popcorn/160 employees/certification > 2 years/ISO 9002)

"Most of the people don't understand the overall system. If you ask them about the quality policy, they'll recite the company rules." (123/Germany/egg products/100 employees/certification < 2 years/ISO 9002)

Initially, there was great difficulty getting staff to accept ISO. It was easier at a management level to change procedures. It was much more difficult to do this at the operative level. *"When you get down to the second level of ISO documentation i.e. work procedures, and operating procedures it is difficult to inform and train staff in recognising the need to change. They found it difficult to accept why the change was required i.e. customer driven. Staff had to go through a process of retraining on product quality, quality control in general, and safety. It had to be explained that the consumer had changing requirements. It was a slow process. All management levels were involved in the development of ISO. Delegation of tasks took place. Two days information training sessions were set up at the start. Delivery was provided by the Quality Control manager and the Production staff. Customers were invited to give an input on these sessions. These sessions were conducted during the off season period from November to January. This training programme was supplement with a*

follow-up one day training session.   Quality management and new developments were discussed,   and any changes to the business."
(422/Ireland/butter/49 employees/certification > 2 years/ISO 9002)

"The training of the personnel on issues that concern quality takes place every six months in groups consisting of 4 or 5 employees. After the end of the training period a testing procedure takes place in order to show how capable of those issues the employee has become...." During the last two years the company has covered the basic issues of training employees. All the employees should be trained in the future on issues such as: new techniques in quality control, deep knowledge of quality problems faced by all the departments of the company (purchasing, production). The employees of the company should have an overall view of the implementation of the Quality Assurance system in all the departments of the company. That would help them to fully understand the meaning of Quality. *(322/Greece/toast/258 employees/certification > 2 years/ISO 9002)*

"Training is always on-going for all staff as different aspects of quality management 'are rolled out'. Training might be needed to cover new weight control networks, on-line product testing and auditor training."
(725/United Kingdom/peanut butter, gales honey, tablet jelly/300 employees/certification > 2 years/ISO 9002)

The company puts particular emphasis on the training of internal auditors. During the introduction training for the ISO system especially good and committed people were called into the team of internal auditors. Auditor training - with external support was carried out with them. A team of 10 internal auditors came out of this involving a steering group of three at management level. It is particularly for these employees that training must take   into   account   the   constantly   changing   requirements.
(124/Germany/roasted ground coffee/70 employees/certification < 2 years/ISO 9002)

Training of process competence

The relatively young quality management theory to develop not only product but also process-oriented quality awareness meets with the approval of a striking number of experts in SMEs of the food industry. This is based on sector-specifics.

• The achieved - increasingly technology based - networking of all business and management processes also in the surveyed SMEs makes the organisational optimisation of theses processes the centrepiece of the efforts to improve the results. Achieving market- and customer-oriented quality aims - availability and freshness, quick response in the market to new customer demands and consumer wishes - as well as achieving economic aims - cutting cost for manufacturing supplies, transport, storage etc. which itself has effects on the product and environmental quality - lead to process optimisation.

- At the operative level of the performance process the integration and automation of the materials flow, processing and inspection processes brings about that process monitoring becomes the main work task and process competency becomes the decisive qualification of staff. A reliable quality assurance of the raw material assumed, process quality and stability are decisive in the internal performance process, product nonconformities increasingly result from process nonconformities.

- Consumers and the general public increasingly define product and company quality as the proved responsibility for all process steps within the entire food chain.

Companies respond to this with continuously seeking to improve processes, identifying more or less staff and their qualifications as human resource involving them more or less systematically into the continuos improvement process.

Training measures in those interviewed companies which - relying on the technologically assured process quality - focus on training staff in hygiene and safety as well as in the correct handling of the equipment and fulfilment of the documented job instructions are to be assessed as rather restrictive. But already in this field those companies show examples of good practice

- demonstrating formal hygiene requirements in their relevance to critical points of the food processing and ensuring the specialist and product knowledge which is required for the understanding of this relevance

- demonstrating formal safety requirements in the broader context of work, process and product safety and ensuring the knowledge on the process technology which is required for the understanding of this context

- substantiating instructions for the equipment handling by sufficient understanding of the process technology and the critical product specifications in the processing. (Companies get sensitised to the fact that this sometimes requires rather extensive knowledge by experiences that product nonconformities identified by staff with insufficient understanding of the process technology lead to very costly incorrect interventions or to unreliably documented corrective action of process parameters or that an insufficient understanding of critical product specifications lead to far-reaching nonconformities in the manufacturing process, for example at cleaning or adjusting of the equipment.)

- directing training measures and contents with improvement aims of the company, opening up training in the direction of problem-related improvement discussions and feeding back the results of such discussions into the planning of training.

Training of specialist and generic knowledge as well as of quality knowledge, on the one hand, are the basis for process competency; on the other hand, these training programmes can be opened up towards an internal improvement process.

Those companies in the sample striving within a more comprehensive understanding for the training aim of process awareness and improvement competency of staff do not pursue this aim, at least not exclusively, through training but in independent organisation forms of a more or less continuos and systematic internal improvement process.

- In some companies quality management has initiated the revival and extensive establishment of a traditional internal suggestion system.

- Working groups for the development and implementation of the ISO system continue with new tasks as CIP groups very often particularly to de-bureaucratise and make the quality system efficient in practice.

- Teams for the ongoing tackling of current quality management tasks get the competency to develop improvement suggestions for the processes of their work area apart from case-related quality decisions.

In these approaches the development of company-specific process competency and its implementation into company-specific improvement of processes and the quality system are combined in these companies.

Case examples and statements

"At a basic level - i.e. operatives and packers - a greater knowledge of processes and production methods is needed." Having a greater general knowledge of the composition and production of the products would, it is felt, improve the feeling of 'ownership' and responsibility for products which the company is keen to foster. This is seen as essential to instil the feeling that quality management is everybody's concern. *(722/United Kingdom/children's sugar confectionery/610 employees/certification > 2 years/ISO 9002)*

"The production staff must understand the feed formulation. They must know the negative consequences if this is not done. The operatives must understand why certain mixes of feed causes problems in animals i.e. Pigs, cows - monogastrics or ruminants. They must understand the need for hygiene and safety, as they are dealing with products that go into the

*human   food   chain."   (421/Ireland/animal   feeds/39-44
employees/certification > 2 years/ISO 9001/2)*

The staff also became more aware of the importance of customer
requirements. They began to realise the significance of their responsibility
towards their jobs as what they did was part of the human food chain.
*(423/Ireland/full range of fresh dairy products/246 employees/certification
> 2 years/ISO 9002)*

*"It is a major mistake on the part of management to assume that their staff
understand the business in which the company operates. Therefore,
training should take place, even at a basis level of explaining the
company's business and the markets in which it operates."
(424/Ireland/full range of milk products/343 employees/certification < 2
years/ISO 9002)*

Currently, a major project is underway involving all staff. The objective is
to revisit the standards and procedures in operation with a view to
improving them. This task involves splitting staff into small groups,
comprising of management, supervisors, and staff within each of the
functional areas. A certain number of staff have been trained in facilitation
and presentation skills. It is their role to lead the group. Areas for
improvement are being identified and recommendation put forward. These
are then discussed at the management level to discuss the cost/benefits and
to establish the areas which are to be affected. Before any change is
implemented all staff are notified by their managers. *(424/Ireland/full
range of milk products/343 employees/certification < 2 years/ISO 9002)*

Training of social competencies

A large number of the interviewed managers concedes in open conversation that
social key qualifications such as the capability to communicate, the capability to
learn, team capability, responsibility, problem-solving competency and capability
to make decisions are crucial in the implementation of quality management and
considers training measures for the achievement of a high degree of fulfilment as
absolutely necessary.

In many interviewed companies these issues are a main subject particularly of
external training of staff. Target groups are above all

• the senior management in business-administrative, planning-developing,
  personnel-and quality-managerial functions

- the middle management

In the new methods of working of the senior management itself which are more strictly geared to principles of a cross-functional project management, the reorganisation of business processes makes social key qualifications an essential cross-functional qualification of managers along with their normally existing and continuously up-dated specialist qualification. Significantly less wide-spread was the opinion among the interviewed experts, that especially quality management requires these social competencies of leading staff also in the implementation of decisions of the leading management in the company and in personnel leading. This was recognised in some companies during the implementation of the ISO system in the task to convince employees and the employees representation of the sense and benefit of quality management. Example of good practice was found in companies where the "responsibility of the leadership" was defined as an internal customer relationship, the tasks of the customer comprising an examination on whether the orders were executable by the internal suppliers and preventive assurance of the necessary implementation conditions as regards material and personnel.

At the middle management level the interviewed experts very often identified barriers for the implementation of quality management in a lack of social key qualifications. This was particularly true for supervisors advanced from the production line with partly very high specialist qualification who were to take over the extended tasks of up-stream quality assurance and especially the respective personnel development. It turned out to be problematic to delegate, with very little precautions for the personnel development at the company level, the responsibility for the identification of training needs of staff to supervisors at the line without being aware of the demanding nature of this tasks and without providing sufficient know-how about management of human resources for appointed staff. An important outcome of the expert interviews seems to be the experience of some interview partners that especially at this level of middle management, prior to learning quality-promoting social skills, "dis-learning" of old established instruction-execution and monitoring-execution behaviour patterns has to take place, which would otherwise be a barrier. Hierarchy-based instructional behaviour patterns devalue specialist authority and hinder staff bringing in their competencies co-operatively for the identification and solution of quality problems; due to the old division between monitoring and execution under reorganised responsibilities the paralysing confusion between the self-responsibility of staff for the identification, documentation and elimination of nonconformities with personal liability lives on. Examples of good practice can be found in companies

- deliberately focusing training of the middle management on redefining its responsibility from the handicraft-technical specialist to the multiplier of the internal quality knowledge and to the moderator of quality competency of staff

- integrating this social qualification dimension right from the start into the training of new specialist staff for the quality management such as internal auditors.

This survey critically assesses the frequent emphasis on the social key competencies of operatives by many interviewed managers. Focusing the aim of quality-promoting personnel development on social key qualifications of staff does not seldom arise from the wish for a passe-partout replacing the company's expenditure for the training of staff as the supporters of the quality systems and the improvement process. A critical analysis is particularly appropriate when above all "the daily routine in the company", "by work", "ongoing training" etc. are indicated as the company-specific training methods of social key qualifications and when the modern technological provision for the quality assurance and clear-cut job instructions are pointed out. On the one hand, it is true that social skills develop only within a practical social context. But, on the other hand, the intended results of quality-oriented collaboration, problem awareness and improvement responsibility of staff cannot be achieved without expenditures of the company for the development of the required skills supposedly automatically resulting from the ongoing work routine in the performance process.

From examples of good practice, the necessary interplay of the following factors can be pointed out:

1. "Social competencies" of staff are a prerequisite in order to establish a company-specific quality system with the support of staff in order to carry out the necessary learning and dissemination processes among the staff and to implement the new quality knowledge into the everyday work routine.

2. At the same time, without the imparting of operationalised and understandable quality aims of the company, of all quality-related knowledge elements, particularly about the critical characteristics of the product and the process technology, appeals to "staff motivation" and "self-responsibility", "quality awareness" and "team spirit", "problem awareness" and "capability to handle conflicts" remain without substance.

3. Social key qualifications require their integration into institutionalised information and organisation channels of the company in which they can actually be "filled with life".

Case examples and statements

"Changes have to take place at management and supervisory level first, and then the rest should follow". (423/Ireland/full range of fresh dairy products/246 employees/certification > 2 years/ISO 9002)

"... there is a 'deficit' on professional training of the intermediate management in the areas of organisation, attitude and behaviour ..." *(521/Portugal/milk products/281 employees/certification > 2 years/ISO 9002)*

"The executives of today have different tasks than they use to have. Today they are moderator and coach. If you have the responsibility for staff it is also your duty to ensure training. Also to the personnel department! This falls under our broad understanding of "responsibility of the management". Supervisors are then also in charge of controlling the employee training. People who have personnel responsibility need to be trained in conflict management, in moderating techniques. These are current training issues." *(125/Germany/frozen products/688 employees/certification < 2 years/ISO 9001)*

"As to quality issues, the most important one is that the internal inspectors be trained so that they can behave properly and are not able to abuse the authority they have." *(323/Greece/puff pastry, strudel leaves, frozen vegetable, pizza/231 employees/aspiring certification/ISO 9001)*

More training needs to be undertaken for management. The company are now embarking on a personal development programme for font line managers. This will involve teamwork approaches, and facilitation skills. This will be done on-site using external providers. *"Changes have to take place at management and supervisory level first, and then the rest should follow".* *(423/Ireland/full range of fresh dairy products/246 employees/certification > 2 years/ISO 9002)*

"There is a 'Management of Self' and 'Management of Others' programme." This programme is delivered off-site, over a two/three year day period, for managers, supervisors and skilled workers. This programme is delivered by external consultants who were given a specific brief to make it relevant to the company's operations. *(425/Ireland/canning of food and vegetables, beverages, packing dry pulses/295 employees/aspiring certification/ISO 9002)*

"One of the most important aspects to take into consideration is certainly the interpersonal relationship, concerning the daily problems, in particular, for which the 'bosses', regardless their position in the

company's hierarchy, should be the main responsible, since I think that the direct leadership is one oft he best tools of the human resources management. From this derives the importance that, in my opinion, should be given to this kind of training." (522/Portugal/milk/ 406 employees/aspiring certification/certification > 2 years/ISO 9002)

"There are many different areas where professional training could fall upon, but I would like to emphasise:

- *Motivation of the senior staff*

- *Transmission of the company's culture*

- *Acquisition at the internal and external levels of the know-how to supply quality products and to allow increasing the global worth of people*

- *Categories management*

- *Participatory management" (523/Portugal/coffee/ 297 employees/ certification < 2 years/ISO 9002)*

"Management and Supervisors are undergoing training with external training providers. After each training session, a meeting is held to review the quality of training. The facilitators' brief is to help staff improve communications; to understand customers' requirements – both internally and externally; to establish what needs to be done in order to meet these requirements; and to move towards a cultural change. Each manager is charged with the responsibility for ensuring their staff are trained. The Personnel section expects each manager to maximise the amount of time and money they spend on training. Some sections assign four mornings a week, consisting of three hours as part of the continuous improvement process." (424/Ireland/full range of milk products/343 employees/ certification < 2 years/ISO 9002)

Training methods and training conditions

On average, also in the organisation of the training and with a view to the training methods, the strict division between the commercial, managerial and planning functions, on the one hand, and the operative-productive functions, on the other hand, as well as the strong gradation of qualification levels of staff of these two functional areas are reproduced in the surveyed companies.

Formalised training schemes separated from the work are mostly left to the management and the specialist staff of the laboratory area. This group of personnel is also the main target group when companies utilise external training provision or organise internal training programmes with external training bodies and consultants. This is at least true for formalised training programmes within the framework of an ongoing more or less strategically planned training policy of the companies.

For the majority of the operatives of the interviewed companies, training is carried out mostly internally.

On average, formalised training schemes for the operative personnel detached from work is limited to

- retraining in hygiene and safety according to legal regulations and for the preparation of external audits in the ISO routine
- settling-in new regular and seasonal personnel
- rather unique training campaigns i.e. for the implementation of a quality system, within the framework of a reorientation of the company e.g. with company co-operations and combinations.

Operatives receive ongoing training in the sense of a personnel development through further training mostly

- close to the workplace and
- directly related to the job

The statements of many interviewed experts indicate the decisive reasons of the companies:

Training

- needs to justify itself in the face of the limited resources of time and money
- is to be company-specific and of direct benefit to the company.

The pressures of competition and costs in the European food industry define the framework conditions for employee training in the interviewed companies. Several of the interviewed managers concede that under cost pressures expenditures for employee training are first of all treated as "the first victim of a cost cutting exercise". The efforts of companies to fully utilise their plants which have been modernised with sometimes considerable investments limits free periods for training. This tendency also counteracts the practice of SMEs of the food industry with seasonally varying orders to place training programmes into the low-season. In addition, the interest of many companies in flexibly employable staff leads, on the one hand, to the identification of a broader qualification and training needs, but at the same time, the more flexible employment of staff limits the times for training of at least larger groups of staff.

The majority of the interviewed companies seek the solution of these goal conflicts in an internal and workplace-related organisation of the training of operatives or in the external recruitment of more highly qualified personnel. A critical comment in this context is to be made that interviewed experts supporting an improved public basic vocational training were exceptions to the rule.

In-company training methods and training conditions

The expert interviews showed that the implementation of quality management does not only demand employee training as a merely formal requirement. A growing internal awareness for the need and the benefit of quality-oriented training efforts was obvious. The translation of this awareness into the establishment of an internal training system is still either in its beginnings or in the stage of experiment in all interviewed companies. This is proved by the following tendencies:

Ongoing further training and particularly initiatives of a more strategic personnel development have so far been reserved mostly for specialist and managerial staff. The identified main subjects, however, indicate a changing tendency. Particularly the modern management qualification acknowledged by the companies as being necessary contain elements qualifying the specialist and managerial staff as organisers of internal learning processes and disseminators of company know-how. According to the findings of this survey, the practical implementation of this management know-how is however limited mostly to the work methods of the management level itself. At this level internal know-how transfer and learning processes take the form of internal training and working in project teams. The task of a broader personnel promotion is - if at all - delegated to the middle management and has rarely been supported by a continuing personnel development strategy and organisation of the companies so far.

At the operative level the internal training efforts need to be improved particularly with a view to a long-term personnel development policy. Restrictive planning of time and resources seem to be the decisive reason in the choice of work-integrated or work-related methods. The interviewed experts showed only a rudimentary problem awareness of the conflicts between the rather restrictive budgeting of the training efforts as a practical guideline and the frequently mentioned demanding aims of the implementation of quality management and the continuous improvement of self-responsible staff.

Internal programmes of employee training at the operative level are on average restricted to

- training on recruitment for regular and seasonal staff
- (re)training in hygiene and safety according to legal regulations and for the preparation of external audits in the ISO routine

- rather singular training campaigns i.e. for the implementation of a quality system, within the framework of a reorientation of the company for example in company corporations and combinations etc..

On the other hand, the findings of this survey suggest that in the food industry the implementation of quality management as such has a certain personnel developing effect. In comparison with personal job instructions by supervisors, the documented procedure and job instructions represent more extensively the work steps within a comprehensible wider context. For that reason, the understanding of the documented procedure and job instructions covers at least those vocational qualifications which are directly required by the workplace. The risks of a personnel policy of companies, which for that reason regard personnel development as unnecessary have already been described. On the other hand, observations in the expert interviews prove that good quality documents with an assured understanding of staff allow new forms of a combination between work and learning in the companies. This is not only the basis for

- especially institutionalised quality circles of CIP groups

which in addressing current quality issues are learning at the same time. Several interviewed experts pointed out that on this basis

- permanent co-ordination groups of the direct performance organisation

can operate as learning groups beyond their immediate technical organisational tasks.

Case examples and statements

"Most of the training is organised by our own staff. Every person gets familiar with his or her work through guiding and tutoring. That way we guarantee the multidiciplinary skills, to work in many occupations. Also we are using rotation. We have trained 15 employees to be trainers. They have responsibility to train all personnel to get familiar with our practices." (221/Finland/salads, meat products/40 employees/certification < 2 years/ISO 9001)

"As a result of the recent BSE scare and the superlevy, production in the company is down by 25%. Training is always the first victim of a cost cutting exercise." (421/Ireland/animal feeds/39-44 employees/certification > 2 years/ISO 9001/2)

Providing training for all staff is not seen an easy task. There are high cost implications i.e. having to replace people during the training period. *"The company cannot shut down business (milk) to carry out training. It has to be delivered on a continuous basis."* This delivery takes place in short, sharp sessions on a regular basis, for a period of a half an hour to an hour. This allows for a particular line only to be shut down while this training is provided. Through overtime the company are able to make up for the down time. Where two to three days off-the-job training is required (first aid, fort lift truck driving) the company employ people from a panel. *(424/Ireland/full range of milk products/343 employees/certification < 2 years/ISO 9002)*

"Initially the company tried to incorporate the process of quality training in the way that the company handled the planning of the production training. The basic problem was and still is the lack of time since the employees are called to be trained on areas that are out of their everyday duties, at the time of their work. Therefore the training mainly took place outside working hours." Training basically takes place out of working hours in the form of internal or external seminars. Training suggestions are mainly made by the managers of the departments. The technological changes created the need for training of the personnel, since new employees were hired in a factory where new machines were introduced. The new employees follow a basic training, whereas on quality issues they are trained afterwards. *(324/Greece/pasta, tomato products/336 employees/certification > 2 years/ISO 9002)*

"Our big problem with training needs is getting it engineered - that is the problem on this site. It's not identifying what people need - we've got succession plans, appropriate people have got training needs plans - it's getting it done that's the problem. Both financially and time-wise. One of the first things that gets cut is training." (723/United Kingdom/infant and dietetic foods/280 employees/certification > 2 years/ISO 9002)

"We've still got a long way to go on training. We do struggle with lack of space or somewhere to do it. And just the nature of the business does mean that it's hard to take people away from the shopfloor to give them any training." (724/United Kingdom/edible cake decorations, sugar and chocolate confectionery, popcorn/160 employees/certification > 2 years/ISO 9002)

Quality management leaders were appointed from the staff. Training was delivered by external providers. They received additional training over a two day period. These leaders have formed quality teams which come together from time to time to discuss relevant quality issues. A company-wide survey was recently conducted to identify if staff required further training. The results of this are being co-ordinated by the Training Officer and will be analysed by the Training officer and the quality teams in conjunction with the relevant managers. From this it is hoped that a training plan for further training will be identified. *(422/Ireland/butter/49 employees/certification > 2 years/ISO 9002)*

"Staff cannot be expected to change to a new way of working without providing proper training and support. To do this there has to be ongoing training. A member of the management team has the responsibility of co-ordinating training at the plant. With his help and that of the Quality Manager and the plant manager, small groups of workers (nine to ten) are being brought together for further training. The focus of this training will be work responsibility and teamwork." (423/Ireland/full range of fresh dairy products/246 employees/certification > 2 years/ISO 9002)

External training

Specifically for the achievement of quality aims in the wider sense and closer to the implementation and improvement of their quality system, the majority of the interviewed companies resorts to external training provisions.

In those cases where the companies explicitly and in a systematic way use external training for their need or organise internal training schemes with external training providers and consultants, managerial and specialist staff of the laboratory area are the main target group. External training of operatives focuses on cases of specialist qualifications requiring certification or it is based on the support of individual interest in further training of staff.

Main subjects of the, in the broader sense, quality-oriented external further training of managerial and specialist staff are:

- market and marketing knowledge for the improvement of the customer orientation
- management and personality training for the reorganisation of the work methods of the management
- developments in dietetics, the food and process technologies, the guidelines for "good production practice" and "good laboratory practice", legal standards.

The input of external quality knowledge in the narrow sense, of quality systems and quality techniques, quality assurance systems such as HACCP and of environmental management systems into the companies results from

- recruitment of externally trained quality managers
- external training of managerial staff as quality managers and auditors

- seeking the support of external consultants.

The interviewed companies are predominately satisfied with the external provision of general know-how for managerial staff about quality systems, especially about the ISO system as regards the availability, contents and the cost-benefit ratio. The wave of ISO certification has created the provision and frequently the certification bodies are involved in the provision of quality management training.

Significantly often the interviewed managers criticised the external training programmes for a

- lack of sector-, procedure- and product-specific implementation knowledge of quality management as a support for company-specific improvement programmes,

- lack of external training support for a sector-, procedure- and product-specific adaptation of modern quality methods, techniques and technologies,

- lack of quality-related sector, procedure and product knowledge as such.

These points of criticism have been indicated in companies of all European partner countries participating in this survey. Country-specific reasons seem to play a role in the degree of the dissatisfaction with the abstractness of the externally provided quality management knowledge as well as in the extending the criticism to the public vocational training. Regional factors play a role in companies located in rural areas while training providers are located mostly in urban centres. Most explicit, however, was the criticism of small companies which consider the task to develop a tailor-made company-specific training programme together with external training providers and consultants to be too big.

Many interviewed companies use or at least expect concrete quality knowledge particularly from sectoral organisations, supplier companies - above all from suppliers of laboratory and process technology - and from partner companies, especially those abroad. An example of good practice are training networks among companies resulting from the co-operation in consulting networks for the implementation of the ISO system, among them particularly those which had been supported by national or European funds. Examples of good practice can also be found in companies deliberately changing over from a reactive policy towards the public food monitoring authorities and towards complaints, demands and audits of customers to a proactive involvement of these instances for the quality-related qualification of staff.

The direct involvement of operatives into the quality training using external know-how could be found particularly in the latter cases. This was normally based on a conscious methodological decision of the company: External trainers i.e. for hygiene and safety issues, for example from the public food monitoring authorities, represent for staff an authority based on specialist knowledge as opposed to hierarchical authority, the same is true for representatives of supplier and customer companies as trainers.

Case examples and statements

"A lot is no help for self-help. Examples from the practice of other companies are good." (124/Germany/roasted ground coffee/70 employees/certification < 2 years/ISO 9002)

"It is not easy to find training suitable for us. There is no material addressed to our needs to this particular production we have. Convenience food branch is quite new." (221/Finland/salads, meat products/40 employees/certification < 2 years/ISO 9001)

"Most of the consultants have an –ism that they promote. They have no ability and they are not willing to make synthesis of different managerial approaches and apply them to acute situation of the organisation. The training situations give an header to different ideas or substance but they can't teach anything. The institutions that give training make markets to consultants." (222/Finland/ice-cream/250 employees/certification > 2 years/ ISO 9001)

It is explicitly pointed out that external further training programmes do not address the specific problems of the food industry. The big providers, especially those from the sector of the certification institutions, still impart the implementation of quality management mainly on the basis of technically clear and stable processes in the metalworking and chemical industries. *"External provisions as regards quality management topics for the food industry are rather scarce. Most training programmes are oriented to the automobile and plastics sectors."* Not enough implementation knowledge is provided for processes in the food industry which cannot be as technically schematised. Experiences of food-processing companies with the implementation and the effects of quality management would be useful. There is also a need for food-specific inspection and statistic methods. Standard procedures are not suitable for natural products. *"Know-how for the sector-related handling of personnel development and training would be also necessary. How do you deal best with the wide range of personnel qualifications, how do you identify reliably personnel development needs?"* One reason for the under-representation of the food industry in the topics of the external training programmes: *"The sector association is too small to meet the sector-specific needs through self-organised further training and not strong*

*enough to have an influence on existing training providers."
(121/Germany/spices, spice mixtures/160 employees/certification > 2
years/ISO 9001)*

*"The training about quality management is at its 'childhood', being at the
same level with the employees usually trained."* There should be different
levels of training according to the level of the audience (target group) and
the training content should include practical examples of all sectors (
products/services). *(321/Greece/ice-creams, fresh juices/437 employees/
certification < 2 years/ISO 9002)*

*"The externally-provided training is satisfying. However the training
content is general and mainly concerns the phase of the preparation of a
company to implement a Quality system rather than the phase of its
function." (322/Greece/toast/258 employees/certification > 2 years/ISO
9002)*

*"The content of externally - provided training is general as to Quality
issues. All training programmes avoid giving specialised knowledge. An
issue in which there is insufficient training is HACCP. Seminars that
concern HACCP have such a form that they are directed to those who
know nothing about it, without analysing in depth." (324/Greece/pasta,
tomato products/336 employees/certification > 2 years/ISO 9002)*

External training programmes for quality systems are viewed critically.
*"Especially the big providers often have quite a different way of thinking
than those who work in the production. They have a very schematic way of
thinking. That's what we found when we introduced HACCP.
Organisations of the sector and the food inspection authorities have a
much better understanding of the practical processes and problems in the
companies. They know much better what the companies need and think."* ...
*"A lot is no help for self-help. Examples from the practice of other
companies are good." (124/Germany/roasted ground coffee/70
employees/certification < 2 years/ ISO 9002)*

There was also criticism that the academic training of food chemical
engineers did not give sufficient attention to quality management.
*"Although the majority of the graduates find jobs in the business sector, the
generic training contents at German universities is still mainly oriented*

*towards legal knowledge for employees of public authorities."
(124/Germany/roasted ground coffee/70 employees/certification < 2
years/ISO 9002)*

External trainers are used from time to time. Evaluations are always
conducted after each training session to assess the views of the participants.
The company see the need for external trainers to be more flexible and to
design content specific to the company's business. *(422/Ireland/butter/49
employees/certification > 2 years/ISO 9002)*

There are two factors which limit the possibilities of the company to
systematically make use of company-specific suitable external training
programmes:

The company is located in a rural area, providers of suitable further
training are mostly located in urban centres.

This kind of specialised companies are rather rare and scattered all over the
country. Due to a lack of concentration of prospective customers company-
specific suitable knowledge is seldom provided externally. *(123/Germany/
egg products/100 employees/certification < 2 years/ISO 9002)*

*"As a whole, there is a lot of training available. The problem is to find
trainers that are familiar with the conditions within the food-processing
industry." (621/Sweden/wheat and rye flour, rice, peas, beans/95
employees/certification < 2 years/ISO 9002)*

For the company the price of the providers is a problem. But external
quality-related know-how can be acquired at low cost from supplier
companies i.e. for detergents, spices etc. running special events free of
charge within their product promotion. The provision of big supplier
companies get good ratings. *"Sure, this is advertising. But there are
scientists giving good special lectures. The working groups are rather
small so that you can talk about specific problems." (122/Germany/tinned
fish/12 employees/certification < 2 years/ISO 9002)*

There are very few external trainers who provide courses specifically
geared to the particular needs of the food industry - most of the external
provision available is 'off-the-shelf'. Much of the training the company
requires is highly job-specific (e.g. the training needed for a spray drier

operator is different to that required by a packing operative) so is best provided internally - generally on-the-job. The company's microbiologist has been trained (through a Training the Trainers course) to do basic hygiene training and so she provides this rather than an external trainer. She is able to 'skew' the training to suit the food industry (and this particular branch of it). *(723/United Kingdom/infant and dietetic foods/280 employees/certification > 2 years/ISO 9002)*

"We have received a financial contribution from the European Social Fund , the Objective 4 programme. The aim was to make a total plan for the whole company regarding the need of further development in competence of the whole personnel. Today, thanks to this, we have a strategic plan for all the training required". (622/Sweden/ice-cream & frozen desserts/91 employees/certification < 2 years/ISO 9001)

For more specific training needs, the company would enlist the services of experts from the Food Research Association in the south of England: *"Related to quality, we went to a very specific specialised trainer - in fact it was our Food Research Association down in Leatherhead - and they actually came up here and did the training that we wanted. We were able to talk about what we wanted and it helped that the guy that we were talking to was ex-sugar confectionery anyway. He knew what was required." (722/United Kingdom/children's sugar confectionery/610 employees/certification > 2 years/ISO 9002)*

"The hygiene training is not specific to this sort of industry - it's very catering-oriented. We've got to try to turn it around and make it a bit more relevant. Which is a shame really because you're paying for the package and to have to modify it again. You can get companies who will do it for you but, again, they charge you for it. There are courses run for the industry on chocolate confectionery and sugar products and things like that which it would be nice for people to go on. It's the BCCA - the Biscuit, Chocolate and Cocoa Confectionery Alliance - or something like that - it's called. They do courses where you get a workbook and a video and an audio tape and you work on your own but there's a tutor and you've to put so many hours. And a few staff have said they'd like to this and I think it'd be a good idea - they cover everything - you can do QA ones, you can do hygiene and they're very specific to the industry which I think would be a good thing." (724/United Kingdom/edible cake decorations, sugar and chocolate confectionery, popcorn/160 employees/certification > 2 years/ISO 9002)

"There are many externally-provided offers for training but they do not provide any specialised knowledge though that is what the company needs. The company is saturated with general knowledge and desires insight in pork meat Quality (issues of hygiene, production, quality control). Those issues are covered with the help of experts coming from abroad (England, Germany, Spain) who are well -informed about those matters. The company invites foreign experts for the training of employees on special hygiene and quality issues. It also makes use of EU-funded seminars for improving the qualifications of the staff on basic as well as on quality and hygiene issues." (325/Greece/cooked pork meat/226 employees/certification < 2 years/ISO 9001/2)

A "technical know-how" contract has been established with a company in Holland. This ensures that the company always keeps abreast of nutritional know-how as this Dutch company claims to be five years ahead in technology know-how. It is difficult to *"develop within yourself as you can become too insular"*. The Mill Manager believes the company should be seeking other European countries for similar "know-how" contracts. *(421/Ireland/animal feeds/39-44 employees/certification > 2 years/ISO 9001/2)*

Training needs have been researched in every group of employee. Results of research were evaluated and the training programme based on the evaluation was build to whole company for two years. It is scheduled and there is institutions and schools taken part in the implementing the programme. According to the evaluation main areas where training is needed are;
• telematics
• management
• production
• quality
• work environment
• sales
• economics
• marketing
• logistic
• environmental management
• vocational further training. *(223/Finland/milk products/289 employees/ certification > 2 years/ISO 9002)*

Five years ago in conjunction with the parent company and the other subsidiary companies a CBT training packages was developed for basic food safety. Every member of staff had to undergo this training programme. The programme consists of ten modules. Each module must be successfully completed before proceeding to the next module. The company believes that while this involved an initial heavy expenditure, it has had a high return on investment over the years. Also management and supervisors undergo an Advanced Food Safety programme. There is also a Risk Management programme in place for managers. This programme is delivered on site by company staff and also staff from the parent company. Staff from the parent company are also used to deliver training sessions. *(425/Ireland/canning of food and vegetables, beverages, packing dry pulses/295 employees/aspiring certification/ISO 9002)*

"The marketing department played a role in improving interdepartmental communications. Their style was to bring customers into the factory to meet the operatives if there was a problem. Nowadays, the Plant Manager involves his staff directly with the customer if there is a complaint. This has now become part of the culture of the company." (422/Ireland/butter/49 employees/certification > 2 years/ISO 9002)

"The issues which training might address is about attitudes and customers demands. We can probably work this out with training within the company by bringing people from the production with us when meeting the customers. This will give them a direct communication with our customers and their demands." (621/Sweden/wheat and rye flour, rice, peas, beans/95 employees/certification < 2 years/ISO 9002)

For hygiene issues external experts are invited to give lectures on germs and critical dangerous points of micro-biological contamination. *"It is also more motivating if you can see the connections and understand the reasons for the instructions." (122/Germany/tinned fish/12 employees/certification < 2 years/ISO 9002)*

The advantage of external trainers is of *'being seen as an expert and having greater credibility than someone from inside'.(725/United Kingdom/peanut butter, gales honey, tablet jelly/300 employees/certification > 2 years/ISO 9002)*

"It is more true when someone else than the quality manager gives them training. At occasions like this we always get the help from an external trainer".   (622/Sweden/ice-cream   &   frozen   desserts/91 employees/certification < 2 years/ISO 9001)

Quality and personnel concepts of food-processing SMEs
Summary

Relatively stagnating demand, concentration tendencies, modernisation of the process technology and rationalisation, on the one hand, new consumer habits and increasing quality claims by consumers and public, on the other, are the framework conditions for SMEs of the food industry on the European market. The tendency towards ISO certification, existing also in SMEs, is to be seen as a trial to respond to the traditionally high and increasing quality demands of different instances of the business environment.

Competition & quality management

The ISO system is not regarded to be optimal. Points of criticism are (1) the pressure to formally conform to the system instead of securing concrete quality aims in customer-supplier relationships, (2) the overrating of standardisable and measurable quality characteristics, (3) elements extraneous to the sector and (4) its having an element structure instead of a process structure. In spite of all criticism, quality management according to ISO 9000 is gaining ground due to its recognition in the increasingly globalised market and the suitability of the ISO system as a framework for the integration of further quality-relevant systems such as HACCP and environmental management. But the quality management of SMEs is currently mainly dealing with the introduction and routinisation of the ISO system and, especially, with the implementation of the new European law for the food industry. Improvement of the internal operations and the management are the present main aims of the companies.

In spite of criticism: ISO 9000

Quality-oriented restructuring currently focused on management & laboratory

The restructuring of the quality-promoting organisational and operational structures and forms of work is currently centred on management and laboratories for development and quality control. Inter-functional management teams in the food industry guarantee especially stability of products with naturally varying raw materials, development of products under the condition of naturally varying raw materials and with regard to produceability, acceleration of product development close to the market and customer, planning of production, purchasing and storage with the aim to achieve an optimal capacity utilisation.

Technical modernisation and rationalisation prevail at a co-operative-productive level

At the performing level the work organisation is decisively determined by technical modernisation and rationalisation. Also in SMEs quality management meets with a work organisation which is characterised by automation of the production processes, by technical merging of production with distributive functions and with purchasing, storage and material flow, and by computer-aided production planning and process control. Currently, quality management is formalising only the jobs in this modernised work organisation, but including technologically based inspection and monitoring tasks at the production line. This "friendly" technical basis also reduces the bureaucratic work of quality management. But it also contains a possibly sector-specific "trap" for the extensive implementation of quality management: External or internal "ISO specialists" develop the quality system along technical flow processes; quality is concentrated on technical parameters and it focuses on the stability of the process; the technical logic of the process quality does not show the employees the advantage of the quality system for product quality and customer satisfaction. Insufficient understanding of customer expectations, product characteristics, the production processes and the quality system prevent staff from internalising the seemingly "simple" and thanks to the documentation seemingly "clear" tasks. Quality-promoting measures of reorganisation are, if at all, organised mainly beside the direct performing processes, e.g. in form of internal improvement groups.

For the implementation of quality management, two tendencies are emerging in the external customer-supplier relationships. On the one hand, the awareness is increasing in the companies for the responsibility for the total food chain, not only due to the modern quality concept of the ISO standard, but mainly due to demands of the well-informed consumers, the public and the "sectoral code of practice". In addition, food scandals prove the vital economic importance. On the other hand, SMEs are compelled to take essential external functions and thus responsibilities out of source or transfer them to commerce or to holding and group structures due to cost pressure and competitive and concentration processes in the food industry and commerce. In these relationships, regular high quality demands are made on SMEs, not least a certified quality system is required as a condition of marketability, but not always quality co-operation works free of frictions, and not always the strong external partners support the company in quality matters, which would be appropriate to their quality demands.

External customer-supplier relationships and food chain

Currently, first tendencies towards a more profound and more sector-specific implementation of quality management are emerging:

Sectoral tendencies & future

- Retraceability, improvement of internal operations, preventive and in-process quality assurance

- Quality control of automated and computerised flow-line processes and purchasing/marketing networks

- Customer and consumer satisfaction and customer flexibility of the companies

- Cutting quality costs, economising resources, environmental management

In future it is to be expected: Automated and integrated flow-line production in modern chains of purchasing and distribution logistics require as quality management in the food industry inter-functional and inter-company mastering of processes, thus process quality.

Sector-typical personnel structures & quality management

The task of personnel-related implementation of quality management meets in SMEs of the food industry with sector-specific personnel and qualification structures:

- Strong division of commercial and planning functions from operative-productive functions

- Strong spreading of qualification levels

- Great share of part-time and seasonal work

The majority of companies has a regular personnel department. From the mainly clear functional structure and the industrial mass production processes of the food industry result relatively clear long-term job profiles of the staff. The organisation of employee training required by the quality system is in most cases a responsibility of the personnel department. But a tendency can be identified that in comparison with a rather administrative function of the personnel department, an essential impetus to personnel development emanates from the people responsible for quality management.

Limited effects of the ISO system on personnel development

Due to the fact that the implementation of quality management currently consists in the introduction and routinisation of the ISO system, the consequence of quality management for personnel development policy is, on average, limited to the following two tendencies

- The identification, reorganisation and documentation of the company operations faces the senior and middle management with extensive new tasks. All respondent companies identify skill needs at the level of management, naturally in quality management-related know-how, but mostly also in generic management know-how.

- For the other employees, the introduction of the ISO system results in a formalised description of the job requirements and thus at least in a basis for a more precise definition of necessary skill profiles.

A majority of the respondent company experts denies that the introduction of quality management led to such changes of the processes and the work organisation in their companies, that it resulted in skill shortages with the operative staff and necessity for corresponding training programmes. The SMEs of the food industry implement quality management as defined by the ISO system essentially in the existing work organisation and process technology. Thus, in relation to the direct performance process of the companies, what takes place in the companies is not so much reorganisation but rather redefinition of the tasks of the functional areas. This is true of the laboratory, whose tasks are widening from quality control to planning and evaluation of preventive inspections. At the operative-productive level modern process technology defines the work organisation and tasks combined in activities and behaviour which are essentially quality assuring: monitoring and controlling process parameters, monitoring product specifications and sorting, hygiene and security.

The present specialist employee training in the companies clearly has quality implications, but it is not yet done within the framework of a quality strategy. Skilled staff of laboratories for product development and for quality monitoring and skilled staff for purchasing and marketing need to constantly update their knowledge of international developments in dietetics, food and process technologies, the guidelines for "good production practice" and "good laboratory practice", legal standards etc. as well as of the output markets and, above all, also the input markets with regard to the specific products and processes of the own company. The training needs of these employees increase in companies which practice extended quality agreements with suppliers and a consulting service or which extend their service to customers. Increasing importance is gaining with specialists in purchasing and marketing, apart from commercial knowledge, the know-how in modern marketing and transport logistics systems including their basis in information technology.

Current training in specialist skills

For a large part of the operative staff, most companies identify on the basis of their modern material flow and process technologies occupation-specific training needs mainly in the fields of hygiene and safety as well as machine operation and product handling. Increasing technology-based elements of self-inspection at the flow line require training in handling test instruments and in test methods, in inspection routines and documentation according to plan. This training is currently mainly limited to critical adaptation skills in the companies.

Present cross-occupational training

In the field of generic training the companies currently identify a clear need to train management in methods and techniques of teamwork and project management, often in connection with social behaviour and in personal pattern of leadership. Increasing importance is gaining training of managerial staff for handling integrated information technologies and company-specific software packages.

Also at the operative level are crucial quality tasks *per se* inter-occupational. But solutions are seen for the time being by most companies for the flow processes and for the information flow as well as reliably documented job instructions. On this basis, the training of the operative staff is restricted to familiarising with workplace-specific routines and assimilating basic computing knowledge

Present training in quality system knowledge

In their current quality training many companies are still struggling with a "gap" between overview training in the quality system and training of staff in quality tasks of their specific work area. But two sector-typical tendencies to the integration of system knowledge and vocational further training are already emerging:

- It is particularly in the food industry that training in the system or in system components of the quality management of the companies covers essential elements of the required vocational qualifications and thus of personnel training in the first place.

- Many companies train internal auditors. This suggests the hypothesis that with these internal auditors a new type of specifically qualified staff develops in the food industry. System control, problem identification and solution in co-operation with operative staff increasingly seems to replace traditional foreman tasks such as output and work monitoring.

Current approaches for the promotion of process competence

The relatively new imperative of the quality philosophy to develop not only product-oriented but rather process-oriented quality consciousness of staff meets with the approval of strikingly many interviewed experts in the food industry. At the administrative-planning level there is an understanding of the necessity of an appropriate management qualification particularly for the assurance of the food chain, the acceleration of market- and customer-related product design and a production, purchasing and storage planning with the aim of an optimum utilisation. At the operative level of the performance process the technological integration and automation of the material flow, processing and the inspection processes lead to the result that process monitoring becomes the essential work task and process competence becomes the crucial qualification of staff. As opposed to the recognition of the aim, the implementation in terms of personnel development is on average still in its beginnings.

Interpersonal key qualifications such as the "ability to communicate", "ability to learn", "responsibility", "problem solving ability" and "capability to decide" rank foremost in the personnel implementation of quality management. In many surveyed companies these are the main topics particularly in external training of staff. Target groups are currently mainly **Social key qualifications**

- executives in business-administrative, panning-developing, personnel and quality-managerial functions

- the middle management

At the operative level interpersonal key qualifications still occur more as requests for appropriate behaviour than as operationalised training aim. It appears to be typical for the companies of the food industry that there is a strong new approach of collaboration of staff for the solution of quality issues besides the technology-determined performance organisation. Within this organisational framework sector-specific key competencies of employees in the European food industry materialise to some extent: e.g. the ability to use product knowledge for the identification of hygiene-critical points, to apply work experience for the improvement of process weaknesses etc. The establishment of quality circles and improvement groups characterises at the moment the trailblazers of the implementation of quality management among the surveyed companies. The influence of such quality organisations on the direct work organisation is still in its beginnings.

The pressures of competition and costs in the European food industry define the framework conditions for personnel training in the interviewed companies. Under cost pressures **Limits of the internal training** expenditures for personnel training are mainly treated as a flexible quantity. The efforts of companies to fully utilise their plants, which have been modernised with sometimes considerable investments, limit seasonal free periods for training. Restrictive planning of time and resources ultimately appears to be the decisive factor in the choice of work-integrated and work-related methods. In addition, the interest of many companies in flexibly employable staff leads, on the one hand, to the identification of a broader qualification and training need, but at the same time the more flexible employment of staff limits the training times for larger groups of staff.

Benefits and deficiencies of external training

Many interviewed companies use or at least expect concrete quality knowledge particularly from sectoral organisations, supplier companies - above all from suppliers of lab and process technology - and from partner companies, especially those abroad. An example of good practice are training networks of companies resulting from the co-operation in consulting networks for the implementation of the ISO system, among them particularly those which had been supported by national or European funds. Examples of good practice can also be found in companies deliberately changing over from a reactive policy towards the public food monitoring authorities and concerning complaints, demands and audits of customers to a proactive involvement of these instances for the quality-related qualification of staff.

Significantly often interviewed managers criticised the external training provision for

- lacking sector-, process- and product-specific implementation knowledge of quality management as a support of company-specific improvement schemes,

- lacking training support in the sector-, process- and product-specific adaptation of modern quality methods, techniques and technologies,

- lacking quality-related sector, process and product knowledge as such.

It is a weakness of the personnel strategy of the surveyed companies that it is oriented towards the organisational division of functions and range of qualifications, thus reproducing them, and that it only reacts on average to external requirements and internal reports of an already critical need. A systematic identification of existing human resources and a more proactive personnel development strategy guided by internal company aims which integrate external requirements in the long run is on average not very common. Cross-functional management teams are becoming common for the organisational implementation of quality management, this does not take place for the personnel-related implementation of quality management - the human resources management. Company-specific needs profiles based on long-term company aims are most likely to be used in recruitment. A systematic evaluation of personnel development measures has also so far not been very common. In cases where such arrangements could be identified they were most of the time reserved for cost-intensive external training programmes.

Weak point: personnel strategy

This is to be expected in the future: After the devaluation of craft-based skills, requirements of inspection and control of quality-decisive product and process parameters define **process competence** as the modern vocational profile of skilled workers in the food industry. Target-oriented understanding of customer and consumer interests and of tasks of cross-company assurance of the food chain and of environmental conditions is more and more required. Process-related learning suggests internally cross-workplace learning organisation - e.g. in improvement groups.

Sectoral tendencies & future

Literature

CEDEFOP: Vocational education and training – the European research field, Background report, Volume 1 & 2, Luxembourg 1998

Europäische Kommission (Hrsg.): Panorama der EU-Industrie 93, Luxemburg 1993

Europäische Kommission (Hrsg.): Panorama der EU-Industrie 95-96, Luxemburg 1995

IRDAC-Report: Quality and Relevance", 1994

Europäische Kommission (Hrsg.): Eurostat Jahrbuch '96 - Europa im Blick der Statistik 1985 - 1995, Luxemburg 1996

Europäische Kommission (Hrsg.): Erhebung über die berufliche Weiterbildung in Unternehmen 1994 (CVTS), Luxemburg 1996

List of figures and tables

Figures

Tables